woman
on the
verge
of a
nervous
break-
down

*life, love and
talking it through*

lorna martin

JOHN MURRAY

First published in Great Britain in 2008 by John Murray (Publishers)
An Hachette Livre UK company

1

© Lorna Martin 2008

A CIP catalogue record for this title is available from the British Library

Hardback ISBN 978-0-7195-2451-6
Trade paperback ISBN 978-0-7195-2421-9

Typeset in Sabon by M Rules

Printed and bound by Clays Ltd, St Ives plc

John Murray policy is to use papers that are natural, renewable and
recyclable products and made from wood grown in sustainable forests.
The logging and manufacturing processes are expected to conform
to the environmental regulations of the country of origin.

John Murray (Publishers)
338 Euston Road
London NW1 3BH

www.johnmurray.co.uk

For my mum and dad

This is a true story,
although some identities have been changed
to protect people's privacy.

The state of being in love . . . is psychologically so remarkable and it is the normal prototype of the psychoses.
Sigmund Freud, *Totem and Taboo*

Frequently paraphrased as:
One is very crazy when in love.

Prologue

I was going to be late. Again. Even though I am devoutly agnostic I was praying while on the Gatwick Express. It was my only hope of getting to the airport for 7.45 am, the latest I could check in for my flight home to Glasgow. But it wasn't working. The train seemed to be moving at a slower pace than a brontosaurus.

Suddenly, an image of the White Rabbit from *Alice in Wonderland* appeared in my mind. He was clutching a large, golden pocket watch while huffing and puffing, 'I'm late! I'm late!' My own version of the frantic refrain started playing on a loop: 'Come on, come on, please God, come fucking on. I'm late! I'm late! I'm LATE, LATE, LATE, LATE, LATE, LATE, LATE. Arrrrrrgggggghhhh!'

Every few minutes I tried to distract myself by reading a news-paper or listening to my iPod, but it was futile. The words I was staring at disintegrated en route from my retina to my cortex. They could have been written in Chinese or Arabic for all the sense they made to me. So I tossed the newspaper back into my bag. As for my 'favourites' playlist, I could only tolerate the first five seconds of each tune before fast forwarding to the next one. My top twenty tracks were condensed into one hundred seconds. I couldn't concentrate on anything other than time. Every ounce of my energy was devoted to trying to deliver subliminal mes-sages to the train driver to crank up his speed. When I closed my eyes, I saw, seared into my inner lids, a giant egg timer with lumi-nous pink grains of sand trickling away at what seemed like an ever-increasing rate. When I opened them, I stared psychotically at the clock on my mobile phone and watched another precious minute as it disappeared.

I'd already missed two flights the previous week. This would make it three in ten days. Somehow, this seemed slightly too chaotic. As was the fact that I had also, the previous week, picked up my ninth penalty point for speeding and narrowly escaped having my driver's licence taken away altogether. In the 'losing it' stakes, this wasn't quite on a par with Britney Spears shaving her head in public, but I can see now that I was obviously trying to communicate something.

My sister, Louise, and our mutual friend, Katy, who both work as therapists in the famous Priory chain of private psychiatric hospitals, (Britain's answer to the Betty Ford Clinic for people with addictions, depression and other mental health problems), and who have an annoying habit of being right about most things, have always inferred a lot from my perpetual lateness. They say it's a sign of repressed anger and inherent selfishness, and they look at me with pity when I insist it's just because I am hopelessly disorganised I don't like to wear a watch ('I don't want my life to be ruled by time,' I once declared, provoking widespread ridicule).

This issue had reached its tearful nadir a few years ago during a night out to celebrate Louise's upcoming wedding. I burst into the restaurant, over an hour late, with a gushing apology and a rosy glow on my face: I'd been having fun, and lots of it, with my lovely new boyfriend. It was the first time in six years that I'd managed to sustain a relationship for more than half a dozen dates and the sense of achievement together with the early flush of love was making me feel somewhat euphoric. But I was brought quickly back to earth when Louise and Katy launched their verbal assault. Could I be any more selfish? How special did I think I was? Did I not realise that my constant tardiness indicated passive-aggression and an overdeveloped sense of self-importance combined with massively low self-esteem?

'I just lost track of time,' I whimpered pathetically. 'I was having fun. With my new boyfriend. I thought you'd be happy for me. And anyway, this is Louise's second wedding. It's not that big a deal. Surely.'

I tried not to think about their comments (or mine) that morning as the Gatwick Express approached its destination. Instead, I noticed that my heart was pounding, my palms were sweating and I had the first signs of a self-induced tension headache coming on. Breathe in, hold, breathe out, I coached myself while I waited for the train to stop. Before the doors were even half open, I had squeezed through them like a greased weasel and was running as fast as I could towards the lift and escalator. They were jam-packed. I eventually arrived, breathless and perspiring, at the check-in desk, only about thirty seconds late. I actually felt quite pleased. Compared with my recent form, this was progress.

When the assistant said the flight was delayed for forty-five minutes, adding that she'd ask her supervisor if I could slip through, I was ecstatic, filled with hope and optimism and thanking my lucky star or whoever it was out there who always seemed to bring me back from the brink of disaster. Unfortunately, the good vibes ended abruptly moments later when she sauntered back with the bad news.

'Please?' I looked at her beseechingly. 'It's an emergency. You see, I'm a journalist and . . .' I paused. 'And I have a really important interview to do with, er, um, er, the First Minister of Scotland.'

I said this in the sort of tone that would be better suited to someone who had just landed a world exclusive with Osama bin Laden.

But even if I had had a date with the world's most wanted man, I doubt it would have made any difference. Judging by the expression on the sales assistant's face, she was not about to be swayed by the highly pressured demands of my chosen profession.

So I changed tack. 'This isn't just about my job,' I lied frantically. 'I absolutely need to get home as a matter of urgency because my . . .' I hesitated for a moment, crossed my fingers inside my coat pocket, then continued. 'I need to get home urgently because my gran's, um, my gran's been taken ill.'

She looked at me with sympathy. Or perhaps it was pity. 'I'm sorry,' she said, 'but my supervisor said no. And she told me to point out that our check-in desks close exactly thirty minutes before the scheduled departure of the flight and that we do strongly recommend checking in two hours before then.'

I opened my eyes as wide as they would go and didn't blink for a while in an attempt to stop the tears of self-pity that were threatening to erupt and were already blurring my vision, which probably made me look deranged. 'Please? I know you probably get a lot of chancers concocting all kinds of ridiculous excuses to try to get through. People who think they're so special that the normal rules don't apply to them. That they're somehow exempt. But I promise I'm not making this up. My gran's just had a . . .' I paused. 'My gran's just been rushed to h . . . h . . . h . . .'

No. I couldn't say it. I couldn't say that my little old gran, an amazing ninety-three-year-old woman, had been taken to hospital with something terrible in case she ever was and I'd have to shoulder that terrible burden of responsibility for the rest of my life. Imagine the bad karma.

The assistant looked at me with a knowing smile. 'There's another flight in three hours.'

'THREE HOURS?' These two little words sent a signal straight to the floodgates, bursting them open. 'Three hours? My gran could be d . . . d . . . d . . .' I sobbed and stuttered.

Carried away by my own performance, I'd apparently managed to convince myself that my grandmother, who would have been at home doing her knitting while waiting patiently for *This Morning* to come on, had actually been taken seriously unwell. 'My gran. Three hours. Anything can happen in three hours. My gran's ninety-three. Nine. Three. Can you imagine being nearly a hundred years old, sitting in your high-rise, lonely, waiting for, you know . . . just waiting? Your time, your precious time, running out.'

I went on to rant about the unfairness of it all: about passengers getting penalised when they're late, but the airline getting off scot-free when it's delayed. 'It's a travesty,' I said, my lips quivering.

I wiped the snot dripping from my nose with the back of my hand before storming off to the bar, still sobbing and mumbling an ignoble string of obscenities under my breath, not giving a damn who saw me or how demented I must have looked.

The targets of my rage included: budget airline companies for their double standards and appalling inflexibility, the check-in assistant for not being able to persuade her jobsworth supervisor to let me through, and Britain's entire railway network for failing in its duty to get me to the airport on time in the first place. *This would never have happened in fucking Germany or fucking Switzerland, with their super-efficient, integrated and well-invested transport systems*, I thought, as I fleetingly considered moving. *And it wouldn't have happened if I'd been travelling with British Airways*, I thought, vowing never to travel budget again. *And if it wasn't for that supervisor being such a petty bitch, well, I'd be sitting on that plane – that one out on the tarmac, right now. The one that's not going to take off for another fucking hour.*

It was everyone's fault, anyone's fault, but my own. Scapegoats were my best buddies. I was surrounded by them and, oh, how I loved them. Blaming them was my default position and was far easier than facing up to the uncomfortable and inconvenient facts: that I had a complete and utter lack of personal responsibility, that I'd wasted hundreds of pounds that I could ill afford on unnecessary flight changes and hotel bills in the past few weeks as a result, and, worst of all, that I'd just invented a desperate and morally indefensible lie in a vain attempt to save my own skin.

Five minutes later, I had broken my rule of never drinking before lunchtime and was sinking into the soothing embrace of a lovely, strong gin and tonic. The scapegoat was swiftly demoted to second best friend. While the early morning alcohol began to course through my veins, the rest of the world went about its normal activities around me: businessmen and women talking on their mobiles as they rushed to catch a plane; friends squeaking excitedly as they waited to go on holiday; young couples with their hands entwined, in love, talking and laughing and gazing adoringly at each other, oblivious to everyone but each other. *They're going to get fucking married and have fucking children and live happily ever fucking-well after*, I thought, struggling to stop myself from resenting complete strangers. Then I quickly soothed myself with the comforting thought that it wouldn't last, that he'd soon get bored and run off with someone else – a younger, prettier model – because that's what always happens.

Would I ever be able to form a normal, mature, functional relationship with the male of the species? I wondered. I'd been offered this and more, but, when it was there on a plate for me, I had bolted, too afraid and not yet ready, willing or able to give up my cherished freedom and independence. Instead I'd chosen to walk open-eyed into the most destructive relationship of my life.

In the recesses of my bag my mobile phone still held a saved message from Emily, one of my best friends. It was a week old. I opened it and read it for something like the 200th time. 'Sorry Lor. But u asked 2 be told. They were seen having another v cosy tete-a-tete ystrday. Also heard she spent the morning in his office. Blinds closed!'

I read it again. And again. And again, before hurling another silent stream of obloquy, this time directed at the two villains referred to in the message: Christian, a handsome, intelligent lawyer, who happened to be married, and Charlotte, a legal trainee, who happened not to be his wife.

Although I'd never laid eyes on Charlotte, I had several well-informed sources who spent their days in the city's law courts and their evenings in the bars around the Merchant City area of Glasgow to help me fill in the blanks. According to these informants, Charlotte was stunning and clever and so petite that she had to buy all her clothes from kiddies' departments. (She didn't like to keep this burden to herself, however, and apparently made a point of telling every woman she met.) Being a size sub-zero wasn't the only cross she had to bear, though. It seemed she had no girlfriends because, as she reportedly repeatedly explained:

'I'm so pretty. Girls don't like me. They feel threatened by me. Which is why I prefer to play with the boys. It's why I'm a man's girl.' Oh, and Charlotte currently worshipped the ground Christian walked on. The problem was: so did I.

I know this is no defence or excuse, but I had spent my entire adult life regarding adultery as a crime almost as heinous as murder. Although I'd never exactly advocated death by stoning, I wasn't far off it. I held extreme views on this particular sin. During wine-fuelled conversations with my friends, I was the one who would vow with all my heart never, ever in a million years to cheat on a guy I was with or to inflict that kind of pain on another woman. I knew from experience the agony of betrayal and I had often pledged, with 100 per cent total and absolute conviction, that I wouldn't do it. That I couldn't do it. It was immoral. I looked down from my perch on the Other Women as pathetic, predatory, perfect-marriage-ruining homewreckers. (The guys? Well, guys are guys, aren't they? How is a poor, helpless man supposed to resist when a devious, shameless woman's throwing herself at him?)

And yet, and yet . . . there I was, the third point in a messy love triangle that appeared to be on the verge of flourishing into a thoroughly unholy love quadrangle.

Once I had crossed the line, I kind of split into two for my double life. When the two Lornas collided, the bad one told the good one that everyone was doing it – 80 per cent of people at some point in their lives, according to one convenient (if unscientific) survey I'd discovered – and, most importantly, that I had complete control over my feelings. 'I'm just having a little fun,' the devil said to the angel. 'I don't want him. I don't love him. I'm just being a little naughty for once in my life. Don't worry. Chill out. It's all under control.'

But when I found out about Charlotte, the Other Other Woman, I started behaving like a betrayed spouse in a novel, declaring my undying love to a bewildered Christian, and even scheming to ruin his life by telling his actual wife everything.

I knew my reaction was not only tragically ironic – other

adjectives which came to mind included inappropriate, dispro-
portionate and completely misdirected – but I felt as if I was on
the moon looking down at the earth through a telescope and
eavesdropping on a story of someone else's screwed-up life. Only
I wasn't. It was my screwed-up life.

A tear plopped into my gin and tonic. I was in serious danger
of turning into the kind of pathetic person I'd always despised.

* * *

Two years earlier, I'd landed my dream job with the *Observer*, the
oldest Sunday newspaper in the world. My family had been
thrilled and proud. When I told my gran, she was more excited
than I was. She said she couldn't wait to tell the family, the neighbours, the health visitors and the district nurses, then she asked if
I'd get to meet the Pope. She was visibly disappointed to learn
that it was THE *Observer* (circulation nearly half a million;
famous writers: George Orwell, Michael Frayn, Hugh
McIlvanney, et al) and not the (Scottish) *Catholic Observer* (circulation 16,000; famous writers: the local priest).

Although I too was initially ecstatic about my new job, I was
also plagued by the never-ending feeling that I wasn't good
enough for it, that they'd made some terrible mistake in appoint-
ing me. My sister, in an attempt to be helpful, would say things
like 'dare to be average' or 'wake up to the fact that you're not
that important', or she would point out something she'd read
recently stating a little-known law of the universe: 87 per cent of
all people in all professions are incompetent.

Terrified that I might be exposed as one of the 87-per-centers
(even though I told myself I was one of the lucky 13, or should
that be unlucky 13?), I often fantasised about quitting, especially
in the wake of the whole Christian debacle. And it wasn't as if I
lacked other offers. Only a fortnight earlier I had been asked to
move to Egypt to live with a lovely wealthy man I'd met on a
family holiday who wanted to 'take care of me forever'. But, since
I wasn't absolutely convinced that I wanted to be taken care of
forever, even by a sexy Egyptian, I reluctantly turned him down

and instead contemplated moving to a war zone to try my hand as a foreign correspondent. When it dawned on me that I was more au fait with the complete recordings of Take That than the events in the Gaza Strip, I reconsidered again.

* * *

Slurping down the remains of my early morning refreshment, I realised that I was the only woman I knew in her mid-thirties – in fact, my thirty-fifth birthday was exactly one week away – who had neither a partner, nor mortgage nor even a cat. I was more commitment phobic than most of my male friends. Like many women my age, I had wildly conflicting fears: of being trapped in a relationship with someone I wasn't truly, madly, deeply in love with and of being alone; and of wanting to settle down and have children, but being afraid of giving up my beloved freedom and independence.

In the previous few weeks, several close friends and colleagues had gently suggested that I might want to think about 'seeing someone' (a shrink as opposed to a new love interest). But my view of the whole therapy culture was not benevolent and fell somewhere between ridicule and revulsion. Why pay someone to tell me that I use humour, or at least try to, as a defence mechanism? Or to tell me why I don't let anyone get too close? Or that I want my father's approval? I already know all that. 'In therapy,' Louise once said, 'all that you thought you knew – about yourself and others – will be turned on its head.' Maybe that's what happens to other people, I thought, but not me. I know myself better than anyone else can ever know me.

That morning, however, I was no longer so convinced. I decided that I didn't want to spend the rest of my life never letting anyone in.

I thought again about my gran, who, when she was in her thirties, was raising nine children single-handedly in a cramped tenement while her husband fought a war and worked in the dockyards. I compared my life to that of my own mum, who, when she was my age, was working until dawn, doing the night shift as a nurse on a geriatric ward and raising her two daughters while she coped with a husband who often worked away from home. I also remembered some of the remarkable people I'd been privileged to meet through my job as a journalist – individuals who had survived wars and genocide and who had suffered unimaginable losses in their lives, but had found incredible strength and resilience to carry on. The words of one man, who had lost a child in the most appalling circumstances, were indelible: 'Life cannot be postponed, it must be lived *now*. Do not wait for something to happen, for some future illusory event to take place; do not wait until it's too late to learn how to live.'

When I thought about him, I felt even more ashamed and guilty. What exactly was I waiting for? Is it one of the cruel ironies of being human that something terrible has to happen to you before you can really start to appreciate this one short life? I had a great job and great friends and perfect health, and yet I kept running away. From love. From commitment. My life was not tragic, but I was not happy and I was out of gear, and I decided I was going to have to do something about it.

I opened a notebook I'd bought on my way to the bar. My intention had been to write to 'the authorities' about the country's transport problems. Instead I wrote *Notes on a recovery* on the first page and started to scribble. At the end of a twelve-page stream-of-consciousness ramble, I scrawled: 'I think I might need help.' It felt much easier to write than to say. But I knew I needed to do more than just commit my thoughts to paper. So, before the moment passed, I called Katy and asked for the number of the best therapist in town.

in
denial

January

There's Nothing Wrong with Me

There's nothing wrong with me. Seriously. Nothing, nada, zilch, bugger all. I'm not a chronic alcoholic, drug abuser or anorexic. I wasn't locked in a cupboard under the stairs during my childhood or beaten to within an inch of my life by an evil step-parent. Nor have I ever been in a war zone or on a hijacked aeroplane or suffered a great whacking loss that has left me traumatised. I've never even been in hospital. As a patient, I mean. And my friends and family are all in good health, as far as I know. So, you see, there's absolutely nothing wrong with me. And I definitely don't need to be in therapy.

That's exactly what I would have said if the anxious chatter in my brain had found its way to my lips. It was 7.20 on the third morning of the new year, twenty minutes before my first therapy session was due to begin. I was sitting in my car outside a grand Victorian tenement building in the West End area of Glasgow revising and rehearsing what I was going to say to the woman I was about to enter into a close personal relationship with. As the early morning darkness began to lift, it was possible to make out a thin blanket of frost covering everything, from the huge Gothic steeple of the city's ancient university on the horizon to the steps leading up to her consulting room. There was hardly a soul to be seen, apart from the occasional jogger and dutiful dog walker. It was beautiful and serene. Inside my car, however, it was an altogether different story. I station-hopped frantically before settling on *Good Morning Scotland*, turned up almost to full blast in an attempt to drown out the incessant chit-chat in my mind. But the radio, even at high volume, still wasn't loud enough.

Perhaps I shouldn't bother going in? It's not as if anyone's forcing me. It's not as if I've been sectioned or anything. But that would be a real cop out. Plus, I've waited weeks for this appointment. Maybe I should just go for one session? She'll probably burst out laughing and tell me that, compared with all the other bonkers people she sees, I'm the sanest, most together woman she's ever met. Yeah, I'll go for one, even if it is just to be told that there's nothing wrong with me. That this is normal. That I'm normal.

I had woken that morning at around 4 am with my heart racing, the nape of my neck damp with perspiration, and was unable to get back to sleep. As I contemplated spilling out my most intimate and embarrassing secrets, I began to wonder what I was letting myself in for and what exactly it was that I was hoping to achieve.

I'd always been a major therapy sceptic. Apart from for those who had suffered some major traumatic event in their lives, I'd always dismissed the so-called talking cure as an extravagant con for weak, pathetic, self-indulgent losers who had lots of time and money on their hands but nothing more serious to kvetch about than the terrible hardship of having nothing particularly serious to kvetch about. In other words, people who wanted to whine about their weight/self-esteem/alcohol/commitment problem while blaming their emotionally absent father and/or overly critical mother. I was all for scapegoating when I missed a flight, but pinning the blame for everything on my own flesh and blood seemed a bit harsh.

No doubt my blinkered attitude had something to do with Louise and Katy, who had, for years, been spouting annoying psychobabble to explain just about everything, including, for instance, the screwed-up personalities of warmongering politicians ('It has nothing to do with oil, weapons of mass destruction or ending despotic regimes and everything to do with unresolved daddy issues and a neurotic craving for power and control').

'Yeah, whatever,' I would say to them.

'Everything that drives us, that motivates us, is hidden away in storage,' went their refrain. 'Everything that's ever happened to us.' Until these unconscious factors are brought to our awareness, they insisted, we're doomed.

'To what?' I'd occasionally, and foolishly, ask.

'To an inauthentic life. To living a lie – never being who you really are. To making self-destructive choices and decisions. To being driven by jealous, competitive, manipulative and control-ling impulses that you're not even aware of but that run our lives in unsuspected ways. To remain an eternal child or adolescent, imprisoned by the personality your parents inadvertently imposed on you.' Case solved, apparently.

'Who cares what makes you the way you are?' I'd often protested. 'It's just the way you are. You can't change it. You can't do anything about it.'

'Not with that attitude, you can't.'

And so it went on.

Adding to my conviction that they had crossed that fine line between sanity and madness was their unyielding insistence that *everyone* would benefit from a bit of therapy. During their most fervent sermons, they even used to suggest that a spell on the couch should be compulsory before a person has children. 'If we don't *become* who we really are before we reproduce,' they would say, 'then we just pass all our shit, unconsciouisly, onto the next generation.'

Unlike them, I'd had no time for rummaging around in the past. At least, not in front of an audience. And certainly not one I would have to pay for. Of course, I thought I knew myself. In fact, I'd always thought I was pretty well advanced in the self-awareness stakes. Who doesn't? But I preferred to do my soul-searching and navel-gazing in the privacy of my own home. Or, if I felt the need to share, I had my friends and family to talk to. Therapy seemed to me a convenient excuse to evade responsi-bility. Life's too short and too precious to waste time poring over ancient history that can't be changed, I'd often said.

Yes, I had a couple of battered old suitcases bulging with emotional baggage packed away, but, again, who doesn't? I'm a doughty stoic Scot. We don't do touchy-feely. Scottish men pride themselves on being the least emotive and communicative in the UK, if not the world. We pull our socks up and we get on with things. There are members of my extended family who think the word 'shrink' means only something that happens to a carelessly washed item of clothing and who think the word 'depression' should be capitalised and preceded by the definite article. Repression of our feelings is a survival trait. Clearly, Louise and Katy were national traitors, because, generally speaking, unless intoxicated we Scots would prefer to eat the deep-fried limb of a child than talk about emotional stuff.

If you've got a problem, deal with it. That was what I liked to say and that's exactly what I thought I had been doing. Change your job. Get out of a relationship. If that's too difficult, distract yourself. Get drunk. Do some exercise. Read a good book. Immerse yourself in a worthwhile project. Travel to a foreign land. Go to the movies. Set yourself a goal. Do a detox. Listen to Abba. Think of people worse off than you and start counting your blessings, as my mum would say. Get yourself a wee hobby or some fresh air, as my gran would say. If you absolutely have to, then pop some happy pills, but don't waste your time, your money and your one and only life confessing all to a stranger and then spending the rest of your days blaming your parents for your problems. That was what I thought.

But that was before I kind of lost the plot.

During the previous few months, as if the missed flights and the repeated speeding fines weren't enough, I'd found myself unable to stop crying. I shed so many tears that I began to think about the history and culture of tears: where they came from, why some people cry easily and others don't, why women cry more than men, whether I was going to dehydrate or if, indeed, as I was beginning to suspect, my reservoir was bottomless. Crying became a sort of second career. I sobbed like an abandoned, inconsolable toddler in my editor's office, in the HR department, in the pub with my friends, in The Coach and Horses in front of colleagues from the *Observer* (some of whom I hardly even knew), in the swimming pool changing rooms, and in my bed at two, three and four in the morning. One day I saw an old man sitting alone in a bar with a half pint of Guinness. When he lifted it to his lips, he lost his grip and spilled it all over his trousers. I helped clear it up, then ran to the ladies' for a good bubble. An elderly busker playing the violin, appallingly, just about liquefied me entirely. And emptied my purse.

On another occasion, when I was in London and had missed another flight, I begged an *Observer* columnist not to take advantage of me because I was a little bit vulnerable. In the unlikely event that he hadn't heard or understood me, I repeatedly told him that he *musht pleashe not take advantage of me cosh little bit vulneable* as we walked to his home. When it became clear he had no intention of doing anything other than very kindly letting me sleep in his spare room, I saw the chance for some more quality sobbing, and I took it. Why, why, why, I blubbed, didn't he want at least to *try* to take advantage of me?

During this time, I also made several slightly hysterical phone calls to Christian, pleading with him never to go out with That Charlotte Girl again and threatening to tell people what had happened between us if he did. The rational part of me knew that not only was this insane, but that I had as much chance of changing his behaviour as I had of changing the weather, but the irrational part of me was in the driving seat and refused to budge over.

So there I was, effectively blackmailing a man who was another woman's husband because I simply couldn't bear the thought of him falling in love with Another Other Woman. Jerry Springer would probably have taken my calls. I was ashamed and thoroughly disgusted with this person I had become.

Before the trio of missed flights, I had turned to my tried and trusted arsenal of self-soothing strategies – I forced myself to go for swims, I disappeared for long bracing walks in the wild Scottish hills, I threw myself into work, I got drunk, I abstained for a month,

I thought of people worse off than me and counted my blessings, I scribbled in my notebook and wrote truly appalling poems about the agony of unrequited love, I went back on Prozac – but this time nothing seemed to provide the refuge, escape or tranquillity I needed. This time, I knew I was going to have to do something much more drastic.

It was now 7.35 am – a time at which, under normal circumstances, I'd still be in my bed. I felt as if I were a pupil about to start a brand new term at a brand new school, albeit with much nicer shoes on. But this was worse because I was here through choice and seriously sleep deprived. In fact, it felt more like being a married man visiting a sleazy sex den for the first time – as if I were up to something dirty and forbidden, and terrified I was going to be caught in the act. I considered going home, disappearing back under my duvet, spending the large sum of money I'd borrowed to pay for therapy on something much more immediately satisfying, like a wardrobe full of expensive new clothes, a giant plasma-screen TV or an exotic holiday. Or all three. Partly to stop myself changing my mind and partly to avoid the risk of being seen, I sprinted from my car, up the stairs and pushed the buzzer. Only a dirty old mackintosh would have enhanced my furtive demeanour.

The door clicked open and, following the instructions I'd been given over the phone, I walked up three flights of stairs, opened another door, and sat down in a small empty hall area that had been converted into a waiting room. I took several deep breaths – the smell of coffee was so rich I could practically taste it – and scanned my surroundings. There was a dark green armchair and two brown ones, and tan wide-plank pine flooring. Four landscape photos hung on one wall – the first I recognised immediately as the snow-capped Torridon mountains, probably Scotland's most spectacular range, another looked like Loch Lomond at dusk. It was enveloped by that lovely pinkish-purple glow that made you want to get into your car and drive there immediately. The other two were of a beautiful isolated and rugged beach. I think it was Luskentyre on the Hebridean island of Harris – frequently voted one of the world's top twenty beaches.

Down a hallway was a framed black and white picture of an elderly bearded man. Was it Freud? Surely that would be too flagrant a disregard for cliché. It certainly wasn't the famous one of him holding a cigar. Whoever it was was sitting at his desk looking baleful. His gaze was harsh and disconcerting. Surely it couldn't be Freud? Wasn't he a bit of a cowboy? And a sex-obsessed, misogynistic one at that, who believed women suffered from penis envy and hated their mothers for sending them into the world 'insufficiently equipped'? Oh deary me, as my friend Emily would say. Now I really was wondering what I was letting myself in for. Perhaps the photo was of my therapist's grand-father, I consoled myself.

Alongside a water cooler were two bundles of well-thumbed magazines: the *Atlantic Monthly* and *National Geographic*. I looked at the familiar yellow border and picked up the top copy. It was from 1985 and had a cover story about the famine in Ethiopia. This confirmed my view that this was a place for people obsessed with the past. It also reminded me how trivial my 'prob-lems' were. And it made me think back to 1985. I would have been fifteen – the end of the world as I knew it, although I didn't fully realise it then.

After a few minutes, I heard another door open. A slender woman, of average height, who looked to be in her mid to late fifties, appeared and offered her hand. 'Lorna?' she asked, with the faintest trace of a smile, and then introduced herself.

'Hi. Really lovely to meet you,' I said, shaking her hand firmly. 'Thank you very much indeed for agreeing to see me,' I added gratefully.

I thought it was a bit strange and disconcerting that she didn't smile brightly and say: 'You're welcome, my dear.' Instead, she turned and strode away along a corridor. I dutifully followed her. I'd imagined her as a bit of a hippy type with long, unkempt Kate Bush-style hair, charity shop clothes and the sort of sensible shoes my gran wears. But, on first impressions, she seemed more like a head teacher or an executive with her dark grape-coloured suit and dusky pink jumper, her carefully styled shoulder-length light brown hair, the wire-rimmed glasses and her formal, businesslike manner. The overall effect was of a grimmer Helen Mirren. In her portrayal of Her Majesty, The Queen.

'Please come in,' she said, opening the door to her consulting room and gesturing towards two leather armchairs situated across and at slight angles to each other. I sat down and glanced around the room. There was a couch – *the* famous couch! – placed against one wall. I have no idea whether it was a black leather one like I'd imagined, because, like the famous one, it was draped in a dark Persian rug. It was armless and backless, making it look more like a small single bed or a bench than an inviting, comfy sofa. A box of tissues lay strategically on the floor. They must be for the really damaged people, I thought, glad and relieved that I wasn't one of them.

I favoured her, Dr J, with a warm, friendly, smile. She reciprocated with an inscrutable expression – maybe a half-smile. It certainly didn't reach her eyes. How unfriendly, I thought uncomfortably. I suavely attempted to break the ice by thanking her again, and commenting on the wonderfully rich and soothing smell of coffee hanging heavily in the air between us, practically obliging her to offer me a cup. She didn't, but I got a tight little nod as a meagre consolation prize.

I'd been eagerly anticipating her enfolding me, her dear child, in a warm embrace and cooing that I didn't need to worry anymore because she was going to take care of me. 'Everything's going to be okay now; Dr J is here to look after you. Nothing bad will ever happen again. Dr J will see to that,' I'd imagined her saying. But I was clearly in the early stages of a rude awakening.

Unlike life coaches, self-help books, glossy magazines and inspirational speakers, Dr J didn't pledge to free me from my fears, unleash my true potential, help me realise my dreams and make me happy, rich, successful and fulfilled by the end of the year. She didn't even offer to help me find a new boyfriend. In fact, Dr J didn't promise anything or offer any guarantees. She simply sat in silence, looking at me with an unreadable expression on her face. It felt weird. Very, very weird. Like nothing I'd ever experienced before in my life.

Surely, I thought, she must be wondering why I'm here – what it is that's wrong with me, that's brought me to therapy? Surely she must be dying to ask me some questions? To find out all about me and my life? Apparently not.

When the sound of the silence became deafening, I gave her another big beseeching smile. Still nothing. I considered thanking her once more . . . Instead, I scanned the room again. On her large mahogany desk, which was situated behind her and in front of a large window, there was a computer, a neat pile of journals and the back of two photo frames. On the wall to the left of her desk were what looked like several framed degrees and diplomas with glittering gold-embossed lettering. I also noticed a mother-and-child sculpture. To my left, opposite the couch, there was a bookshelf, full of unreadable books, which rose to the ceiling, and, alongside it, and slightly behind me, a large earth-coloured print bedecked the wall.

I looked at her and wondered what her story was: whether she was married – there was no ring – and whether she had children.

Eventually, just before I broke out in a nervous rash, I spoke my opening line, which defined everything, really. 'I'm sorry. I'm not really sure what to do?'

There was more than a trace of desperation in my voice. She blinked a couple of times, but said nothing.

Thanks to Hollywood, I was familiar with the caricature of a shrink as someone who sits in silence, expressionless, stroking his chin and occasionally asking: 'Why is that, do you think?' Or 'What does this bring to mind?' But that's exactly what I thought it was: a caricature.

I was no longer so sure.

What the hell's going on here? I thought. What am I paying for? It was excruciating. I smiled nervously, crossed my legs, uncrossed them, scraped at the skin round my thumbnails, twisted my hair around my finger, then, just when one of my legs was about to start twitching, I tried again. Sounding a little like the verbally incontinent Vicky Pollard, I began to spew: 'I'm really sorry about this. It's the first time I've ever had this kind of therapy and I'm not really sure how it works. I don't really know what to do or say because, the thing is, I don't have any real problems, as such. There's nothing really wrong with me. Seriously.'

I laughed and nodded vigorously to reinforce my sincerity. 'Honest to God,' I said, as I prepared to recite a version of the speech I had prepared earlier. 'I'm not a chronic alcoholic, drug abuser or anorexic. I wasn't starved or abused or beaten as a child . . .' I continued until the conclusion: 'So, you see, I don't think I really *need* to be in therapy.' She gazed at me austerely before the corners of her mouth edged up a millimetre or two to form an offensively weak smile.

Because I couldn't bear another silence, I quickly continued: 'What I'm trying to say is that I know there are people in the world much worse off than me. People are dying. People are starving. Terrible things are happening all over the world. And I'm here. It's utterly pathetic, I know. My life is a walk in the park. I have a great job and great friends. And perfect health. I'm ashamed to be here because I know that life has its ups and downs and it's not always easy. I sometimes think I'm just not very well equipped to deal with it. Perhaps I should just go home and count my blessings or get some fresh air or a new hobby? Or do some voluntary work in the third world?'

This entire ramble was delivered as one big question in the hope that she would either guide or reassure me. She did neither. She just nodded almost imperceptibly and said: 'Hmmmm.'

* * *

This wasn't what I'd ordered. It was all so different from the initial consultation – it is normal practice in the UK to be seen by someone other than the therapist who will eventually work with you. My assessment had taken place a few weeks earlier with the head of one of the country's largest private psychoanalytic psychotherapy services, which has its main offices in London. I had timed the consultation to coincide with a work trip to the capital. The psychiatrist who saw me was a lovely, warm, avuncular man, who got down to business by asking gently: 'Well then, my dear, what ails?' I wasn't sure whether to say 'everything' or 'nothing', so I said: 'Everything', then a moment later added, 'Nothing', then burst into tears. He smiled sympathetically and I toyed with the idea of moving to London, or commuting three times a week, so that he could be the one who would take me into his arms and save my life.

Once I'd pulled myself together, he scribbled furiously as I answered his questions about my family, my job and my relationships, already feeling slightly as if I was being undressed.

Towards the end of the consultation, he said: 'Why now?'

'It's a last resort,' I admitted, after a brief pause. 'I've tried everything else – fresh air, pills, exercise, changing jobs, drinking, not drinking, going out, staying in, new hobbies. I have no energy and no passion anymore and I'm afraid of the way I'm feeling.'

He nodded.

'And,' I added, tentatively, 'I've been having, you know, bad thoughts. I'd never do anything, but I can't stop wondering what the point is in anything in carrying on. I feel as if I'm having that horrible adolescent "why am I here, what's the point of living if we're all going to die anyway" phase all over again. Only it's worse because, well, I was an adolescent two decades ago.'

'Anyone who thinks about life contemplates the alternative,' he said, matter-of-factly. 'And, believe it or not, there are a lot of people out there who may look like adults but who are, underneath, still angry teenagers.'

'I'm not angry,' I said gently. He gave me a sad smile.

After around ninety minutes, he took off his glasses and placed them on the notebook on his lap, then he put his palms together, rested his chin on the tips of his two index fingers and closed his eyes. I felt as if I were waiting for the results of an important exam. A few seconds later he looked at me with a nod and a sympathetic smile. 'I think,' he said, in his soft and compassionate voice, 'that you might find psychotherapy quite helpful.'

I replayed his words a couple of times in my head. He *thinks* I *might* find psychotherapy *quite helpful*. Was that it? *Might* be *quite helpful*? I'm a journalist, I love drama. I'm used to sensation and hyperbole and screaming headlines that promise miracle cures for ticking time bombs. Just as well he's not the public relations chief for the union of headshrinkers, I thought. It wasn't exactly the ringing endorsement or lucrative incentive I'd been naively expecting. But, even without a hype-laden promise that I was going to be instantly healed and transformed, I couldn't help but feel a little bit triumphant. I was more than capable of providing the hype myself. Once I put my own spin on his prognosis, I began to feel slightly giddy, as if I'd been given an injection of adrenaline and amphetamine.

I'm a suitable candidate for psychotherapy, I praised myself. *Hallelujah! I'm taking control of my life. I'm getting myself sorted out before it's too late. I'm going to find peace and happiness and contentment and meaning at long last. And probably even a new boyfriend. A fabulous new boyfriend. And we'll have gorgeous, perfect children and live happily ever after, just like in the movies. This is a wonderful day. I am a suitable candidate of intensive psychoanalytic psychotherapy. Halle-bloody-lujah!*

I wanted to kiss him, but even *my* sense of drama had its limits, and, as if he could read my mind, he hastily said: 'Just a few more things. First, tell me what you hope to achieve from therapy.'

I decided against sharing my romantic fantasy and instead carefully pondered his question for a long time. What exactly was it that I was looking for? To be as happy as a swallow and as carefree as a child? Freedom from all my fears? A trouble-free, struggle-free life? Not quite. I wasn't that detached from reality. I knew that struggles and troubles and sadness were part of being alive. I had all my favourite life-affirming quotes pinned above my desk, after all. 'But a lifetime of happiness! No man could bear it; it would be hell on earth.' George Bernard Shaw, one of my favourites. I knew that the pursuit of happiness for its own sake was self-defeating. But I had never felt so hopeless and directionless and devoid of energy, enthusiasm and passion. Nor had I ever felt so terrifyingly out of control of my own feelings.

One of the things that had turned me from arch sceptic to potential convert was observing the transformation of a good friend from in-depth psychotherapy. She'd changed from a highly strung, unhappy woman into someone who was clearly much more contented, light-hearted and at peace with herself. She seemed as if the weight of the world had been lifted from her shoulders and was a very compelling advert.

But there was something else too. All my life I'd felt not quite good enough. Not smart enough. Not attractive enough. Not funny enough. Not anything enough. Not everything enough. I didn't know where it came from, because I didn't have high-achieving, pushy or over-critical parents. In the past, I'd looked on the positive side, reassuring myself that it's 'just the way I am' and that it was far better to be a driven, insecure, goal-setting, perfectionistic Type A personality than an under-achieving, lazy Type B one. But the truth was that it was beginning to cripple me. I was exhausted and fed up with persistently striving for some elusive goal. In addition, there was the depressing realisation that the self-protecting boundaries I'd set up for myself at the age of twenty-five – never allowing myself to get too close to anyone for fear of losing someone I loved ever again – had been counterproductive. What I had thought was self-sufficiency, I was beginning to see as self-deficiency. Many of my friends were settling down, getting married and having children. I felt as if time was running out for me. But, before I jumped into another dysfunctional relationship, I wanted to find out a bit more about myself, in particular why I had been repeating self-destructive patterns in relationships and what was behind my fears of love, loss, rejection, failure and commitment. I suppose my ultimate hope was that the next time the opportunity for real love came my way, I would be in a 'better place' and wouldn't be so quick to let it pass me by.

'I want to want to live again,' I said. I knew it sounded melodramatic, but it was the best way I had of describing how I truly felt. 'I want to get my passion back. I want to love life again rather than feel that it is an unbearable uphill struggle.' The psychiatrist leaned forward in his chair, looked at me with his kindly eyes and smiled knowingly. I, naturally, burst into tears again.

'There are no quick fixes for the human condition,' were the first of that lovely old man's final words to me. He almost whispered them, as if he were conveying a secret of great significance. 'Psychotherapy will be difficult at times. It will be painful and it will be frustrating. You will see things in yourself that you don't want to see, but, in the long run, I think you will find that it has been worth it.'

I knew this kind of therapy was expensive, so I asked if there were any trainee analysts available. It's not that I'm parsimonious. I've never been a £900 shoes and handbags woman, but I wouldn't think twice about investing what might seem like an obscene amount of money on a new Clarins moisturiser or a lash-lengthening mascara. Nor would I flinch at spending my hard-earned cash on regular haircuts and highlights, massages or a gym membership that at times was so embarrassingly under-used it ended up costing close to £100 for a monthly sauna. But the idea of paying someone more than my rent simply to have a conversation with them still seemed somewhat absurd.

There were, however, no low-cost amateurs available, and I was eventually referred to Dr J, a highly experienced professional with an excellent reputation. It was recommended that I see her three times a week for an open-ended period of time, but a suggested minimum of one year. Although a long-term commitment is required for this kind of therapy to work, it's not like a gym membership. You don't sign up to anything and lose your money if you bail out. You simply agree to turn up at fixed times and pay your bill at the end of each month. You can walk away at any time. I put aside a lifetime's worth of misgivings and took out a bank loan for eight thousand pounds, telling the manager it was for 'home improvements', which I thought sounded a bit better than 'mental health improvements'. It was enough towards a down payment on a flat, a new car or a round-the-world trip, but none of those things held any allure. All I wanted was to find out what the hell was going on inside my head.

* * *

Now, as I sat across from Dr J, I was beginning to think maybe I was crazier than I'd first thought. A mannequin could have performed the same role as her. She seemed to have taken a vow of silence, which I was paying for, and managed to make someone like Margaret Thatcher seem like a fluffy agony aunt.

I decided to try again and to be assertive about it. 'As I mentioned, I'm not really sure what to do here,' I said desperately. 'Should I just carry on telling you a bit about my life or would you prefer if I sat quietly for a while and you could ask me some direct questions?'

After a moment's pause, during which she never took her eyes off me, she said: 'Do whatever is agreeable for you.'

I let out a strange sound, combining a snort of derision and a grunt of sarcastic laughter. 'Sorry?'

'There is no need to apologise,' she said, before repeating, in the same level tone of voice, 'Do whatever is agreeable for you.'

'Do whatever is agreeable for me?' I parroted, with a very sceptical frown, as if her words were from another language. Which, in a way, they were.

She nodded.

'Well, okay,' I ventured hesitantly, tucking my hands underneath me. 'Would it be better for me to lie on the couch or just sit here? What difference does it make? What do your other clients, patients, whatever you call them, what do they do? What gets the best, the quickest, results?'

Dr J took her glasses off and consulted the ceiling for a moment. I followed her gaze. When she brought it back to me, I leaned forward. She replaced her glasses. 'Either or,' she said. 'Whatever is agreeable for you.'

'But what do your other clients do?'

'Why do you care?'

This is totally weird. I was just looking for a little bit of guidance. That's all. A little bit of freaking assistance. Is that too much to ask for?

But because I'm instinctively averse to any kind of open confrontation, I didn't say that, of course. I just smiled as politely as I could manage under the circumstances and fleetingly pondered the possibility that this might be my first and last session. It was way too crazy for me.

Not wanting to walk out or sit in silence or give her the opportunity to use her catchphrase one more time, I started to ramble about my fears of becoming dependent on therapy (even though I knew I wouldn't).

'Okay, well,' I said, remaining seated, 'I've heard about people ending up in therapy for years.' I laughed nervously. 'I'd hate to turn into one of those weak, needy women. I despise women like that.'

'Despise?' she said, as if she'd never heard the word before.

I nodded enthusiastically.

'It's a strong word for a woman who, in your eyes, is weak or having difficulties,' she said, missing the point entirely.

'Okay, maybe not despise,' I immediately conceded, feeling a little reprimanded. 'But hate. I hate weak, needy, pathetic, helpless women.'

'Hmmm,' she said, resting her chin on the thumb of her left hand and gazing at me in a way that made me feel as if I were an unusual exhibit in a zoo.

I remained on the same hobby-horse for the rest of the session, telling her I was afraid of getting brainwashed in therapy, because I thought of it as being a bit cult-like; I was afraid of turning into someone I'm not, losing my sense of humour, hating my parents, turning into a man-hater. I'd read about people who had recovered false childhood memories during therapy and I was terrified this would happen to me. Finally, though I didn't know a great deal about Freud, I knew enough. I was worried that this kind of therapy would make me want to murder my mother and sleep with my father. I pulled an ew-yuck-gross-vomit-can you imagine? face then giggled. Dr J continued to stare at me, as she had done during this entire monologue, as if it were I who was now speaking in a foreign language. Swahili or something.

I paused for breath.

'We have to stop now,' she said.

As I picked up my bag, I said: 'Thank you. Thank you very much indeed,' though I had no idea what exactly it was that I was expressing so much gratitude for. 'See you on Friday,' I added, pulling on my heavy winter coat. 'At 7 am?' I checked, even though I knew for certain that was the ridiculously early time we'd agreed. They were the only times she had available: Mondays at 7.40 am, Wednesdays at 6 pm (but not this first week) and Fridays at 7am. 'I'd normally still be in my bed at that time,' I said finally, trying to engage in a bit of normal, friendly chit-chat, 'but I'm totally committed to this, so see you at 7, then?' She responded with a single formal nod of her head and a weak non-committal smile.

I ran down the stairs, sprinted to my car and sat in it for a few minutes in a state of utter bewilderment. 'My therapist is a total fucking mental case,' I texted Katy.

'Projection,' she texted back. 'Your vast reservoir of repressed anger hurled onto her. Poor woman.'

'Stupid cow,' I mumbled, as I pressed delete. Still in shock, I headed to Kember and Jones, my favourite delicatessen, for my breakfast and to try to concentrate on reading the papers.

* * *

The following morning I was on the shuttle to London for a weekly editorial meeting at the *Observer*. Journalism gets a bad press at times, but, as a way to earn a living, I thought it was hard to beat. Compared with all the other mundane jobs I'd done, life under a constant deadline surrounded by some of the smartest and wittiest people I'd ever met was terrifying, exciting, stressful and addictive. I loved it. Everything about it. But every ointment has its fly, and mine was editorial meetings, which I dreaded and usually managed to avoid. The thought of having to give my uninformed opinion on the rest of the Sunday newspapers and then discuss world affairs in front of some of the most talented journalists in the country never failed to make me feel physically sick. As did having to suggest and talk through story ideas for the next weekend's edition.

Although I'd managed to be on time for once, I simply couldn't face it that morning. So I decided to make myself late by whiling away half an hour in the Costa Coffee outside Farringdon tube station nursing a mug of sweet milky tea.

When I eventually rushed in, I discovered, to my dismay, that the editorial meeting had been postponed. My boss and some reporters were in the newsroom, though. Offering a flurry of muffled apologies, the first thing I registered was someone saying: 'We should probably do a big piece on Travis this week.'

'Yeah, that's a good idea,' Tracy, the foreign editor, agreed. 'A big profile would be great.'

I thought it seemed a bit random but, always eager to please my superiors, I decided to volunteer. After all, my official role is Scotland editor and Travis *is* a Scottish band. 'I could do it,' I said chirpily, as I dropped my bag and jacket over a chair. I was used, in my job, to hiding my natural state of mild terror behind a mask of professional faux confidence, which had the undesired but frequent side-effect of rendering me dizzyingly verbose. 'So what's the hook? Have they got a new album coming out or something? I mean, it will be difficult for them following "Why Does It Always Rain On Me?" I love that song.' Any moment I was about to break into the chorus. 'I just loved those heartfelt lyrics. We could include a bit about the inspiration for that track. And I think the lead singer's a dad now. We could do something on how becoming a father has changed him and influenced his songwriting. And we could do a panel on other . . .'

I halted mid-sentence when I realised something was wrong. Where were the nods of agreement or thanks?

'What the hell *are* you talking about?' Tracy said, half-laughing but at the same time shaking her head in confusion. 'Has *who* got a new album coming out? *Who* has become a father?'

I hesitated. 'Er, Travis,' I said faintly. 'I thought you wanted a big piece on them.'

There was a moment's deathly silence. '*Chá-vez,*' she said slowly, emphasising each syllable. 'We're talking about Hugo Chávez, the president of Venezuela. We're thinking of doing a piece on him after the fiasco of last month's parliamentary elections and ahead of the presidential one.'

'Ah.' A fiasco? Hugo didn't know the meaning of the word. Ground – open up and take me away to a better, safer place.

Some faulty transmitter in my brain told me it would be a good idea to pretend that no one had heard me, even though my face was cooking with mortification. And so I managed to dig myself in a little bit deeper: 'Ah yes, of course. The election was indeed a fiasco. A total fiasco. Didn't that happen somewhere else, too, recently? Bolivia or Nicaragua or America or Scotland or somewhere like that? All these elections are like that. Ha ha ha. Right. Great. Chávez. Hugo Chávez. Elections. Venezuela. Brilliant. Right, must go to the ladies'.' I continued laughing nervously as I walked backwards out of the newsroom. Tracy, who knows what's happening in every corner of the globe, was left looking as if she didn't know whether to laugh or cry.

I rushed to the ladies and locked myself in a cubicle. God-All-fucking-Mighty, what the hell is wrong with me? Now, on top of everything else, I was going to have to look for another job. I'd never be able to face these people again. I'd have to start afresh. Somewhere new. Somewhere where no one knew me, or my inability to detect the difference between Chávez and bloody Travis. First, though, I had to attend the editorial meeting that I'd hoped to miss and pretend that I wasn't a complete idiot.

I slumped into a seat at the back of the room and tried to hide behind the political editor and the investigations editor. Kamal, who was a good friend as well as my boss, was at the head of a large desk and Lucy, his deputy, and another great friend, was sitting to his left. The table was strewn with all the Sunday papers, the sight of which sent my nerves into sudden overdrive. After they had discussed them all (apart from me, who hadn't said a word), the focus turned to the week ahead. Someone had an exclusive interview with the Prime Minister; the investigations editor had discovered that British officials had allowed the export to Iran of a cargo of radioactive material that experts believed could be used in a nuclear weapons programme. Round the table it went, with people pitching all their great ideas.

'Lorna, anything exciting happening with you this week?' Kamal asked. Shit. I'd been hoping, because I'd managed to avoid eye contact with him, that he might have forgotten about me. I had nothing. I frantically racked my brain for inspiration. Silence. Kamal looked at me expectantly.

I don't want to make the people I work with sound like a bunch of intimidating tyrants. They're anything but. Many of them are very good friends as well as colleagues. The terror, fear, inferiority complex were all in me. Since the day I started working there, they had been supportive, helpful and encouraging.

'Er, well . . . I've had a lot on my mind recently but the, er, smoking ban is going to destroy the environment. Apparently.' I ventured warily. Kamal looked at me quizzically. I told him that I'd heard that all these outdoor heaters would lead to a massive rise in greenhouse gases. 'We could do Planet Up In Smoke.' There was a moment's awkward silence. Kamal didn't actually say 'That sounds fucking ridiculous', but I could tell by the look on his face that that was the gist. 'Hmm. Anything else?' he asked.

With a rush of blood to the head, I said: 'Actually, I might have something. I've got this friend. A girl – single, thirty-something. On the outside she has it all – great job, great friends, perfect health. There's nothing really wrong with her life, but, then again, there's nothing really right with it either. For so long, she's been going around smiling and pretending nothing's up. She pretends to be all confident and happy but the facade is beginning to crumble. So, anyway, although she's a real sceptic, she's decided to go into therapy. Not just once a week, or for eight or ten weeks – that's kiddies' stuff. There are no quick fixes for the human condition, you know? There's a lot going on in our unconscious that we're not even aware of but which drives us in unsuspecting ways. She's going for the real deal – on the couch, three times a week. And she's got this absolutely intense, terrifying therapist, who's like the devil crossed with a Trappist monk. This is going to be a year that will kill her or cure her.'

Silence. Everyone turned to look at each other, then at me. 'It's not me, if that's what you're thinking,' I brayed nonchalantly. Then I pulled an apologetic face that said: 'Christ. Is it *that* obvious?'

Kamal smiled. He'd been one of several *Observer* colleagues who had very patiently mopped up several bouts of tears during the previous weeks and months, and who had gently suggested that I might find it helpful to talk to someone.

'Anyway,' I continued, 'this, er, friend of mine, well, she might be up for writing a piece about it. But we'd have to change her name. She won't want people knowing she's going to see a shrink. It's not that she's ashamed. There's no shame in it. But you know what people are like – they can be so judgmental. She won't want people getting the wrong idea and thinking she's nuts. Because she's not. There's absolutely nothing wrong with her.'

Suddenly the line sounded a bit unconvincing. 'Actually, there probably is something wrong with her,' I added hastily. 'But it's nothing serious. So she's got some issues. *Minor* issues.'

'Who hasn't?' Kamal said. 'But it takes strength to admit that and even more to do something about it.'

After the meeting I had a long chat with him about writing the article. He said he thought issues such as relationships, mental health and emotions were extremely important but difficult for many people to talk about. He also said he thought it would be brave to write about it, but urged me to think about the possible pitfalls of opening myself up.

I did and, a few days later, I called him and said I would like to write about going into therapy and would use my own name rather than a pseudonym. 'It might help other people, and challenge the stigma,' I said. At the time, I honestly thought these were my only motivations for sharing such an intimate secret with a potential audience of more than one million *Observer* readers.

* * *

The next night I was in one of my locals, Chinaski's, a hip bar in Charing Cross, minutes from my flat, with my friends Rachel (Thirty-two, works in TV. Tall, curvy, long dark curly hair. A great friend. We used to work together and have known each other for about eight years), Emily (Thirty, a stunning lawyer, looks like Jennifer Aniston, only more attractive. I met her on a post-graduate journalism course which she quit to pursue a legal career) and Katy (Thirty-six, the therapist, tall, great legs, shoulder-length brown hair, cool fringe. Although Katy had been my sister's best friend since they were teenagers, we'd gravitated towards each other over the past eighteen months simply because we were both single thirty-somethings). I decided to tell the rest of them – only Katy knew so far – that I was in therapy.

'Therapy?' shrieked Rachel. 'Are you joking? You've always said you thought it was a total con.'

'I did,' I said, nodding. 'I think I still do.'

'You know what they say,' Emily chipped in, throwing back the remnants of her wine. 'Anyone who would go to see a psychiatrist ought to have their head examined. Ha ha ha.'

I was just about to launch into my slick justification for going into therapy – possibly casually throwing in the famous Scottish psychiatrist R.D. Laing's maxim that, while we all like to think we know who we are, many of us are in fact strangers to our true selves; or my other one, from Socrates, about really knowing yourself before you can transform yourself – but I didn't get the chance. Katy gleefully took the opportunity to jump onto her soapbox. 'I think it's great. There's not one person around this table – in fact, there's probably not one person in this pub – who couldn't benefit from a bit of therapy. Look at us.' She was being polite. She meant: 'Look at you. Plural.' 'Smart, successful, independent women, but when it comes to relationships – total fuck-ups. We always blame the guys for being emotionally stunted or commitment phobic or for having arrested development, but, let's stop kidding ourselves, we're just as bad.' There were a few angry protests, including some from me, but she raised her voice to an embarrassing level and continued. 'Sadly,' she shouted, 'most people behave like children in relationships. They manipulate, they coerce, and they don't communicate openly and honestly. They seek out a mother or father figure. They repeat unhealthy patterns. They're passive-aggressive. They stay with people they don't really love because they're so fucking narcissistic they think the other person's life won't be worth living without them. Or they stay with people they don't love because they can't bear the thought of being on their own or of someone not liking them or feeling angry with them. Psychoanalytic therapy frees you from all that and enables you to form healthy, adult, equal relationships.'

Suddenly, forgetting about my bizarre and uncomfortable experience the other morning with Dr J, and the transient thoughts I'd had about not returning, I started grinning excitedly. It was going to be so brilliant to be cured. But my happy bubble was burst almost immediately when Rachel finally managed to get a word in edgeways.

'If therapy is so fucking wonderful, then how come you've not found Mr Right, married him and had his fabulous children?'

Good point, I thought. Very, very good point.

Katy shook her head wearily and rolled her eyes to the ceiling. 'There are other, equally fulfilling ways to live happily ever after,' she said airily.

'Really?' I asked in complete amazement. I wondered what they were. I glanced around our table and was pleased to see that Rachel and Emily looked as baffled as me.

So we ordered another bottle of wine and talked about something much more interesting: the emotionally stunted and commitment-phobic men in, or at least on the periphery of, our lives.

* * *

Despite my reservations, I went back to Dr J for more of the same. My next few sessions proceeded the same way. All the normal rules of polite society were left outside the door to her consulting room. We didn't 'chat'. She didn't ask any probing questions. She didn't offer any advice or recommendations. I sat down, smiled, waited for her to say something – 'tell me about your day, your mother, your father, your sexual fantasies, your love life, your dreams, your earliest memory' – anything, but she never did. So I began to yammer. And I continued. Going on. And on. And on. About whatever was at the forefront of my mind. Until she said it was time to stop.

If the average person talks at a rate of around 180 words per minute, then during these early sessions I reckon I was notching up somewhere between an excited auctioneer's 250 wpm and the average 350 wpm spoken by an enthusiastic government policy debater. The words were pouring out of me in barrages like machine-gun fire. Allowing for tear breaks and the occasional silence, I must have been spewing out around 14,000 words (that's a novelette) during each of those fifty-minute sessions. Dr J, meanwhile, was going at a rate of less than one word per minute. 'Please come in . . . We have to stop.' Occasionally, if she was in a talkative mood, she'd home in on one word, which often seemed an irrelevant one, and steer me off in a completely unexpected direction. It was all very odd.

* * *

One morning, when the snow outside her window was falling in merry chaos, I was telling her about my previous dabbling in therapy. It was of the cognitive behavioural variety (CBT), the most widely practised and popular of all approaches in the western world. This kind of treatment is short-term and much more structured than the kind I was now having. In CBT, the therapist plays more of a friend or 'life coach' role and has no interest in what's going on in your unconscious, but simply aims to change the way you think, feel and behave by teaching you to challenge automatic negative thoughts. I had five sessions a couple of years ago when I was suffering from nothing particularly interesting or debilitating; just the same, but less acute, fears and anxieties that were bothering me now.

At the time, I had not long joined the *Observer* and, although I went down to London once a week, the rest of the time I was working from home and had found the change from the busy hustle and bustle of a city centre newsroom to virtual isolation really difficult to adjust to. I remember reading somewhere about the first year of motherhood being the loneliest in a woman's life, as she is cut off from work colleagues and friends with little adult company, and I felt a bit like that. Obviously, I didn't have the sleepless nights or hormonal hell, but I hadn't realised the extent to which we are social animals and I'd taken colleagues for granted. Like most human beings, I was used, from the age of five onwards, to spending most of my days surrounded by and talking to people, whether it be at school, college or various workplaces. For the first time in my life, I was facing every day with no colleagues and only my own four walls for company.

But, after five sessions of CBT, I quit.

'It's a load of crap,' I said to an expressionless Dr J. 'It's superficial and simplistic. You have a negative thought, you challenge it, and replace it with a positive one. Smile and you'll be happy. Commit an act of kindness. Write down a list of things that went well today. It's no more than a band-aid. It papers over the cracks. Any loss is reinterpreted as a gain; a rejection as an opportunity. You feel good for a little while, until you realise that the power of positive thinking isn't all it's cracked up to be. It's delusional to think positively all the time. In fact, you realise that positive psychology is a pile of total bullshit.'

'It seems to work for some,' she said annoyingly. To my ears, her words sounded cold enough to have come straight from outside the window behind her.

In contrast to CBT, psychoanalytic psychotherapy, the kind I was having, started with the discoveries of Freud a century ago, and assumes that unconscious motives influence how we function. It includes the impulses and ideas, the wishes and fears which operate out of sight and awareness, but exert a powerful influence over our attitudes and behaviour. This kind of therapy is, according to some information I'd found on the Internet, the most ambitious and most complex of all the 'talking cures' and is intended to help people understand and resolve their problems by increasing awareness of these subterranean motivations and how they affect relationships, both past and present. In some ways it's the opposite of positive psychology – rather than ignoring negative or uncomfortable feelings or immediately transforming them into positives, the aim is to get in touch with deeply buried difficult or uncomfortable emotions and become better equipped at handling them. It differs from other therapies in aiming for deep-seated change and emotional development. It is ultimately about exploring why we feel what we feel, fear what we fear, think what we think and do what we do. All the literature stressed that 'the relationship with the therapist is crucial'. But I seemed to be having a bit of a problem forming any kind of meaningful connection with Dr J.

After sharing my previous brief experience of therapy, I told her I had interviewed the 'grandfather' of CBT in New York a few years ago.

'He called me a crazy fucking love slob,' I said, trying to force Dr J to crack a smile. 'But then he said all human beings are out of their minds. Screwballs, he said, every single one of them. And that's from a top psychotherapist!'

She didn't ask for more information – she just sat staring at me like I was some kind of unusual creative – but I gave it anyway.

Albert Ellis, who was ninety-one when I met him and who died recently at the age of ninety-three, had been described as one of the world's most eminent psychotherapists and was ranked by the American Psychological Association as the most influential of the twentieth century (after Carl Rogers and ahead of Freud).

After I interviewed him, I attended one of his infamous Friday night workshops. Described as stand-up psychotherapy, Ellis had, for thirty years, demonstrated his unique technique on two volunteers in front of an audience of up to one hundred. He was also the exception to the rule that CBT therapists were generally friendly and supportive, though he certainly made up for it with charisma and entertainment value. I decided that this was a once-in-a-lifetime chance. And, since I was thousands of miles from home, I volunteered. I climbed onto the stage. I told Dr J about my 'session' with him, which he gave me a tape of and which went like this:

ME (shouting into a microphone, as Ellis is hard of hearing): I think I might have a bit of a fear of rejection.
ELLIS: Give us an example.
ME: Well, I would never ask a guy out in case he said no. And I would never let a guy know that I liked him in case the feeling wasn't mutual.
ELLIS: How would you feel if a guy rejected your advances?
ME: Oh, you know, just crap, really. Humiliated, not good enough, just, you know, rejected. Embarrassed.
ELLIS: You know what you are? You're another crazy fucking love slob. This city is full of them. Yours probably is too. A screwball with a dire need for other people's love and approval. Why should everyone love and approve of Lorna, huh? It's a pretty Godlike demand you're after. You're like every other human being: fucked up. Of course some guys are going to reject you. The way to get over your phobia of rejection is to get used to it. If someone turns you down, it doesn't mean you're a worm or a louse. When someone rejects you, you have a choice: you can feel sad and say too damn bad or you can whine and scream endlessly, like you obviously like to do, and say it's awful, I'm no good, I can't stand this, I'm a reject, a no-goodnik. Nobody loves me. Nobody loves poor Lorna. Boo-fucking-hoo!
ME: (stunned silence)

ELLIS: Don't worry, I think I can probably make you saner, but you're going to have to work your ass off.

ME: (still stunned, still silent)

ELLIS: First, we're going to have to get you desensitised to rejection. When you get home to Glasgow, go into a bar and pick a few men that you're pretty damn sure will reject you. Ask them out and get yourself rejected. Then pick another ten men and get rejected ten more times. Do it again and you'll start to see that being turned down isn't nice, but it isn't fatal either.

ME: Hmm.

ELLIS: I think you'd also benefit from trying some of my shame-attacking exercises.

ME: Huh?

ELLIS: Get on a bus or the subway and yell out the stops at the top of your lungs. And just pretend it's completely normal behaviour. What are the stops on your subway?

ME: Er, Hillhead, Partick, Buchanan Street.

ELLIS: Right, so you get on and yell at the top of your voice: HILLHEAD. And everyone stares at you, because they think you're crazy. But you're not embarrassed, you're amused. Or walk into a store and shout the time: 'Ten thirty-three and all's well!' These exercises can show you, like they've shown hundreds of my clients, that no one can make you feel ashamed or embarrassed or humiliated or angry or anxious. No one can make you feel almost anything unless they take a baseball bat to the side of your head. You control your inner states of feeling and you have a choice about how you feel.'

ME: Righto!

ELLIS: By the way, don't worry too much: you're not alone. Practically all human beings have strong, innate and learned tendencies to act like babies all their lives.'

'He was a crazy old guy,' I said to Dr J, who had remained silent and expressionless throughout. 'Do you know,' I continued, 'when I returned home to Glasgow, I actually took him literally and tried to do it – to get myself desensitised to rejection. But I didn't manage to ask one person out, never mind ten. My worry wasn't just that I would be repeatedly turned down, I was also afraid that someone would actually say yes. I was afraid that I'd go for one casual drink with a guy who was meant to reject me and end up stuck with someone who wasn't the love of my life for the rest of my life. What's that all about, then?'

Ignoring not only my question, but everything I'd said in the last fifteen minutes or so, she gave me a Paddington Bear hard stare and said: 'How are you feeling just now?'

I tried not to frown, even though I thought her question was somewhat odd and irrelevant. 'Fine. Great, thanks,' I automatically replied.

Silence.

'How are you feeling about me and you?' she said a moment later.

I glanced around the room, felt my thumb heading towards my mouth (not to suck – I'm not that screwed up – but to bite my nail). I have no idea why her question made me feel so uncomfortable, but it did. 'Fine,' I repeated, shrugging my shoulders and trying not to look alarmed.

'Are you sure? Any other feelings? Any hostility? Or anger? Or frustration?'

'Nope,' I shook my head. I was raised to be polite. I wasn't going to tell her that I thought she was totally mental and had a strange way about her. 'I honestly feel pretty good. All this talking, this therapy stuff, it's fantastic. Just getting everything off my chest. Yeah, it's great. It's helping a lot.'

'Hmmm,' she said, her chin leaning on the thumb of her left hand. 'You're not putting a positive spin on how you're really feeling.'

'No,' I said, feeling increasingly like a guilty criminal under investigation.

I got the feeling she didn't believe me. But I wasn't joking. Although I thought she had terrible social skills, I *had* been feeling much better of late. Despite the staring and the silences and the general weirdness of if all, it was great to talk uninterrupted and unchallenged for nearly three hours a week about me, myself and I, or anything else on my mind. I left the sessions during the first three weeks feeling a mixture of confusion combined with giddy exhilaration and relief. It was strangely seductive to unburden myself of all my woes and to have someone's undivided, rapt attention. It felt, initially, like confession for non-believers, but without even the punishment of having to say a few Hail Marys; of the soothing reward, if you're that way inclined, of being promised a place in heaven.

In fact, I'd been feeling so good that I was beginning to think I was cured already. I've always been a quick learner, I praised myself. Maybe it's just other people who need months or years of this treatment? Maybe I only needed a few weeks to get it all out?

I was thinking it might be time to say goodbye to Dr J and blow the rest of my bank loan on a luxury holiday and a fab new wardrobe. I thought this until I was sent to Koh Samui in Thailand for work and I did something so mindlessly, insanely dumb, that I realised the surface had barely been scratched.

February

Is it Good to Talk?

I arrived at Koh Samui Island Airport, four flights and two days after I left Glasgow, at around 10 pm local time. I was dressed in jeans, my favourite black woollen polo neck, a hand-knitted cardigan, a fleece, thermal gloves and a pair of furry boots. It was snowing when I left home, but I quickly discovered that, in Thailand, it was summer almost all year round, not to mention nearly twenty-four hours a day. By the time I collected my somewhat conspicuous suitcase on wheels – every other item of luggage appeared to be a large backpack – I resembled a rickshaw operator after a long shift. Although I seldom look my elegant best drenched with sweat and with damp hair plastered to my head, the heat was only one of my problems. There was also the small nagging concern that I had nowhere to stay.

When my boss, Kamal, had asked two and a half days earlier if I wanted to go to the island, immediately, to write a feature about the myth of paradise following the murder of a young backpacker and numerous alleged rapes, I said yes before he'd finished the sentence. I very rarely said no to anyone and certainly not to my editor. Plus, I regarded foreign assignments as golden opportunities to be seized with both hands before they were offered to someone else.

But, in my heart of hearts, as I repeatedly thanked Kamal for offering me this fabulous assignment, I knew that I was also jumping at the chance of putting 6,000 miles between me and the Christian affair. To my shame, I was still playing the role (emotionally if not physically) of the other woman – or one of them, at any rate. I'd even phoned him the day before I left in an anxious frenzy after I'd heard that, despite his assurances to the contrary, he was still seeing Charlotte.

'This is history repeating itself,' I sobbed at him before he'd even said hello. 'Why do you have to be so weak? Why do men have to be so weak? Why can't you just say no to her?' I attempted to regain some poise by paraphrasing a great line from George Cukor's classic bitch-fest movie *The Women*, about a man having only one escape from his old self – to see a different self in the mirror of some other woman's eyes. But it came out all wrong and Christian burst out laughing and said: 'What the fuck are you talking about? I've told you a hundred times: there's nothing going on. We're just friends. We hang out. We go for coffee. We have lunch. We discuss briefs.'

'That's what I'm afraid of.'

'Ha ha, Lorna. But seriously. You're imagining things. I could have her if I wanted – it's there on a plate – but that's why I'm not that interested. As you know only too well, I prefer a really tough challenge – someone who tries so damn hard to resist me but then eventually crumbles. So, please, will you calm the fuck down.'

I apologised tearfully for being such a nightmare. I was no match for the persuasive reasoning of a highly successful lawyer, especially one that I was still hopelessly in love with.

I shook my head to dislodge the memory of that unpleasant conversation, and grabbed my laptop, mobile, notepad and a couple of changes of clothes. Here's to another stamp on my passport, I thought. When I'd gushed to my sister Louise about the week-long trip, she laughed and said I'd do anything to avoid journeying inside my own mind. I forgave her, knowing that her blatant jealousy was only natural. After all, when she wasn't work-ing, she was stuck at home all day with her cute but conversationally challenged twenty-month-old son, Lewis, affectionately known as King Lewis. He calls me, to the great amusement of the rest of my family, 'uh-oh', which is very sweet and wouldn't bother me at all if it weren't for the fact that he can say a much less ambiguous version of everyone else's name – Mama, Dada, Gannee, Ganda, even Kitee. And there is, of course, also the fact that 'uh-oh' is the internationally recognised term for 'here comes trouble'. I've invested countless hours trying to teach Lewis to get his tongue around the letter 'L', so that he can perhaps manage the faintly exotic sounding Lo-lo or Lola or even La-la, which has marginally less disturbing connotations. But to no avail. It's beyond his grasp. He looks at me with a baffled little frown on his brow, which breaks into a grin as he points a chubby finger directly at me and, unfooled, says: 'Uh-oh'.

Fully living up to the name, I was now standing, gently steaming but trying against all the odds to maintain my cool, in the tiny airport terminal, wondering what to do next. I was supposed to have asked the newsdesk administrator to arrange accommodation, but hadn't, deciding instead to find somewhere when I arrived. I'll be fine, I told myself. I'd turned up at far-flung destinations before and not had any problems finding a place to stay. Plus, it added to the image I liked to hold of myself as an adventurous, brave and fearless journalist in pursuit of truth and justice. Or at least a good story.

But even I was beginning to think that I'd have done better to plan ahead. A glut of taxi drivers swarmed around me, all wearing the famous, if slightly disconcerting, 24/7 Thai smile. I scanned their faces and, based on little more than his cool little pony-tail and beanie hat, nodded like a prom queen choosing a dance partner at a young man who introduced himself as Burut. When he grabbed my suitcase, I noticed that his eyes had the far-away rheumy glaze of a methadone addict, but it seemed too late and too much hassle to change my mind. As soon as we closed the doors on his dilapidated cab, though, he calmly unfolded a clear bag full of large green leaves, took one out, rolled it up and started chewing. He then raised an eyebrow and extended the bag to me. I shook my head and swallowed hard. I later found out the leaf was Ton Lamphong, a highly toxic plant that many Thai men chew constantly. Although legal, if you're not used to it, it can turn you into a hallucinating zombie, I discovered in my *Lonely Planet*. Figuring me for a boozehound instead, Burut offered me a can of lukewarm Singha beer, which I accepted, to make up for rudely refusing to partake of his drugs. Then he cracked one open for himself.

'Okay. You go where?' he asked, in his broken English.

I showed him the four hotels I'd highlighted in my out-of-date guidebook and asked which one he'd recommend.

He laughed. 'Full, full, full, full,' he said, pointing at each one on the page. It was high season, he explained, adding that the island was so busy that some 'farangs' – foreigners – had been found sleeping in the sacred temples.

To stop myself from panicking, I told myself that Burut was probably just fooling with me. The Thais are well known for having a cheeky sense of humour. I smiled knowingly. He was probably on commission from the owner of another hotel. 'Can you suggest somewhere?' I asked with a grin. He shook his head, then shrugged his shoulders and said: 'Beach hut?'

Had it not been in and around the beach huts that the recent attacks had occurred, I'd have gladly slept there. Taking my horrified silence as an answer, Burut escorted me around the island for the next two hours, skilfully, if drunkenly, negotiating the pot-holed narrow roads. Somehow he managed to avoid several head-on collisions with jeeps travelling in the dark without lights, flotillas of motorcycles and numerous overloaded tuk-tuks all honking furiously along the way. I begged one hotel manager after another to give me a roof over my head for the night. A cupboard, or even a manger would have done by this point. But Burut clearly hadn't been joking: there were no rooms available. I sat in his cab with my head in my hands, repeating: 'What am I going to do? What the fuck am I going to do? This is a nightmare. I am a complete fucking nightmare.'

Incongruously, a vision of Dr J came unbidden into my mind. She was raising a sardonic eyebrow.

By now it was around one in the morning, 6 pm in the UK. I could have phoned my mum or my boss or Louise, Katy, Emily or

Rachel and asked them to go online and help me out, but I was too embarrassed to tell anyone about my crass stupidity. The faintest hint of smug righteousness in anyone's voice would have been more than I could bear.

So when Burut eventually said: 'You come stay with me?' it didn't seem as utterly insane as it does now that I agreed. In my defence, he did assure me that he had an English girlfriend. I asked if I could speak to her, but he looked at his watch and shook his head. It was too late, he said. She'd be asleep and he didn't want to wake her. Plus, he added as an afterthought, they'd had a bit of an argument and weren't on speaking terms. At least I think that's what he said.

My only other valid option at this point was a little hut on the beach. Because of recent events, the latter seemed too risky. I'd spent the last three hours with Burut and he'd been nothing other than the perfect, if awesomely drunk and wasted, gentleman. Plus, I was a well-travelled, highly experienced journalist from the world-famous London *Observer*, for God's sake. I'd been an honoured overnight guest in households before while reporting from Bosnia and parts of Africa. (I'd been with other people on those trips, mind you, but I conveniently glossed over those not insignificant details for the time being.) I don't need to stay in a westernised, sanitised five-star hotel when I could experience the real Koh Samui, get under its skin, hang out with the locals, get the true story behind the picture postcard image. This is hard-hitting cutting-edge journalism; I might even get an award for it, I thought, beginning to get slightly carried away with excitement at the very prospect. As I drained my second Singha, crumpling the can, I wondered what dress I'd wear to the awards ceremony, whether I should put my hair up or wear it down and what I'd say in my thank-you speech.

Are you out of your freaking mind, you lunatic? Don't you realise this guy could be an axe-murderer? And that not a soul in the world knows where you are right now? All questions I'd have done well to have asked myself at this point.

Instead: 'Do you absolutely promise to God that you have an

English girlfriend?' I beseeched Burut, momentarily forgetting that, had he been a homicidal maniac, he probably wouldn't have had too many qualms about telling a little lie to the next victim about his relationship status. He nodded and scrolled through the contacts stored on his mobile phone to show me that there was indeed a Linda in his address book and a text message from her. This was the name he'd mentioned earlier so, in my desperate and brainless state, I took it as convincing evidence that he was a trustworthy and upstanding member of the local community. I heaved a huge sigh of relief, apologised for asking so many intrusive personal questions and accepted the invitation.

I must have retained a smidgen of common sense, though, because I asked if he would give me his number so that I could text it to a friend. I sent Rachel a message with his name and number. To everyone else back home, I sent vague texts saying things like: 'All well. Will call ltr x'.

Any negative thoughts about what I was doing, or about the not so trivial subject matter I was there to report on, were automatically, conveniently pushed to the farthest recesses of my mind.

Burut sang during the half-hour drive inland through lush mountains and over a hair-raising single track road to his house. I drank two more Singhas, figuring that the best way to get through this was in a slightly drunken haze. I even contemplated chewing a couple of his leaves, which had certainly taken him to a very happy and chilled-out place. Eventually, he pulled up outside one of a cluster of Portakabins in the middle of a forest. It was now around two in the morning. He unlocked the front door and I stepped into a small living room, with an even smaller kitchen area off to the side. He started rolling a joint. When he offered it to me, I shook my head and asked where I would be sleeping. He showed me a tiny spare room with a single bed and not much else. I closed the door, collapsed on it and fell asleep.

The next morning I met Linda. She looked much older than Burut, but, after an initial frostiness, seemed happy enough to play hostess to an unexpected visitor. She suggested that Burut should act as my driver and 'fixer'. She'd give me a good price for his services, and for the room, which she said I was welcome to have for another night. From this distance, it seems too insane to be true, but now fancying myself as a cross between an adventurous journalist and an overgrown gap-year student, I gratefully accepted.

That afternoon, Burut drove me around the island and I met some people I could interview later for the story. Burut chewed his leaves and drank several Singhas. At night, we went into the main town of Lamai and had dinner. He left me to explore and said he'd pick me up at a cafe at midnight. The town was teeming with traffic, the air thick with dust and petrol fumes. Stalls offering lethal local whisky and fake designer goods competed for pavement space with stray dogs and street vendors selling chickens and ducks. On the narrow road, hundreds of motorcycles tried to out-do each other by constantly blasting their horns, while dilapidated jeeps crawled along, their tannoys blaring adverts for the best foam parties in town and Thai lady boxing.

In and outside the freak show neon-lit 'lady bars', paunchy, balding, middle-aged western men in their ghastly leisure-wear paraded young, beautiful Thai women on their arms with unashamed pride. The world is a crazy place, I thought. I spoke to several backpackers, then, at around midnight, Burut and I headed back to his home.

Burut was, by that stage, even more wasted than he'd been the previous night. Every so often, on the drive home, he would take his eyes off the road, turn to look at me, and start grinning. I smiled back nervously, then fixed my gaze on the road ahead so that I could alert him to any looming hair-pin bends, or grab the wheel if necessary. When we entered their house, he put his finger to his lips and pointed towards his and Linda's bedroom.

I quietly put down my bag, bent over to get my contact lenses case and then, holy bloody fucking Christ. I felt something. It was a hand, undoubtedly the same one that had so recently been rolling those large green leaves, placed gently but firmly on my backside. I froze. HolymotherofGodAlmighty. What was I going to do? I wondered whether I had the strength and speed to run for

my life. But where would I go? I glanced around to see if there
were any sharp implements to hand. There weren't, so I inhaled
deeply, stood up and turned around 180 degrees. He didn't lunge,
probably because he was too spaced out. Instead, he sort of
swayed towards me, a bit like a zombie, with his arms outstretched and his unfocused eyes and open mouth inches from my
screwed-up-in-horror face. I threw my hands up over my nose
and mouth and adroitly swerved towards the kitchen area in
desperate search of a weapon of some kind.

While I was rifling through a drawer hoping to find a rolling
pin, I snuck a quick glance back into the living room area, fully
expecting to see my host advancing towards me with his trousers
round his ankles. But thank God for the miraculous properties
of Ton Lamphong and Singha: he had collapsed on the sofa, his
mouth still wide open. Calm, calm, calm, I urged myself, as I crept
back into the living room towards my bag. Shit! I nearly stood on
a kitten. There was a high-pitched meow, which woke Burut
up. He looked irritably at me, mumbled something incoherent
under his breath and stumbled off to bed. I, meanwhile, spent
the rest of the night sitting frozen still in a chair, feeling a com-
bination of relief, shame and utter dismay at my own spectacular
stupidity.

In the morning, I gave Linda a wad of cash and asked if she
could phone me a cab to take me into the main port town of Na
Thon. She wanted to wake Burut so that he could drive me, but,
thrusting another couple of thousand Baht into her hand, I managed to convince her that it wasn't a good idea. I suggested that
because he'd had two late nights driving around the island, he
should be left to sleep. She eventually agreed.

At Na Thon, I went to an Internet cafe and, after a couple of
hours surfing and phoning, eventually found myself a room: in
the most expensive hotel on the island. Very westernised. Very
sanitised. My intrepid girl-reporter pose had evaporated. And it
was destined to become even less tangible when, later that
evening, my mobile phone, my lifeline, was stolen while I sat at a
bar, relaxing for the first time since I'd arrived. Fortunately, I was

waiting to meet a photographer who'd come down from Bangkok. When he appeared, I wrapped my arms around him and clung to him in a bear hug. 'This cannot get any worse,' I muttered into his shoulder. 'It's only a phone,' he said, whilst trying to extract himself from my embrace.

We managed, over the next three days, to find enough people to talk to for the story. I interviewed businesspeople, backpackers and the head of the local police force. But on the Saturday morning, now five days after I'd arrived on the island, and just as I was about to file my story, my laptop crashed and I lost all my work. I had no backup. I called Kamal in a tearful frenzy. He was as cool, composed and encouraging as ever. But it didn't change the fact that two blank pages were waiting to be filled. I had ninety minutes to write 3,000 words from scratch using the Internet in the hotel lobby. Some journalists are naturals who can dash off finely tuned prose as effortlessly as I can burst into tears, but I'm not one of them. Somehow, I got the job done without even splitting an infinitive, but I was beginning to wonder if I was cut out for this journalism malarkey. I felt as if I'd aged a decade in that hour and a half.

The story safely, finally, sent, I headed straight to the hotel bar, and drank a Singha and a large tequila. Mid-afternoon, thoroughly exhausted and slightly tipsy, I staggered outside and fell asleep, fully clothed (thankfully) on a sun-lounger. When I woke up, in the early evening, having dreamt of being chased around a kitchen by a giant knife-wielding green leaf watched by a laughing Dr J, I could hardly open my severely sunburnt eyes.

The following day, as I boarded the plane home, I told myself that I didn't look ridiculous, even though I had bright pink dabs of dried-on calamine lotion covering my lobster-hued swollen eyelids. I looked like I was wearing a vivid shade of scarlet eyeshadow to which I'd had a nasty allergic reaction. But though redder, I was also a little wiser. I was beginning to realise that what I liked to call spontaneous and adventurous was really nothing more than reckless and irresponsible. And I seemed to have learnt the hard way that running away from the difficulties in my life wasn't going to be the answer. In fact, as I looked out of the aeroplane window at the paradise island of Koh Samui, I could hardly wait to get back to cold, wintry Glasgow and, strangely enough, to Dr J.

* * *

'Of all the world's wonders, which is the most wonderful? That no man, though he sees others dying around him, believes that he himself will die.' I recited this quote at my next session with Dr J. It's from *The Mahabharata*, a Sanskrit epic from ancient India. I told her I'd found it in a magazine I'd read on the plane home. 'That's what I was like in Koh Samui. I just thought nothing bad would ever happen to me. The terrible things I read about and sometimes report on – they happen to other people. Not me. I was like a naive teenager, still thinking I was immune to the dangers of the world. Thinking, you know, that I was in some way special. And therefore invulnerable.' I shook my head.

I'd been anticipating therapy with so much eagerness that I'd conveniently forgotten that there would be no warm welcome. When I told her about Thailand, she neither sympathised with nor criticised my behaviour. Nor did she express relief that I was still alive or laugh at my sunburnt eyelids. She simply sat and listened, with that disconcerting, expressionless stare, saying 'hmmm' and nodding every now and again.

After recounting all the details, a lot of the time with my head half hidden behind my hands, I told her that it had made me think very carefully, for the first time in my life, about the motivation for my behaviour. In the past, if I'd given any thought at all to it, I'd have said that I just had to get the story, it's my job, it's just the way it is, it's just the way I am. But, on the long journey home, I thought about all the times I had put my life in danger, without giving so much as a fleeting thought to the potential consequences.

I didn't really understand how the relatively short spell of therapy had made me think about this, but for some reason it had.

'I'm not trying to make myself sound like Martha Gellhorn or

John Simpson, or any of the hundreds of other journalists who risk life and limb reporting on wars and investigating human rights violations in far-off countries,' I told Dr J, 'but I have taken a lot of risks – unnecessary in many cases – in my career. For the first time I thought, really thought, about why. Why on earth did I do that? Why am I so averse to making plans? Why did I not do what my boss had suggested and ask his assistant to book accommodation? Why did I stay with a taxi driver I'd known for three hours? Why couldn't I ask him if he would mind, at the very least, not drinking and taking drugs while driving? Why? Why? Why? Do I value my life so little? Or do I really believe I'm invincible? I don't know which is worse. Or more stupid.'

If Dr J had her own theory, or was curious about mine, she was keeping it to herself. Indeed, her cards were practically glued to her chest. She hadn't yet shared any opinions, observations, searing insights, earth-shattering observations, or whatever it was she was thinking about me. Somewhat selfish, it has to be said, considering her hourly rate. I was, at this stage, simply paying someone to listen to me. Absurd, I know.

With no other option, I was left to peek around the room looking for clues to Dr J's personality. She was, as usual, immaculately dressed, in another expensive-looking suit and smart shoes, covering feet that she was able to keep absolutely still, without even the slightest fidget. She seemed to have adopted a modified version of *The Thinker*, sitting with her right hand tucked under her left elbow and her left hand crooked under her chin. The room was always quite dimly lit, with two floor lamps, and warm. In one corner, there was a large plant, a eucalyptus, I think. Not much data there. I built up fantasies about the two framed photographs on her desk: sometimes I imagined she had two daughters and the photos were of them. Other times I thought maybe the pictures were of a golden retriever or her husband, if she had one, or her parents. Or Freud. Or her favourite patients.

When it became clear she wasn't going to share her thoughts on the Thailand escapade, I spilled out some more of mine. Not the most disturbing ones, though – I couldn't quite put those into words yet. Instead, I told her that it had also made me think about other stupid things I'd done in the past.

'In the two jobs I had before the *Observer*, I handed my notice in three times at each, even though I didn't have other jobs to go to. If something annoyed me or I was having a crap day, I just thought, right, I've had enough. I'm off. Luckily I had editors who, when I went back to them sheepishly an hour or a day later, allowed me to withdraw my resignation. Like Thailand, I'd always thought this was just about being free-spirited and spontaneous, but now I'm starting to think maybe there's a bit more to it.'

Dr J decided to exercise her vocal chords. 'Impulsive perhaps, rather than spontaneous?'

'Yeah, exactly,' I said, even though I didn't know what the difference was until I went home and looked it up. (Impulse drives the inner brat. Spontaneous people are flexible and like to do things on the spur of the moment. Impulsive people take spontaneity to the extreme. They are ruled by their inner brats. They don't think about the consequences of their actions. They can be naive, like children.)

'But then what's the alternative?' I asked Dr J. 'You never take a risk? You don't go out and explore and experience the world. You stay in, too afraid to venture out in case something bad happens to you.'

After a while, she said: 'Do you think they are the only two options – one extreme or the other?'

There wasn't a hint of accusation or criticism in her question, but it didn't matter. I was offended. 'No. Of course I don't think they are the only two options,' I sniffed. I decided against sharing with her a conversation I'd had earlier that day with Kamal after he'd asked if I wanted to go to China later in the year. 'Absolutely no way,' I replied. 'I don't want to sound ungrateful and thanks for offering, but after Thailand I don't want to leave home ever again. I don't want to do any more foreign assignments. I'm staying in Glasgow forever.'

Because I wasn't used to saying no to my boss, I'd been feeling pretty good about what I had thought was my new-found assertiveness. Now, thanks to this odd woman who was supposed to be making me feel better about myself, the feel-good factor had disappeared. In its place was the realisation that I was indeed an extreme, black or white, all or nothing thinker. Hmmmm.

* * *

Although I remembered the words of that kind old psychiatrist – about not expecting a quick fix – I was still secretly yearning for a fast, tangible transformation: my passport to secular heaven. I'd always been impatient. I wanted to see the fruits of my labour.

But it wasn't until mid-February that I finally plucked up the courage to introduce Dr J to the details of the Christian, Uh-oh and Charlotte axis, the subject about which I'd been obsessing for months and which had led me to her door in the first place. I'd mentioned, during previous outpourings, that I was embroiled in a 'bad situation', but I hadn't elaborated until now.

'My mind is infested with visions of the two of them together – laughing, talking, flirting,' I admitted one dreary morning, after giving her all the sordid details. 'I understand *here*,' I gestured to my head, 'that it's insane and irrational. But it doesn't get into *here*,' I said, pointing to my heart. 'And it's driving me out of my mind. He gets away with everything: he goes out, has a laugh, flirts away with the next stupid woman and I sit at home in tears. And I know I have no one to blame but myself, which just makes it even worse. I'm so angry with myself for ever having been so fucking stupid.'

I saw a wan flicker in Dr J's eyes. 'You are feeling angry with yourself?' She spoke slowly and deliberately, as if every single word she deemed worth uttering had been very carefully chosen.

'Yes,' I snapped. 'That's why I can't stop crying. Whenever I get angry, which isn't often, because I don't do anger, I cry.'

'Is this a pattern – turning your anger inwards?' I looked at her, my face screwed up with a mixture of confusion and irritation, and sighed. She was fanatically keen to focus on anger, but I was having none of it, anger is so unattractive and I'm not generally an angry person (as I was constantly telling her). So I brusquely interrupted her rare attempt at extended speech, and offered my own interpretations.

'I'll tell you about a pattern,' I volunteered. 'I seem to be repeating a pattern of falling for bad boys: the kind who isn't strong enough to say no when another woman comes along, as she invariably will, and flatters his fragile ego. The kind who pretends he's single when he's actually with someone. The kind who needs to keep a constant gaggle of women lusting after him. The jerk.'

'It's always easier to focus on other people's flaws and weaknesses and to blame them,' she said in her quiet, level tone, 'but that means you avoid having to look at your part in this. What's much more interesting for us to explore is why you might have been attracted to that kind of man in the first place.'

I shrugged. 'I once read somewhere that the difference between rats and people is that when a rat gets shocked at one end of a maze he never goes there again. Humans, on the other hand, repeat the same unhappy destructive relationship patterns over and over again, always trying to create a happy ending. I've noticed it before in friends. They always go for the same type. Some want to mother their partners. Others want to control them or change them. I'm only now beginning to see it in myself.'

The only man I've ever gone out with who did not conform to type was my lovely ex, a tall, dark, handsome, witty and intelligent Scot, a top-notch political journalist, who had wanted to settle down and have children. He was completely secure in himself, the kind of guy you just knew would never cheat on you and he made me feel very safe. But I didn't seem to want someone who'd be reliable and faithful. 'I don't know why. I just had this feeling in my gut that he might not have been The One,' I told Dr J, and I had been afraid that if we got married I would either stray and be racked with guilt or stray and be racked with regret. So, when I was thirty-two and after two years together, we went our separate ways.

I bumped into him, for the first time in about a year, a few days ago and he seemed happier than ever.

'Now, I'm all alone and he's all loved-up with his new girl-friend,' I complained. 'He said they were just back from a wonderful mini-break in Amsterdam. Do you think I'll ever be able to go on mini-breaks with someone special? Maybe after, you know, some more of this treatment?'

Dr J studied my face closely for a few seconds before rewind-ing to a previous comment. 'You said you weren't convinced your ex-boyfriend was The One?'

She said the last two words very slowly, as if she didn't know what they meant. I nodded. 'Sadly, I don't think he was.'

'The One?' she repeated coldly. 'What does The One mean to you? What would be different about you right now, about your life right now, if this one, as you say, was part of it?'

I glanced uncomfortably around the room. 'What is The One?' I asked slowly, checking that I'd actually heard her properly. 'What would be different about my life if I was with The One?'

She nodded.

How is this woman ever going to help me if she doesn't even know what The One is, I thought wearily. Eventually, I attempted to enlighten her. 'The One is, you know, The One. The One you think about constantly. Who invades your headspace. Who makes you go weak at the knees. Who renders you speechless. The One is the one you spend hours daydreaming about: running along the beach together holding hands and laughing and then amazing snogging and, you know, carrying on and everything. The One is your soul-mate; you invent your own language; share your own little jokes as well; have stupid names for each other; go on mini-breaks and exotic holidays together. He knows you inside out. He is the one you want to marry and have children with and live happily ever after with. You know, he's The One. He's your everything. And you're his everything. You can just feel it in your bones. What would be different about my life if I was with The One? Everything.'

'Hmmm,' she, said, nodding and biting, ever so slightly, on her lower lip.

We lapsed into a familiar if not especially comfortable silence. I looked out of the window behind her, focusing on the blizzard that obscured everything else.

'You know what?' I eventually said. 'I don't even need a therapist to tell me why I have a problem with commitment. I already know.' And I proceeded to tell her all about Johnnie, my first love, the curly-haired singer-songwriter in a band, who broke my tender heart at the age of twenty-five after eight glorious years together. He was the one I had planned to marry, have children with, grow old with and cycle around the world with. He was the love of my life, my true soulmate, my north, my south, my east and west etc, etc. I thought our love would last forever. I was wrong.

'He used to write songs about me.' I said this in the sort of modest tone that suggested he was John Lennon and I was Yoko Ono but was playing it down. 'His band got signed to Parlophone, the same record label as The Beatles. On iTunes their debut is described as the finest Britpop album of 1997.' Dr J didn't look at all impressed, but I was on a roll: 'We criss-crossed the country in the back of a van and I often tagged along for the ride, playing to the proverbial one man and his dog for years before we were signed. I put all my own dreams on hold and ran their fan club, designed their home-made CD covers, bombarded record companies. When, at last, we got a record deal . . .' I paused to allow reality a chink of light. 'When, at last, *they* got a record deal, well, it was all our wildest dreams come true. I was at Robbie Williams's twenty-fifth birthday party!! There's a little picture of me on the inside of one of their CD covers!! I could bring it in and show you if you like? Or I could recite a couple of verses?'

Dr J didn't say: 'Oooh, would you? That would be marvellous. Ready, I'll count you in: one, two . . .' Nor did she sigh in exasperation. She just sat, taking it all in, presumably, while maintaining her freakily expressionless mien.

She's probably never even heard of Robbie Williams, I consoled myself. *She probably doesn't even know what iTunes is.*

She's probably jealous that she didn't go out with a gorgeous singer in a brilliant band who wrote heart-felt songs about her. She probably only went out with the bongo player from Mott the Hoople. Grrrr.

I was about to rhapsodise some more about my perfect relationship when Dr J said, in her monotone voice: 'How did this relationship end?'

I glanced quickly from side to side, like a guy selling dodgy watches in a street market. I knew therapists liked to look for the negative in everything, but I didn't fancy fielding that question, so I sidestepped it with what I thought was an amusing little anecdote about the first date I went on post-Johnnie.

'After we split up, three years passed before I could stop crying for long enough to go out for a drink with anyone else. That's how long it took me to accept that it wasn't just a little phase he was going through while he "found himself". When this cute guy asked me out, I thought it would be a good idea if I took Johnnie's band's CD along on our date. I described in great detail the stories behind the songs, sang a few verses, and insisted that he listened carefully to every word of every ballad.'

I stopped grinning for a moment and looked sadly at Dr J. '"It's Just not the Same When You're not Around" – is my favourite of their songs. It goes like this . . .' And then I did something I don't recommend to anyone in therapy. I half-sang some lyrics. After the first verse, I interrupted myself to explain to Dr J that: 'The you is me. Seriously.' Then I carried on, half-crooning, half-talking, but wholly out of tune, while she stared at me unblinking throughout.

At the end, as I sat with a sad but self-satisfied smile, I noticed that, for the first time, to my triumph, she seemed to be struggling to keep her calm and composed equilibrium. A crease appeared on her usually smooth forehead. She looked as if she were trying to decide whether to say something or not. She didn't. Instead, she leaned forward slightly and looked at me in a way that made me feel as if I had just grown a second head.

'Anyway, where was I?' I wondered aloud. 'Ah, yes. So I was out for a drink with this lovely cool surfer guy. I told him, half-jokingly that I might break out in a nervous itchy rash, or a dose of hives, because it was the first date I'd been on since I'd started going out with Johnnie when I was seventeen.' I smiled as I shook my head, cringing at the memory. 'It gets worse. Guess what happened next?' I paused momentarily for dramatic effect.

She looked blankly at me.

'He said he was just going to the toilet but he never came back.' I burst out laughing, but if Dr J was laughing along, she was doing it in a silent and motionless way. Like a corpse.

Eventually she raised her right eyebrow by about half a millimetre and repeated her original question: 'How did the relationship end?' I exhaled slowly then chewed my bottom lip. Therapists must get some kind of perverse and cruel pleasure out of other people's pain. There was clearly no escape.

It had ended in the early hours of a January morning a decade earlier. Johnnie had suggested going for a drive. He stopped outside my parents' house, dropped his head onto the steering wheel and mumbled something about 'someone else'. At first, I didn't hear him, but when he repeated it there was no room for miscomprehension. 'Have you kissed her?' I naively asked, thanking him for being honest and telling myself it was probably just an unconsummated crush. He nodded.

'More than that?'

He nodded again.

'How long?'

'A while,' he mumbled.

'How long?

'A year.'

Aaaaaaaaaaahhhhhh! I let out a horrible, feral wail – a sound I didn't even know I was capable of making. That was it, my heart irreparably damaged. The end of first love and its innocence. He unburdened himself of more of the details: she was a sassy, young blonde groupie I'd noticed at a lot of their gigs; everyone in our social circle knew about it and had done for months. I was the last to know. 'So all those times I was in

London trying to help get your band a record contract, all those CDs I sent out, all the time I was recruiting fans for your fan club, all that time, you were with her?' He hid his face and nodded.

I lost myself for a moment in a fit of child-like sobbing. Until I looked across at the driver's seat and noticed Johnnie with his head still slumped on the steering wheel. I leaned over to hug him. 'It's okay. It's okay. It's okay. I understand.' And then I immersed myself in the much more important business of comforting him. 'It must have been so difficult for you to tell me,' I consoled him. 'You poor thing.'

I never once shouted at him or screamed or slapped his face. Nor did I scratch his beloved records, slash his bicycle tyres or harass his new girlfriend (new? ha!). In fact, I actually asked to meet her and, when I did, I embraced her tightly and said something like: 'It's okay. I'm not mad. I understand. He's a great guy, isn't he? These things happen.' Johnnie smiled appreciatively. I knew that there was nothing more unattractive than an angry woman and, since I was still hoping to win him back at that point, the last thing I wanted was to get all hysterical and start making an undignified scene.

When one of my friends called him a two-timing bastard, I immediately rose to his defence. I wouldn't hear a bad word said against him. I made all kinds of excuses: he's the singer in a band; he's gorgeous, talented, a tortured artist; we were first loves, it was inevitable; she ensnared him; he couldn't resist. It was a long time before I could look back on our last two years together and see all the warning signs. From a distance they were so obvious, but I had been blinded by love. I had him on a pedestal and saw only what I wanted to see.

I'd never experienced pain or a feeling of betrayal like it, which was why I'd vowed never to inflict anything like that on someone else. I curled up in the foetal position and didn't function properly for about four years.

After I'd given Dr J the gory details, I concluded: 'I decided that it's not a great idea for a woman to put her dreams on hold while she helps her boyfriend pursue his. On reflection, I think I also must have decided that the only way to avoid the pain of loss is to avoid ever getting too close to anyone. And that's exactly what I thought I'd done. But then the Christian thing happened. Which is why I'm here. I really thought I had control of my feelings. I thought you could choose whether or not to fall in love with someone. And I thought I could stop myself falling in love with someone I shouldn't fall in love with. If you know what I mean.'

Dr J looked at me sceptically. Once again, she pursued what seemed a bizarre angle: 'You described this relationship with Johnnie as . . .' She paused and gazed at her intricate oriental rug as she searched for the right word. 'I think you said blissful. No, glorious. You said eight glorious years together.'

For someone who didn't take notes, she had a very good memory.

'They were the best years of my life,' I nodded. 'Eight glorious, blissful years of perfect, pure and innocent, never-to-be repeated first love when you give everything and hold nothing back. It was a great relationship. We never argued. Not once.'

After a second, Dr J said: 'You never argued.'

What is your major malfunction? I wondered. It was as if she felt the need to question, to test the validity of every single statement I made.

'No, we never argued,' I clarified. 'Not once in eight years.'

'What about when you were angry with him? How would you communicate that?'

I frowned. 'I was never angry with him. I loved him. As I said, our relationship was perfect. We were soulmates.'

She blinked rapidly, resting her chin on her left hand and her left elbow on the palm of her right hand. Eventually, she said: 'But he was seeing someone else . . .' She trailed off, but the implication was clear – *that seems like a pretty massive non-verbal argument to me.*

Determined not to let her spoil my rose-tinted view of the past, I said: 'He was indeed, but, as I said, I've dealt with all that. I cried. A lot. I got it all out, which is what I thought you guys regarded as the most important thing. And I'm not bitter or angry. I don't want to be bitter or angry. You can't make me feel something that I don't feel.'

I sighed mutinously and looked down at my short denim mini-skirt, my thick black woollen tights and my furry boots. (I found myself taking ages to decide what to wear for therapy and changing outfits more times than I would have for a hot date.)

For once, Dr J broke the silence. 'I haven't said anything about being bitter or angry,' she said calmly.

Aaarrrgh!

After a long silence, she said: 'How are you feeling right now? Any feelings of anger or resentment towards me?'

Aaarrrgh fucking squared! 'No, I'm not freaking angry at you, you self-obsessed, deluded fool,' I screamed. (Inside.) Breathe in through your nose, hold it, count to ten, breathe out slowly through your mouth. I repeated the cycle twice before I said, just as calmly as her: 'I'm not angry with you. I don't do anger. It's corrosive, undignified and ugly.' I smiled as serenely as I could manage. But, at the end of the session, I slammed the door a little more forcefully than usual and muttered 'stupid fucking smug fucking bitch' under my breath as I descended the staircase.

* * *

No one said therapy would be easy. But nor did I expect it to be so unbelievably frustrating. That night, I dug out a textbook Katy had lent me.

'The client's experience of psychoanalytic therapy is rarely easy or smooth. She might well feel a good deal of puzzlement or frustration that the therapist does not respond to her in the ways that she would have expected. The client might have hoped for more comfort and reassurance than seems to be forthcoming. It might even seem as though the therapist has answers that are wilfully withheld. The therapist provokes changes by disturbing the client's usual patterns of relating and of understanding herself. To be affected by the therapy she needs, in some way, to be unsettled, challenged, even shocked. It can be a disorienting experience – and it can get worse!'

I closed the book and sighed wearily. I tried to watch a DVD but couldn't concentrate. My head was full of fantasy conversations, not, for once, with Christian, but with Dr J.

* * *

At my next session, I went looking for some answers. I needed to know what was going on inside Dr J's mind. What does she think of me? Am I nuts? Am I like all her other clients or, and this would be good, a little bit different? A little bit special, more interesting? But it would be pointless asking her. I knew by now that she'd turn it round and ask me, in her calm and composed manner, why her opinion of me was so important.

I didn't know why, but it was. Maybe not important, but I was certainly curious. And, anyway, she was supposed to be the expert, which was why I was paying her a small fortune. I simply wanted her to do something, say something, anything, to convince me that I wasn't stupid and that she wasn't a crank.

So, instead of asking her outright, I decided to play her at her own game and challenged her to a silence contest. Surely, I figured, if I remained quiet for long enough, she'd eventually get a bit freaked out and uncomfortable. When it became unbearable, she'd no doubt open up a bit.

Silence.

At first, it was serene. I decided to turn it into a staring competition as well. I looked at her and smiled. She looked back, with her trademark noncommittal half-smile. A long, slow minute passed. The tick-tock of her clock, whose distant sound I'd never previously noticed, was getting gradually louder. I unintentionally looked away, towards the window. Damn, damn, damn. She was good at this. It was a freezing but bright morning. The sky was blue and cloudless. I heard robins singing outside. Again, I'd never noticed them before. In fact, I didn't realise birds sang in wintertime. Chirrup, chirrup, tweet, tweet. I smiled again. She was still looking directly into my eyes, this time with her completely disconcerting blank expression. A dog started barking outside.

The noise – the woof, woof, chirrup, chirrup, tweet, tweet, tick-tock, chirrup, chirrup, woof, woof, tweet, tweet, tick-tock, woof, woof, chirrup, chirrup, tweet, tweet, tick-tock, woof, woof – reached a deafening crescendo.

'Look,' I finally blurted out, after what felt like thirty minutes but was probably closer to three, 'I need to know if I'm doing okay. You know, if I'm telling you the right kind of things. I need to know if you think there is anything actually wrong with me that you would be able to fix. Can you make me better? Or do you think I'm just a bit of an obsessive worrier who should just go away and get on with my life? It would really help me to know what you're thinking about me.'

I scrutinised her face for an indication of what was running through her mind. I thought briefly of interviews I'd conducted in the past as part of my job and how easy it often is to get an idea from someone's face of feelings, such as anger, contempt, disgust, excitement, happiness, confusion, sadness and surprise. Yet Dr J seemed to have an uncanny ability to keep almost all of her facial muscles fully under her control.

After another long silence, she said: 'I'm interested in the question behind the question. I wonder why my opinion of you is so important? Why do you care so much about what I think of you?'

I am not a violent person. I have never lost my temper. (Apart from just before I came into therapy and I went crazy with Christian.) I've never fallen out with my mum or dad. I never argue. Even when I was a secondary school teacher, dealing with adolescents, I never raised my voice. (I ran into the staff toilet in tears a few times, but that's another story.) I'm just not very good at arguments. I'm a conciliatory person. I like everyone to get on well with each other. I shy away from confrontation. But why the hell can't she just answer one simple question? 'All I want to know is if I'm doing okay here,' I said pleadingly. 'That's all. It's a simple question.'

She looked as if she were about to speak, then she thought better of it. Instead, she took her glasses off and turned her gaze to her favourite spot on the ceiling for a long time while, I assumed, she chewed over what she was going to say. I studied her closely. She was wearing a black trouser suit, a magenta sweater and black leather shoes. Her eyes were bright and alert, as blue as the sky behind her. She was slim and healthy looking. What little make-up she wore was very natural and her skin was unblemished. And there was always that heavy, rich aroma of fresh coffee in the air, whether it was one of my two early morning sessions or the evening one. But though I'd have loved a cup, it was clearly never destined to be coffee-time for me.

Eventually, Dr J removed her gaze from the ceiling, replaced her specs and fixed her eyes directly on me. Thank the Lord! I looked back expectantly and smiled.

'Do *you* think you're doing okay?'

That is it. Enough is enough. She's clearly a con artist and I've been duped. Those six words are the last she'll ever say to me. We sat in silence for a very long time, longer than I have ever not talked while with someone, unless taking part in a sponsored silence. I kept thinking about getting up and walking out but something stopped me. I bit my nails, sighed and drifted off to think again about the weirdness of this.

Eventually she cleared her throat and asked how I'd felt after the previous session. I groaned inside. This woman seemed to find it impossible to let sleeping dogs lie. 'Fine,' I lied.

'Not angry, hostile or frustrated when you left here?'

Oh God. I sighed again. 'No,' I said, the tears of frustration stinging my eyes. 'Do you know, my editor once told me that I was always smiling and happy, gregarious and good to have around the office?'

She looked at me as if to say: 'So?'

'Honestly, I am not an angry person,' I said finally.

We spent the remainder of the session in silence until she stole a quick glance at the clock and said: 'It's time for us to stop now.'

Always polite and well mannered, because that's the way my

parents brought me up, I got up and said: 'Thank you very much and goodbye.' As I slammed the front door closed on my way out, I added, sotto voce, in my best Glaswegian, 'CRAZY FUCKING CHARLATAN.'

* * *

You would have thought I'd told Louise and Katy I had irrevocably decided to throw in the towel.

'I'm not quitting,' I protested. 'I'm just looking for a new therapist. Someone with better social skills, with a little friendliness and warmth. Any. Someone who smiles once in a while. And a little feedback would be nice. Everyone needs a little feedback at times. She won't even answer a simple question – am I doing okay?'

They shook their heads in despair. We were in The Wee Pub, in the cobblestoned Ashton Lane, the heart of Glasgow's cosmopolitan West End, as the brochures put it, for our weekly post-wine-tasting bottle of wine. Some people might think it's a bit over-indulgent to go for more grape juice after a two-hour class devoted to it, but they'd be mistaken. So much time is spent swirling and sniffing and discussing varietals and bouquets that hardly any time is devoted to actually getting drunk.

Louise and Katy take wine tasting very seriously; so seriously, in fact, that they would probably describe themselves as compulsive oenophiles. They sit exams and compete with each other over who could coin the fanciest linguistic gem to describe a Pinot Noir.

I, on the other hand, abandoned the official class after only one introductory lesson a year ago when I immediately realised I was never going to achieve an adequate, or indeed any, degree of sophistication. I hadn't been able to progress from 'mmm, that's lovely; please can I have some more?' and my favourite remained New Zealand Sauvignon Blanc. I was far too impatient, and greedy, to spend half an hour in a heated debate about whether something smelled like old leather, black pepper or a freshly mown lawn. But I always met them for a drink afterwards because I was following the tutor's sage advice about practice making perfect.

The Priory Pair, who don't seem to be able to leave their work behind where it belongs, were overanalysing my decision to ditch Dr J while simultaneously doing a blind tasting on a glass of red.

'Look,' I spluttered into my Sauvignon, 'I know she's very highly qualified and experienced and has an excellent reputation, so I'm not blaming her. You should be proud of me, because I'm being adult and mature about this and taking full responsibility. I'm sure she's a wonderful therapist, but I don't like her and I think the feeling is mutual.'

Katy had her nose in a glass: 'I'm getting dark fruits, blackcurrant and maybe some cherry. Dark chocolate, too. Ooh. A wonderfully intense nose. Lorna, this is how therapy works. And no, you're not being adult about it. Can't you see that you're like a little schoolgirl who wants a glowing report card from her teacher? And, when you don't get it, you want to run away because it's so uncomfortable.' She went back to her wine. 'If I dig deep, I think I can get a touch of spice, too. This kind of therapy is about the personal relationship you develop with your therapist, and the exploration of those dynamics. That is what holds the key. It will reveal why you have such difficulties forming close, healthy adult relationships. Why you have such intimacy problems. Why you can only do closeness on a superficial level. Old world. Rhône perhaps?'

Louise shook her head and inhaled deeply from Katy's glass. 'An intense nose all right. Quite a pronounced medicinal edge. Some wood influence?'

'So what are you saying?' I protested. 'That you should stay in uncomfortable situations? If that's the case I'd still be working in a bank and going out with a guy I went to school with.'

'Typical black or white, all or nothing thinking,' they said in unison, while nodding knowingly at each other.

'Lorna,' Louise said, while staring lovingly at Katy's glass, 'therapy of this kind isn't easy. It shouldn't be easy. It's a slow,

painful and rather bizarre process. Think of it as a slow decon-
struction then reconstruction project. And don't expect something
tangible from each session. There will be hours of frustration.
What a beautiful colour that wine is, isn't it? Amazing legs, too.
I'm sure your therapist will become more talkative, but at the
moment she's both challenging you and trying to shine some light
on your unconscious to make the invisible motives visible.' She
smiled. 'Do you know, Katy, that strict Freudians don't offer any
interpretations during the first six months?'

'What?' I gasped. 'What the fuck am I paying for?'

'You'll see,' Louise replied. 'And anyway, she won't be a strict
Freudian. There aren't many left. Right, Katy, let me have a wee
taste.' She took a small mouthful and swirled it around. Then she
closed her eyes. 'Mmmm. A wonderful concentrated palate.
Chunky and juicy. Delicate, but also quite cranky. The other thing
to bear in mind, Lorna, is that people are extremely resistant to
change, even when they say they want to change. Change is terrifying. Ultimately, she's trying to strip away all your defences,
which have built up since childhood, to help you chip away at
your false self. It's a struggle. It's not pleasant discovering that
you're not the person you thought you were. You are one of the
most well-defended people I've ever met and you're going to be
stripped bare before you are built up again. It's not going to be a
walk in the park.'

Katy: 'South African?'

Louise shook her head, advised Katy to taste it – all she'd done
so far was swirl, stare and smell – then demanded evidence to
support my conclusion that Dr J didn't like me. 'She never tells
me what she's thinking. She never smiles, like really smiles, like
from her heart. She seems frigid. She doesn't have a sense of
humour. She never laughs at any of my jokes. In fact, I don't
think she's human. She could be a robot,' I said.

They looked at each other and rolled their eyes.

Katy: 'Argentinian? It's a filthy Argentinian, isn't it? God, I
love it. Sex in a glass. Mmmm.'

Louise: 'Nope! Therapy's not meant to be a barrel of laughs. I

can just imagine you trying to entertain her, jolt her into responding to you in the way you want everyone to respond to you. You
want her validation and approval in the same way that you want
everyone's validation and approval. But, if you stick at it, you'll
realise how life-curtailing that is. I bet you've been going on and
on about Johnnie as well.

'No, I've not,' I protested. 'Well, maybe a tiny bit.' She
ignored me and, in a mocking, sing-song voice, said: 'I used to go
out with this singer in a band. He was gorgeous. He used to
write songs about me. Which means I must be special. I am loveable, Doctor, honest. Someone once loved me. Honest. I can
prove it.'

I threw back my Sauvignon, as Louise continued. 'You'll be
going out of your way to try to be her favourite. Her special
client. We see people like that all the time, don't we? People who
are desperate to be special.' She nodded towards Katy. 'Don't
take this the wrong way, but, because you're so defended, you're
also – and this, like so much of human behaviour, might sound
paradoxical – totally transparent. Put yourself in her shoes. She'd
probably love to grab you by the shoulders and shake sense into
you. Or scream at you, but she's biting her tongue for a reason.'

Katy: 'You're totally transparent to everyone but yourself. New
Zealand? And you know what Freud had to say about jesting,
don't you?'

They laughed and nodded knowingly. I laughed and nodded
along knowingly too, even though I didn't have a clue.

I tried to speak for the defence, but Louise interrupted. 'You
never stick at things if you don't think you're excelling at them,'
she accused. 'This is just another example.' To Katy, she said:
'Yes. New Zealand. Great structure.'

Katy asked if she knew the grape variety. 'It would help if I had
a bit of cheese or chocolate with it. Lorna, all the time I've known
you, the fight or flight, you've always run. Think of all the jobs
you've had. You must have had about fifty jobs. You don't stick at
anything. Pinot Noir?'

'Yes!' Louise said. 'Some Pinots can be a little jammy, can't they? Some lack the subtlety of the great red Burgundies, but this one's superb.'

'I can't believe you think I run away from things,' I said, shaking my head. 'That is complete rubbish.' I recited my all-time favourite quote, which I have pinned in gigantic writing above my desk, but which I also know from memory:

'Perseverance. Nothing in the world can take the place of perseverance. Talent will not; nothing is more common than unsuccessful individuals with talent. Genius will not; unrewarded genius is almost a proverb. Education will not; the world is full of educated derelicts. Perseverance and determination alone are omnipotent.'

When I finished, I smiled proudly: 'I absolutely love that quote. It is my personal overriding philosophy for life.'

A quick pregnant glance passed between them before they burst out laughing.

'Yeah, Lorna. It's a wonderful, life-affirming quote, but that's all it is,' Louise said. 'You are always going on about quotes and words and how wonderful they are. And they are, but remember you can play with them. You can put one in front of the other and make them say anything. You can hide behind words, but you can't hide from feelings. At least not forever. Think about it: you could say to someone I love you, I love you, I love you, or to yourself I love him, I love him, I love him, but it won't bring the feeling if it's not already there. People say things that they don't mean all the time, especially in the heat of the moment. But actions and behaviour always speak louder than words.' They nodded vigorously.

Louise reeled off a catalogue of ill-fated projects I'd embarked on with obsessive zeal then quit because I'd failed to become excellent, or in many cases even competent, at them: running, playing the cello, tennis, pilates, yoga, learning French, German, Italian, Gaelic and Latin, meditation, painting, creative writing, surfing, snowboarding.

Every time I launched myself into a new project, Louise would wearily suggest that, for once in my life, I take the risk of daring to be average, of doing something just for the pleasure of doing it, rather than for some unrealistic end result like getting a winner's medal or becoming the next Jacqueline du Pré. It was an absurd challenge. To me, mediocrity equalled failure. I used to put her contempt down to jealousy and ask her what kind of loser would strive to be middle-of-the-road. She'd look at me with pity and an expression that said: 'There's really no getting through to you, is there?'

'Oh my God,' Katy shrieked, 'remember the running project? That 10K race? How embarrassing was that?'

In my twenties, yes, I went through a spell as a crazy fitness freak who could be seen on a regular basis swimming up and down the fast lane at the local pool or jogging compulsively around the block. Whenever I caught my reflection in a shop window, I saw a finely tuned athlete who was on the verge of breaking free from obscurity and shattering the British 10,000-metre record. Nuts, I know. I'd been jogging for less than six months. But with obsession comes delusion. At the time it was simply about getting A Body and all the associated benefits – fame, unadulterated happiness, gorgeous sexy perfect boyfriend, unparalleled success etc, etc. (Louise and Katy said it was all about control and avoidance.) Eventually, I did get A Body, but it looked more like a Russian shot-putter's than the graceful greyhound's I'd dreamed of. By that point, though, I wasn't too bothered as I was so high on endorphins.

I was almost cured of my exercise addiction, though, after being overtaken in a 10K fun run by Dundee Jenny, a then eighty-nine-year-old marathon runner. This was the first race I'd ever competed in so it was a bit of a blow, as I had already envisaged the headlines in the next day's local paper: 'Unknown novice destroys course record', and a picture of myself, wrapped in a silver foil blanket and crying tears of joy as I accepted a gold medal, a cheque and a bouquet of flowers from the Lord Provost, my sinewy biceps gleaming in the morning sun.

Seconds after the great-grandmother passed me, I had a near-death experience. My face turned scarlet. Sweat was pouring off me. The baby oil that I had brushed through my hair to keep it looking sleek and stop it going curly (for the photographers) was running into my eyes and blurring my vision.

I somehow managed to thud, puff and grunt my way along the Great Western Road, painfully aware that I'd told everyone, including Louise and Katy, about my great expectations for this race and urged them to be at the finishing line by 10.30 am to witness my victory. At 11.38 am I crossed the line, in 3,549th place. There were 3,600 entrants.

Ha ha ha they both laughed at the memory.

Louise reminded me of another occasion when, she said, I behaved like a child. I was working as a journalist with the *Herald* newspaper in Glasgow. They'd just introduced a new staff appraisal scheme and I was given, not a bad, but just not an exceptionally amazing report. An average one. Since I'd just returned from a week in Aids- and famine-ravaged Malawi, and (in my opinion) written a rather moving dispatch about it (it made me cry), I was a bit miffed. So I stormed into the editor's office brandishing a bitter but beautifully phrased letter of resignation. 'It's not a bad appraisal you got,' he said, in a slightly bewildered tone. 'It's the same as everyone else's: average.'

'That's the problem,' I sobbed. 'It's average. Average. Only average. I don't want to work for someone who thinks I'm only average.'

Like so many things I've done in the past, I cringe at the memory.

Maybe Louise and Katy were onto something.

'For once in your life,' Louise pleaded, 'persevere with something. Persevere with something that's not just about testing yourself, but that's also about really finding yourself.'

Sometimes I hated this pair of lunatics, but I simply had to prove to them that I was no quitter, so I decided I had no choice but to give Dr J another chance.

'Anyway, girls,' Louise said excitedly, mercifully changing the subject. 'We're having a little party in April.' Louise's husband, Scott, is an A&E consultant at the city's Royal Infirmary. 'There'll be lots of lovely doctors at it and there's one in particular I want you to meet, Lorna. He's new in town and he's gorgeous.'

Firstly, I'm not interested in new men. Secondly, I already have one doctor too many in my life. Thirdly, why do married people have to plan things so far in advance?

'Great,' I said, rising. 'I'm going for more wine.'

A gallon should probably be enough.

March

The King and I

M onday morning was grey and wet and very windy. As I drove
the ten-minute journey to therapy, I decided that I was going
to start lying on the couch. The topic hadn't been raised since
that first session when I'd asked whether I should lie or sit and Dr
J had freaked me out by saying: 'Do whatever is agreeable for you.'

The previous evening I'd asked Katy about it. She explained that
for some strange reason, lying down and not being able to see the
therapist seemed to make it easier to get in touch with the unconscious forces and hidden motives that influence our behaviour. 'Lots
of people feel far too vulnerable though and prefer to sit,' she
added. On hearing this, I decided, at some level, that I wasn't going
to be one of the vulnerable Other People. Also, although I thought
I'd spilled my guts out during the previous two months, I realised
I'd told Dr J nothing I hadn't spoken about before. I didn't
know if there was any more to say but I knew that drastic measures
would be required to chip away at my thick layer of self-protection
(or, as Dr J would probably see it, self-deception).

It's surprising how quickly you fall into a routine. I parked in
my usual space, waited until three minutes before my appointment
was due to start, before, bunched up against the weather, I sprinted
to her apartment and rang the buzzer. After the door was unlocked,
I climbed the three flights of stairs, took my usual seat in her waiting room, picked up the same *National Geographic* I did every
session, and flicked through it without reading anything. Then I
heard her door click, the soft footsteps, the half-smile, the 'please
come in'.

As usual, I followed her, took my jacket off and dropped it over my bag on the floor next to my chair. She was wearing an expensive-looking beige trouser suit with a brown silk blouse, which looked better than it sounds. It was even chic. I gazed out of the window behind her. The wind-driven rain was streaming relentlessly out of the sky, battering against the glass.

'I think I would like to try lying down,' I said. Although this wasn't technically a question, it was delivered as one and, I'd been hoping, half-hoping, for some kind of response. She didn't say: 'Do whatever is agreeable for you', but she gave me a look that said it. I stood up, took the three or four steps towards the couch and sat on it. Then I tried to lie back, but it felt too uncomfortable. How can lying on a couch possibly be such an ordeal? It's usually so relaxing. I tried again, screwing up my eyes and gritting my teeth, the way I would if I was about to get an injection, to make the anticipated pain more bearable. Now she was behind me, not directly, but behind and to the right. I could no longer see her face or reaction. In a way, it felt like being at the dentist. But instead of someone standing behind me getting ready to probe and poke around in my mouth, it was this anonymous woman preparing to drill into the deep sea of my unconscious.

I know how dramatic and pathetic this must sound, but it was one of the weirdest, most uncomfortable experiences I'd ever had. I tried turning onto my side so that I could at least see part of her, even if it was just her shoes, then I sat up again before finally taking a deep breath and trying again. I didn't think I had 'power or control issues' but, as I lay there, my shoulders hunched up to my ears, my fists clenched, my face contorted, all I could think about was that she now had everything: all the power, all the control. I felt as if I had lost all of mine and was completely at her mercy. For all I knew, she could be laughing, rolling her eyes, yawning, giving me the finger, falling asleep. I couldn't see her but she could watch me, which made me feel far more, er, vulnerable than I'd ever imagined possible.

* * *

I should clear this up before we go any further. It's sort of embarrassing to admit, but I've always been better than my sister Louise. I think that's why sibling rivalry has never been an issue in my family. What do I have to be jealous about? Yes, she's very pretty, with long curly hair, big blue eyes, lovely teeth and dimples. But I'm taller and younger. I have a more exciting job. I'm free and single. And I am definitely more ambitious: I've got better qualifications, I was more academic and all my school reports said my behaviour was exemplary, whereas Louise was prone to distraction. She can't even concentrate long enough to get a driver's licence. And she has one failed marriage behind her. She was a divorcee before she'd even hit thirty. Imagine. Still, it didn't seem to put her off. After a few wild years of clubbing, there she is: married again, this time to a bookishly handsome, gadget-obsessed hospital consultant. Just to show that I am being totally honest and objective, I will acknowledge her strengths: she's endlessly patient, a superb cook and a surprisingly unneurotic mother. I once asked her if she'd like Lewis to be a famous singer, actor, artist or athlete. She shook her head in disgust and said all she wanted was for her son to be self-confident and well-mannered. As I said, she lacks ambition. So she has her good points. Though I'm pretty sure that if I put my mind to it, I could be patient and impressive in the kitchen too.

I can't be bothered, though, so, no, I have no issues with Louise. Which is why – even though I'd fondly imagined I would have a family long before her – she'd never shown any maternal instincts, at least not that I'd noticed, whereas I'd always thought I was born to be a mother – I don't begrudge her in the slightest the fact that Lewis, her beautiful, blond-curled, blue-eyed toddler, appears to be hogging all the attention which I, as the former baby of the family, had grown to expect for myself. It's really been no problem whatsoever.

Dr J approached the whole thorny issue characteristically: with the cunning of a professional sniper.

One March morning, a couple of weeks after I'd started lying on the couch, I was stretched out, examining my nails, which were short, ragged and partly coated in chipped Chanel Rouge Noir. I told Dr J what was on my mind: a song about the weather and the changing seasons. It was my nephew's current favourite and I couldn't get it out of my head. I put this down to the fact that I'd spent the previous day with him, during which I'd sung it with him around maybe one hundred times, and I'd seen some daffodils that morning.

'Spring is in the air,' I said.

There was silence from behind my head. Maybe she was asleep? Maybe she was just bored? But she could at least have rustled some papers to let me know. Or even yawned loudly. Or moved around in her leather seat.

From the weather report, I went on to rhapsodise about how much I adore little King Lewis, as my family calls him, and the special bond I have with him.

'I feel this love like no other. I can't imagine what it must be like to be a mother. I don't know how they do it. I can't say no to Lewis. I get upset when he's upset. I love other members of my family, of course, and I've loved men in my life, and friends. But the love for a child, who's not even my own, but my nephew, it's immense. I'd do anything to protect him. I'm already worrying about when he has to go out into the big bad world. I'm worried about his heart getting broken. And I'm worried in case he gets bullied at school.'

I decided I wanted to show Dr J a picture of him. I got up from the couch, went over to the chair where I left my jacket and bag, and rummaged around for my mobile. I have a particularly cute shot of him – taken when he was laughing so much he gave himself the hiccups – as the screensaver. It's a close-up of his face, with his mouth wide open, his big blue eyes sparkling with joy.

'He's adorable, isn't he?' I said, lying back down and holding the phone out to my right. She said, and I think she might even have been smiling, 'He is a lovely boy.' Babies are amazing: they are like glue or magnets – they bring people together, even if they don't really like each other. Could King Lewis be the magic ingredient that Dr J and I had needed all along? I almost wanted to leap off the couch and hug her; she wasn't a mannequin or a robot after all. She was a real human being, with feelings and emotions. I held back but interpreted her uncharacteristic response as a sign of encouragement.

'I take him swimming on Sundays and to toddlers' group on Mondays,' I said proudly. Now, this wasn't strictly true. I take him to the pool twice a month if he's lucky and I've only ever taken him to toddlers' group once, and that was because my mum, who looks after him two days a week, wasn't well and there was no one else available except, to my mum's undisguised dismay, Uh-oh. However, the words were out before I could stop myself and they did sound good. In case Dr J hadn't heard me proclaiming my saintly credentials, and there was no indication that she had, I repeated them, a little louder, turning my head slightly to the right: 'I take him swimming on Sundays and to toddlers' group on Mondays.'

When it became clear that, if she thought I was amazing, she was going to be keeping it to herself, I changed tack and tried to jolt her into another smile. Even if I couldn't see it, I'd be able to feel the warmth radiating from behind my head.

Not long before Christmas, when Lewis was about eighteen months old, I had him in my arms at the Clarins counter in Frasers department store while two sales assistants were cooing all over him.

'Oh, your wee boy is so gorgeous,' they gushed.

'He's actually my n—' I stopped myself. 'Thank you,' I said instead, beaming with pride. 'Isn't he a little beauty?'

'Oh, yes he is. Look at those curls. And those dimples. What's his name?'

'Lewis, but I call him my wee bobo,' I said, plastering him in kisses.

There were a few minutes of baby talk, during which I encouraged Lewis to act like a performing monkey while I enjoyed the role of doting mother. Then Louise, who was supposed to have been taking the rare opportunity to do some shopping, suddenly appeared.

'Mama!' Lewis grinned adoringly at her, with his arms outstretched.

'Hello, my baby angel from heaven. Come and give your mummy a big cuddle.'

The assistants looked very suspiciously at me as my face went cranberry red, a sure sign I've been caught doing something wrong. 'He is my nephew,' I said in desperation. I then hung around for a while, over-compensating for my criminal actions by spending nearly £150 on completely unnecessary Clarins products.

'It was quite funny,' I said, laughing.

'Hmmm,' I heard from behind my head.

'Lewis's arrival in the world has completely transformed my whole family,' I volunteered after a while. 'My mum and Louise are very close now. Much closer than they used to be. They're, like, all friendly. They're always going out for lunch and stuff. And my dad has changed almost beyond recognition. It's wonderful.'

For the next twenty minutes or so I told her all about this transformation. My father has become proud and animated, with a renewed zest for life now that he is seeing the world through baby Lewis's innocent and curious eyes. After decades of resistance, he has even started going to dancing lessons with my mum. Three nights a week. And they practise their steps in the living room, while drinking champagne. I know this only because last Sunday afternoon, when I was round for dinner, I noticed that the large rug in their living room had been rolled up and pushed to one side and I'd made some enquiries.

'It's been moved because,' my mum said, giggling in the direction of my father, 'your dad's been having a bit of trouble with his bodywork. Tango bodywork. Haven't you, Owen? And we've got a big dance coming up next month. So we've been polishing up our act.'

'Bodywork? Polishing your act!' I bellowed, glancing out of the window in horror. 'You do close the curtains, don't you? Please, God Almighty, tell me you close the curtains. People can see in. Oh my God, there's a couple looking in right now.' I sank into the sofa and out of view.

'Och, that's Yvonne and Ian from number 15,' my mum announced, waving gaily. 'They see us at it all the time.'

I pulled an ew-yuck-gross-vomit face.

My mum and dad looked at each other and laughed like lovesick teenagers. 'We don't care who sees us dancing together, do we, Owen?'

'No we do not, sweetheart,' replied my dad. 'Come on, let's give them a little demonstration.'

As my dad put on a Latin-American CD, my mum explained that: 'The tango is a very passionate, very sexy dance. Which is why your dad, being a Scotsman, is finding it quite difficult. He has to express all this passion and emotion through his body.' My mum looked at my dad and laughed. He shook his head and said: 'Och Rose, you behave yourself.'

I curled up on the couch, hiding my face behind my hands and peeking through my fingers. My dad, a tall, slim man with grey hair, brown eyes and silver-rimmed glasses, put his right hand around my mum's waist and onto the small of her back. My mum, who has short grey hair and green eyes, a little shorter and a little curvier than my dad, reached up, and with elbows jutting out, held my dad's left hand at head level. They were in a close embrace, chest to chest.

'Okay?' my mum said, snapping her head theatrically to the right and upwards. 'Now this isn't fluid like a waltz. It's more . . . How would you describe it, Owen?'

'It's more clipped. More staccato,' my dad – or at least a man who looked like my dad – said.

And with fierce concentration on their faces, they tangoed without restraint around the living room like contestants from *Strictly Come Dancing*. My dad counted out loud: 'Slow, slow, quick, quick, slow. One, two, three, four, slow, quick, quick, slow,' while my mum silently followed. Every so often, she did a quick exaggerated snap of her head, jerking it from the right to the centre and back to its original position. Once or twice, she hooked her leg around his.

The performance ended with a twirl and a close embrace. My father, looking unusually pleased with himself, said: 'God, I love the dancing. I love this woman.' And he gave my mum a kiss.

Then I clapped. Slowly at first, because of the shock. 'You're actually quite good,' I said, unable to keep the disbelief from my voice. 'But this isn't right.'

Before Lewis came along, my dad's only real interests were reading books, particularly ones about the Roman empire, playing the guitar and going to see Celtic football club. Now, he'd rather get down on his hands and knees and pretend he's Thomas the Tank Engine, or tango across the living room with my mum in one hand and a flute of Moët in the other, all the while in full view of the neighbours. What on earth was happening to my family?

I noticed that, in the course of my soliloquy, Dr J had so far said nothing. I thought of her, sitting behind me, maintaining, I assumed, the lazily watchful gaze of a basking crocodile, deciding when to go in for the kill.

'They dance, they hold hands in public, they probably even . . .' God, no, I had to stop myself, that was too disturbing to think about. 'It is weird but it is also wonderful to see everyone so happy,' I ended instead and nodded. Job done.

After a short silence, she struck.

'I wonder,' she said, 'if you feel good about this all the way down.'

I frowned. I was suspicious. It had been a while since she'd strung so many words together into one sentence. Plus, I wasn't absolutely sure what she was getting at. 'What do you mean? All the way down?' I was gazing at the ceiling, my face screwed up in confusion.

She was unusually talkative. 'There has been a major change to your family dynamic. I'm just wondering if you feel wonderful about it all the way down. Or if there are any other emotions that this has stirred up.'

'No,' I said, shaking my head. 'I'm not aware of any others.'

Silence. A long silence interrupted only by the distant ticking of her clock.

'We have feelings we are not aware of,' she said. 'It doesn't mean they're not there. It doesn't mean they're not strong or important. The birth of a baby, as wonderful and joyful as it is, can also bring other feelings. A new arrival can be a disturbing contrast to recognition of your own aging and mortality. I just wonder if there are any feelings of jealousy? Towards Lewis? Towards your—'

I sat up from the couch and turned to look at her.

'Ab. So. Lute. Ly. Not. I am not a jealous person. I don't do jealousy. Like anger, I think it's such a pointless, ugly and destructive emotion. It's a complete waste of time and energy.'

She stared fixedly at me with that look which I used to think was expressionless but which I was beginning to realise was, like her silences, one of the most valuable tools of her trade. In effect, it was her way of saying: 'Think carefully about what you've just said. Think very carefully about it. And this time, ask yourself how true it is. Ask yourself who you're trying to fool, because you sure as hell aren't fooling me. Think about how you really, truly feel. Not what you think you should feel or what you would like to feel, but what you really feel. Not just at the surface, not out there on the top part of the flower, but crawl underneath the dirt and see if you can get in touch with those feelings that are lurking about deep down at the roots.'

I thought about making a joke about maybe being jealous of Angelina Jolie or whoever George Clooney's going out with, but I suddenly felt a bit wobbly and unable to pull off a smile or any faux joviality.

She clearly wasn't going to let this go. 'I wonder whether you've ever felt jealous of friends or other family members?'

'I really don't think I have,' I said a little hesitantly. 'I've always known that it's better to measure yourself against yourself instead of against others. That's what I've been doing. I think.'

'Jealousy has never been an issue for you?' she asked, allowing the tiniest hint of incredulity to creep into her standard monotone.

I thought fleetingly about Christian and Charlotte snogging

each other, but it was too nausea-inducing, so I pushed the image immediately away and said: 'No. I mean, I know people talk about sibling rivalry, but I've never felt jealous of Louise. In fact, and I know this will sound awful, but I've always felt that I was better than her. So there was never any question of envying her.'

After a pause, Dr J said: 'What do you mean by better? In what ways do you think you are better than your sister?'

My voice suddenly seemed small and feeble. 'A lot of very different ways,' I said. I silently ran through what now seemed like a terribly lame collection of petty feel-good items I'd been relying on to bolster what I was slowly beginning to realise was my very shaky self-esteem.

I sighed heavily, lay down on the couch again and thought back to how I had reacted when Louise ended her first marriage when she was twenty-seven. I went with my mum to Glasgow airport to pick her up. She had left everything behind in London, where she'd been living with her husband for the previous six years. When she arrived, carrying her worldly possessions in just one suitcase and looking painfully thin, she burst into tears. Unlike me, my sister rarely cries in public, so this was clearly serious. My mum held and comforted her. I stood in the background growling and rolling my eyes. It was her choice, her decision to leave, I thought. Her husband was wonderful and really loved her. She'd made her vows. I couldn't understand why she was so upset. I dismissed it as a self-inflicted wound and offered her not an ounce of sympathy or comfort, but only thinly veiled contempt. I thought, like some religious fundamentalist, that good, nice people didn't get divorced. She tried many times to explain to me that it was the hardest thing she'd ever done in her life; that she felt she had married too young and that it was better to break an unhappy wedlock than be broken by it. But I wasn't listening. I was on my moral high horse. In fact, I was only just beginning to fall off it.

Dr J jolted me out of my reverie. 'You said earlier that you thought Louise had never shown any maternal instinct, but she is an amazing mother.'

I had an urge to say: 'She's not amazing. If I said amazing, I was probably exaggerating. She's adequate. She's like any other half-decent mother: she cooks lovely meals for her baby, plays with him, sings to him, gets up in the middle of the night to feed him. Loves him unconditionally. Would lay down her life for him. But so would I. It's no big deal. Nothing special. I don't know if I would say she's amazing. She's good but I'm sure all mothers are like that.'

I swallowed hard. 'Yeah, whatever,' I nodded, gazing at the ceiling.

Dr J continued: 'You have talked a lot about Louise and her happy, contented family life. It would be quite normal, perfectly normal to feel some envy.'

I felt tears of frustration welling up in my eyes: 'I. Am. Not. Jealous. Of. Louise,' I said. 'I think Louise is jealous of me. I have my freedom. My independence. A great career. Louise is probably jealous of me. She must be. Surely. She must be.'

There was a long silence.

'I wonder what is so terrifying,' came the quiet, calm voice from behind my head. 'What would it mean for you to acknowledge that you might have these feelings? That you may be jealous of your sister's life, and of other people's relationships.'

I wiped away some tears that had escaped, then I pondered her question for a long time. 'Well,' I eventually said, 'I've always thought jealousy and anger were disgusting, ugly emotions that I didn't have. But more than that, it upends everything. It would mean I've been kidding myself all these years. And if I've been unconsciously deluding myself about this, what else have I been doing it about? I'd always thought I was really honest. People used to say to me that they'd never met anyone who wore their heart so openly on their sleeve. They said I was an open book. That I'd never be good at poker because my face openly transmitted my every thought and feeling. But now I'm having to try and get my head around the idea that none of that was for real. That it was a way of hiding what was underneath. That I was fooling everyone, or at least trying to fool everyone, including myself, but wasn't even aware of it. It is too uncomfortable to think about.'

'The truth often is,' said Dr J.

* * *

Later that night, I called my mum, who was at my sister's for dinner, to see if she'd read something I'd written in the previous Sunday's *Observer*.

Louise and my parents lived five minutes from each other in the leafy suburb of Milngavie, six miles north-west of Glasgow, and were always at each other's for dinner.

'Hello, pet,' my mum sang. 'Louise's just made us a lovely meal. We had' – she asked Louise what it was and relayed it back to me – 'black pudding and scallops with a mint pea puree, then a rack of lamb with a pinenut and parmesan crust. All home-made. And all with wines to match.'

'Oh, very good,' I said

'What did you have for your dinner?' My mum always asked me this. The answer was usually either a ready-made meal for one from Marks & Spencer, toasted cheese or a mixed-grill take-away from Kebbabish, where I was on first-name terms with the owners. That night it was the latter.

'You need to eat more fruit and vegetables, young lady!'

'Yeah,' I said guiltily. 'It's okay, though, I have a smoothie every morning. Anyway, I was just wondering if you read that piece in Sunday's paper.'

'Oh, I just skimmed it, pet. Terribly sad, isn't it? Anyway, your dad and I have been so busy, looking after this beautiful big boy.' She started talking in a baby voice: 'Lewis, it's Aunty Uh-oh on the phone. Do you want to say hello to Aunty Uh-oh?'

A moment later, a cute disembodied voice said: 'Eh-oh, Uh-oh.' Then he blew a raspberry.

My mum took the phone back. 'Oh, he's a cheeky wee thing, isn't he? Who's a cheeky wee thing, hmm? Who's a cheeky wee, cheeky wee thing?' I presumed she was still talking to Lewis.

I cleared my throat. Loudly. 'Oh, sorry pet. Listen, have you heard him say "love you"? It's the cutest thing in the world. He says: "uve 'ou". It'll bring tears to your eyes. Oh, and have you seen him do "eye, nose, cheeky, cheeky, chin, cheeky, cheeky, chin, nose, eye"?' She didn't wait for me to ask what 'eye, nose, cheeky, cheeky, chin, cheeky, cheeky, chin, nose, eye' actually was but said: 'Lewis, what's that? Tell Aunty Uh-oh what that is.'

The phone was given to Lewis again: 'No-isthe,' he said, in his cute little lispy voice.

'Yes,' my mum sang. 'It's Lewis's lovely, lovely nose. Who's got a gorgeous wee nose, hmm? Who's got a perfect little nose like a beautiful little button?' She definitely didn't mean me this time.

I cleared my throat again. 'Mum,' I said, 'see that piece I wrote—'

'It was terribly sad, pet,' my mum interjected. 'Do you know, if you say one, two, he says freeeeee. Listen, ready everyone?' In the background, I heard my mum, dad, Louise and Scott say in unison: 'One, two,' and, on cue, Lewis said, 'freeeeee'.

My mum gushed: 'It's amazing, isn't it?'

'Yeah. It is. Amazing. Absolutely amazing.'

'And he knows some of his colours, don't you, Lewis? Because you're a very clever little boy, aren't you? Lewis, tell Aunty Uh-oh what colour that is.'

'Boo,' I heard a little voice say, before my mum corrected him. 'No, silly cookie. That's not blue. That's green.'

'Did he get it wrong?' I interrupted, my lips curling into an evil smile. Does he not know the difference between green and blue. I thought, before immediately dropping my head in shame. What's happening to me? I wondered.

I let out a sharp exhalation of breath and shook my head. 'Anyway, see that piece I wrote?'

'Uh-huh,' she said, but I could tell her attention was elsewhere. 'It was the saddest story I've ever worked on. And . . . Oh my God, I nearly forgot to tell you, remember that piece I wrote about Srebrenica? The one I nearly won an award for? Well, it was being discussed on an internet forum thing!' I said this as if it were akin to receiving a Pulitzer Prize.

'Oh, that's wonderful, pet.'

'And I've got a really good story for this week. It's about the smoking ban. I've heard, from a very good source, that it could result in total anarchy.'

'Oh, righto,' my mum said, annoyingly, not realising, or, if she did, not caring, that this was only a teaser to whet her appetite. She was supposed to have asked for more details. Which I gave her anyway.

'There are fears that thousands of people will leave their drinks unattended while they go outside for a cigarette,' I said with alarm, trying to make this sound like a potential national catastrophe. 'All these unattended drinks at bars all across the country. Can you imagine? All the drinks getting spiked. It could end up in total anarchy. Everyone's really worried about it.'

'Oh, righto,' my mum repeated. 'Here's your dad. He wants to say hello.'

I heard my mum say: 'Owen, will you speak to her for a minute?' as she passed the phone to him.

'All well?' he asked, but before I could reply there was a round of applause and squeals of delight in the background.

I wondered whether the little curly-haired miracle had just recited the alphabet backwards or said 'Love you, Granny and Granda,' in Latin, or become the youngest person ever to be accepted into Mensa.

But no. Bursting with pride, my dad revealed that Lewis had just put his empty Rachel's Organic yoghurt carton in the bin. 'All by himself,' my dad gushed. 'He did it. All. By. Himself.'

The line went silent.

'Dad?' I asked. 'Dad, are you still there? Dad, remember that piece I wrote about Srebrenica? Dad? The one I nearly won an award for? It was being discussed on an internet forum thing. Dad, do you know that the smoking ban's going to result in total anarchy. Dad? Dad?'

My mum grabbed the phone. 'Your dad just gets a wee bit emotional these days, pet.'

I wondered whether I'd dialled the wrong number and been

talking to someone else's parents for the past fifteen minutes. My dad doesn't do emotional! Unless Celtic win a European cup. Which happens, on average, once every forty-odd years.

I poured myself a very large glass of wine, lit some candles and put on the TV, but I couldn't concentrate. I can't believe my mum and dad are more interested in one toddler who can't even speak properly than they are in current world affairs and the smoking ban and, er, other stories I'm working on. It's Lewis this, Lewis that. Can we take Lewis for a walk? Can we babysit Lewis? Did Lewis eat all his dinner like a good little boy? Does Lewis like this little outfit that his granny and granda bought him today? Or does he prefer the one they bought him yesterday? Or the one they bought him the day before yesterday? Has Lewis got any new words today for his granny and granda? Does Lewis know how much his granny and granda love him? Very, very, very, very much.

I lay down on my living room floor. You are a strong, confident, independent woman, I told myself. You are not jealous of a toddler. You are not jealous of your nephew. You are a strong, confident, independent woman. You are not jealous of a toddler. You are NOT JEALOUS OF YOUR FECKING NEPHEW OR HIS BLOODY MOTHER.

* * *

Over the next few days and sessions, reality slowly dawned. I'm surprised I never crashed my car leaving a session, as I felt as if I was in a completely preoccupied daze. The image I'd always had of myself was beginning to crumble. My world view was being messed with. It was not pleasant. I was angry. I was jealous. And I couldn't decide whether I hated Dr J for revealing these hidden truths to me, or whether I was grateful to her for these insights.

One Thursday night, towards the end of March, I was in Chinaski's with Katy. I'd asked her to meet me half an hour before Emily and Rachel because I wanted her thoughts on the 'jealousy issue'.

'I need to speak to you about something,' I said solemnly, as she brought a bottle of wine and two glasses from the bar. We had our favourite spot – a window booth overlooking the M8 motorway linking Glasgow and Edinburgh, which, for some strange reason, I loved. It was a crazy tangle of concrete flyovers and pedestrian bridges. I suppose I liked watching cars whiz by, wondering who was in them and where they were going. I brought my gaze back inside and leaned forward confidentially, even though there was no one within earshot.

'I think I am, em, I think I might be, well, there's a possibility that I might be, er . . .'

'An alcoholic?' Katy suggested, pouring wine into our glasses.

I smiled sarcastically.

'I think,' I started falteringly, feeling very much as if I were at an AA meeting and on the verge of making the gigantic first step of admitting that I had a problem, 'I think I'm . . . Hello, my name is Lorna and I'mjealousofbabyLewis. There, I've said it. It's out. Right. Very good. Now I'm on the road to recovery.'

'For fuck's sake,' Katy growled. 'You're such a fucking drama queen. I thought it was something serious. Of course you're fucking jealous of Lewis. We're all jealous of him, including his mother and father. A new young life. Full of possibility and potential. The golden days of childhood still ahead of him and not a care or a worry in the world. His every need and want met immediately. Showered with an endless supply of unconditional love. And he's the centre of everyone's attention. There would be something wrong with you if you weren't jealous of him. And, of course, your sister getting in there first. Making your mum and dad the happiest, proudest grandparents in the land.'

'But I didn't think I was a jealous person. Jealousy is disgusting. It's one of the seven deadly sins, you know. The punishment is getting your eyes sewn together with wire.'

Katy chuckled meanly. 'Seven deadly sins, my arse! They should create an eighth one – gullibility. For idiots like you who actually believe that things like anger, envy, lust, sloth and whatever the other ones are, are actually sins. They should be renamed the seven alively, let me think, not virtues, but just, you know, the things that make us fully human. Anyway, back to the point, your jealousy—'

'Alively's not a word,' I interrupted.

'You're so left-brained,' Katy said. 'This is so typical of you. We're in the midst of talking about something emotional, your deep reservoir of repressed anger and jealousy, and what matters most to you is the accuracy of a fucking word. Are you scared that the editor of the Oxford English Dictionary is going to march in here and put us in jail or send us to hell? It's only me and you here. It's not a cardinal sin to make up a word. Did you know that over-intellectualising is one of the most common defences that people use to avoid getting in touch with their emotions? It's like those people who just have to win every argument. They have to be right. Cannot bear the thought of getting something wrong or making a mistake. Well, they might win every argument, but, in the process, they lose every chance at happiness. Anyway, as I was saying, your jealousy. You pretend, you tell yourself, try to convince yourself, that you're not a jealous or angry person because society tells you it's bad and unattractive.'

Yeah, but it is, I thought, though I didn't say anything.

Katy was really getting into it: 'Women aren't allowed to feel these things. We're supposed to be cheerful and happy and positive and smiley all the time. It's utterly fucking ridiculous. It's not bad to feel angry or jealous. It's normal. It's human. Taking a deep breath and counting to ten can help temporarily. As can meditation, yoga, positive thinking or a trip to the gym. Or going on a no-carb diet. Or telling yourself, one hundred times a day, that you're a strong, confident, successful woman who's in control of her emotions and can have whatever she wants. It's all fucking bullshit. The real feelings, the unexpressed ones, are still there. They're repressed so deep that you can even manage to convince yourself that they're not there. You've automatically trained yourself to control them. But you can't hide from them forever. One of the laws of the unconscious is that that which is repressed seeks expression. Why do you think so many women of our generation are neurotic and on fucking anti-depressants? It's because they've got all these repressed feelings inside them, screaming to get out, but, at the same time, they're terrified to get in touch with them.'

Oh God Almighty. I was beginning to wish I'd never mentioned the jealousy thing. 'Do you know what Freud once described depression as?' She didn't wait for a reply. 'Frozen anger. I think that's spot on. And jealousy and anger are two sides of the one coin. This is why so many women are losing it. We've been told since childhood that these are bad. Wrong. They become alienated from their own feelings, no longer knowing what they like or wish or fear or resent. But, instead, trying to fulfil this superhuman role. And you know what Karen Horney had to say about all this, don't you?'

No. Yes. I don't know. Of course. 'Who?' I managed to squeeze in while Katy paused for breath. Ignoring my question, she continued: 'She said our culture places great stress on rational thinking and behaviour and regards irrationality, or what may appear as such, as somehow inferior. Anger and jealousy are regarded as irrational and inferior. It's almost as if we've been forced not to feel these things. We're not allowed to feel these things. Which is, in itself, utterly fucking irrational. Because it is human to feel these things. It is human to have wants and needs and desires and to feel angry and jealous and so on. But we all have to go about pretending not to feel these things and, as a result, they actually become the driving forces in our lives.'

'Right, right, very good,' I whispered, hoping she might lower her voice accordingly. Katy, no matter whether she was discussing female masturbation, sexual fantasies or our biological clocks, was always, to my acute embarrassment, operating at top volume.

'What did you just say?' she bellowed. 'Why are you whispering? Are you worried people might hear me? Are you worried what the people in this pub, who you don't even fucking know, will think? You are, aren't you? I know you are. That's your problem. Always worrying about what people will think of you. Always trying to please: always the good girl, wanting to be everyone's friend, wanting to keep the peace, the people pleaser, the approval seeker. What is this fear in you, this timidity, that won't allow you to just be who you are? If you don't stop worrying about what other people think of you, you can say goodbye to ever being truly happy, because you will never be able to just be yourself.'

'Shut up,' I bleated. 'I'm not like that. I fucking hate nice people-pleasing approval-seekers.'

Katy topped up our glasses and then all of a sudden her tone changed dramatically. 'Oh my God, Lorna. This is actually bloody fantastic. In the past, anytime we've ever tried to talk about stuff like this, you've just gone to the ladies', or gone home, or said 'yeah, whatever' and changed the subject to your work. This is the therapy. It's beginning to work. It's brilliant, isn't it?'

I crashed my head onto the table. 'No, there's nothing brilliant about it. My head is all over the place. I feel as if it's going to explode. I'm not who I thought I was. I don't even know who I am anymore. I don't know how I feel. Apart from totally confused.'

Just as Rachel and Emily arrived, I decided, bolstered by the two glasses of wine I'd had, that it would be a good idea to phone Louise and apologise for my behaviour all those years ago.

It's weird. I say sorry all the time. I apologise for paying with my Switch card rather than cash; I say sorry when a waitress brings the wrong order and I have to send it back; when someone bumps into me, I apologise; I take the blame when I'm in the Levi's shop and the assistant brings ten pairs of jeans but none is my perfect fit. I probably say 'sorry' about one hundred times a day. I'm thinking of having it printed on my business cards. But I was feeling very anxious about saying it now. I drained my glass and went outside.

After asking about Lewis, what she'd had for dinner, what kind of day she'd had and telling her how splendid the Mitchell Library, which is next door to Chinaski's, looked all lit up, I eventually swallowed hard and broached the subject.

'I'm really sorry for making it even harder than it must already

have been,' I said, after reminding her about that day at the airport, and my attitude since. 'At the time I thought it was wrong:
selfish and unforgivable. Now I think it was brave and courageous.'

'Oh, that's okay,' she said. 'I don't think anyone ever goes into
a marriage thinking it will end. But I was emotionally still a child
when I got married the first time.'

Since I was slightly drunk and in confessional mode, I continued: 'I know this will sound appalling, but I'd always thought
I was better than you. I saw only what was negative or what I
perceived to be flaws in you to make myself feel superior.' I shook
my head.

'I know,' she laughed. 'You're so transparent, Lorna.' Ha! That
was all *she* knew. 'But that's what people do, so don't be giving
yourself too hard a time for it. Jealousy is a very difficult emotion. It's there with family, friends and colleagues. The irony is
that the most jealous people try to deal with it by denying it
completely. It stops people having to face their own vulnerabilities
and weaknesses. So they cope by elevating themselves above
others. They need to believe they're better than other people but
they give themselves away all the time, if not by the comments
they make then by their behaviour.'

'Oh God,' I cringed. 'Do you think it would have been dead
obvious to other people? Why didn't you say something?'

'I tried. Well, I kind of tried. But you can't tell someone what
they don't want to hear. You can't point out other people's flaws.
It would be a bit like trying to tell a teenager he's not immortal.
It's futile. He'd rebel even more. You have to discover it for yourself. And many people go through their whole lives without that
self-awareness.'

'Lucky them,' I said. 'What is the point of facing them? I'm
beginning to think they're better avoided. I'm beginning to wish
I'd never gone into bloody therapy. I felt much better when I
didn't know all this. I felt better when I thought I was great – even
if I was deluded.'

'It might be a bit of a shock, even a bit uncomfortable just
now,' Louise said, 'but once you get your head around it, you

will feel completely liberated. Once you actually acknowledge, explore and understand these things in yourself, they become much less destructive. You feel them, which means that, para-doxically, they're no longer the driving force in your life.'

For the first time in my life, I saw my sister in a completely different light. I was filled with guilt and confusion. Who else had I been like this with? I wondered. I was also trying to get my head around the fact that Dr J possibly wasn't a money-grabbing con artist after all.

I weaved back into Chinaski's. Rachel and Emily were at the bar, chatting to the lovely barman.

Katy changed the subject and asked how I was feeling about the Christian situation. To her subsequent regret, she had introduced me to him two years earlier.

I had actually texted him that day, but kept that to myself and instead told her about the last conversation I'd had with him. 'There's definitely nothing happening with Charlotte. He assured me of that, which makes me feel much better. But I'm trying to break the habit. I've not seen him or spoken to him for a while. I'm feeling pretty optimistic about things, especially since he's not seeing Charlotte. It was the thought of them together that nearly tipped me over the edge. I think he's trying to repair his marriage.'

She raised a sceptical eyebrow.

We were joined by the others, who had decided that we should go west for 'one more drink'. Full of high spirits and giggling about nothing in particular, we tumbled out of a taxi and into The Wee Pub. There, in a corner, was a tall, broad man with light brown hair and those huge brown eyes that melted me every time I looked into them. It was Christian, looking gorgeous in a black suit and white, partly undone shirt. My face lit up until, as if in slow motion, I saw a teeny doll-like creature clinging onto him. It could only have been Charlotte.

still in denial,
but not as much

April

Love Quadrangles

If I had been first into the bar, I'd have made the split-second shutter-snap decision to do a u-turn. I'd probably have made an excuse about the place being too crowded. We'd have gone to another pub and I'd have rushed to the ladies' and burst into tears or felt like throwing up. Or both. Then I'd have tried to talk myself into believing that it wasn't really him. Couldn't have been him. Not with her. I only caught a fleeting glimpse, after all.

Earlier in the day, Christian had replied to a text I'd sent him, saying he wouldn't be able to meet me that evening as he was going out with a friend. 'Shld I join u 4 1? Going out with girls but cld meet u ltr' I queried. I couldn't stop myself. As he was trying to withdraw, I was, like a rodeo rider, trying to cling on. 'Call u ltr' was Christian's final reply.

As it was I was last through the door. By the time I'd stepped inside, there was no escape. Katy and Christian, who had known each other not closely, but through mutual acquaintances, for years, had spotted each other. The Wee Pub is cosy and intimate, like a very small living room. It has only half a dozen barstools, three or four high tables and two great window seats for some of the most entertaining people-watching in the city. No more than thirty can fit inside without bodily fluids being exchanged. It's not the kind of place you can avoid someone.

Katy introduced Christian to Rachel and Emily. Although they were aware of what had been going on, and though Emily knew of Christian through legal circles, they'd never met him. When Katy turned to me, she hesitated for a slight, almost imperceptible, moment. She knew everything, but she obviously didn't want him to know that. 'I think you guys have already met?'

Christian made an exaggerated frown then, as if a light bulb had just gone on, said: 'Ah, yes. We were introduced at . . .' He made a small circling movement with his hand to jog his memory. 'Was it Ali and Dominic's wedding?'

I nodded slowly, though I felt as if I'd been electrocuted inside, as if I could very easily stop breathing and keel over.

Ah yes, I remembered it well. I had met Christian two years earlier at a wedding on the island of Arran, on the south-west coast of Scotland. I was there as Katy's guest and knew hardly anyone else. Christian also knew only a handful of the other guests. We found ourselves alone at a table and got chatting about our work. At the time he lived in London. I had not long joined the *Observer* and told him I spent one or two days each week in the capital. We also talked about our mutual love of scuba diving. I'd just completed my PADI introductory course and had completed only six dives – the last of which was at the Blue Hole in Dahab, Egypt and so terrifying that I'd vowed never to dip below the surface ever again – but I managed to make myself sound as if I were Jacques Cousteau's mermaid granddaughter. I noticed that not only did he have a naked wedding ring finger, but that when he talked about all the places he'd been to notch up his near one hundred dives, he always said 'I' and never once referred to the merged 'we'.

I thought he was gorgeous. I also thought he was single. Until he went to the bar and Katy disabused me of that notion. He'd been married for two years. Jerk, I thought. I spoke to him only briefly after that. At the end of the night he gave me his business card and asked for mine, saying his company was involved in some interesting cases that he thought might be newsworthy and that he'd be able to give me the inside track on. I put his card in my bag, intending not to give him another thought. Which was relatively easy until he emailed me a few days later. He said he had a potential story about criminal gangs and suggested we meet for a drink the next time I was in London to talk about it.

When I saw him the following week, I thought he was even more good-looking. Instead of discussing gangsters, we chatted about life, work, dreams (although, looking back, it was mostly his life, his work, his dreams).

Over the next year we met for a couple of drinks every time I was in the capital. But our friendship really began to develop when he moved back up to Scotland. I spent less time in London and more time out drinking with him. We talked about everything. Apart from two topics that we conveniently managed to avoid: one was his wife (all I knew about her was that she was a high-flying management consultant who rarely finished work before 9 pm. He told me this in response to the one question I asked about her, whether she minded that he seemed to be out every Tuesday and Wednesday night. Apart from that, I'm ashamed to say, we behaved as though she didn't exist). The other subject that was off-limits was the thing between us. In other words, we talked about everything under the sun apart from what we should have been discussing. I found him funny and intelligent and passionate and sexy. He was everything I would look for in a man. But I kept reminding myself that a) he was unavailable, whilst affecting not to notice that b) we were, of course, turning into a big fat cliché.

Prospective adulterers are supposed to follow a script, but he never once uttered the well-worn words: 'My wife – she just doesn't understand me', or 'I love her, I'm just not in love with her'. And we managed to maintain our pose as just good friends until last summer. The fault line was crossed one drunken night when his wife was out of town overnight on business. (The script was now being followed with a vengeance.)

We were a little bit drunk, of course. At first, we just kissed. In the hall in my flat. We did that for so long that my lips began to feel numb and swollen. It was amazing. I made a half-hearted protest, saying it shouldn't go any further. But once I'd taken that first bite of the forbidden fruit, well, it required more strength than I had to say no to more. Afterwards, I knew what people in films meant when they talked about feeling as if they'd died and gone to heaven. Or of being on cloud nine. That was exactly how I felt. For about two minutes.

The role of a mistress is, at least in the movies, a glamorous and exciting one. But for a Glaswegian with Catholic roots, the inbuilt guilt destroys any lingering pleasure. Some lovers, in the rosy aftermath, share a cigarette or strawberries and champagne before they start all over again. Some read love poetry to each other. But moments after the end of our first dangerous liaison, when the cocktail of brain chemicals had worn off and the reality of what had just happened began to sink in, I started to panic. I went through to my living room and rummaged frantically in my bookshelves. Had there been a bible there, I'd probably have opened it and started chanting from Exodus 20:14 or Genesis 1:16–17: 'And the Lord God commanded the man, saying thou shall not . . .'

I heard Christian shouting from my bedroom, asking if there was any chance of a Marlboro Light. Leaning against my bedroom doorway, I shook my head and read out a moment-ruining paragraph that I'd highlighted from Chekhov's *The Lady With the Dog*. All my books are marked in the margin at thought-provoking sections. Strange, I know, but surprisingly useful at times. 'Listen to this,' I said, struggling to keep the alarm from my voice. 'Every affair, which at first adds spice and variety to life and seems such a charming, light-hearted adventure, inevitably develops into an enormous, extraordinarily complex problem with respectable people . . . until finally the whole situation becomes a real nightmare.' Of course, I knew this anyway. I knew it intrinsically, but somehow I had to be reminded. I had to see it in black and white.

'What the hell are you on about? This isn't an affair,' he laughed dismissively. If he was burdened by a Catholic or any other guilt complex, he was hiding it well.

'Go, go, go,' I said, ignoring him and ushering him out of my flat. 'This must never, ever, ever happen again.'

'Of course it won't,' he assured me, pulling on his clothes. 'Calm down. That's it out of the way now. We can just be friends without this big thing between us. And if neither of us ever speaks of it, it'll be like it never happened.' Great idea, I thought, nodding enthusiastically.

But as anyone who's ever been in this kind of situation will know, once the line is crossed, it's almost impossible to go back. The line is all but erased. You become like a junkie who gets high on the thrill, excitement, danger and secrecy of an illicit liaison. 'This must be the last time,' is said, if not out loud then at least to yourself, every single time you get a fix until eventually it becomes meaningless. They become nothing more than six little words strung together in a futile attempt to appease your own conscience and delude yourself into thinking that you're in control.

Although my friends knew what was going on, it was only when it started to unravel, towards the end of last year, and I started going crazy, that we spoke about it. Before that, I pretended to them, as I had been pretending to myself, that it was a different Lorna who was in love with someone else's husband. Not the nice Lorna, the good, law-abiding (apart from speeding), well-behaved, moralistic daughter, sister, friend, the one who had vowed with all her heart never, ever, ever in a million years to trespass. Of course, they weren't as dumb as me. They knew when I was lying and, on occasion, must have lost patience with my inability to stick to plans and my evasiveness. But, at the time, I was too self-absorbed to care.

Even after we crossed the line, I never told Christian how I felt about him. Nor did I make any inquiries about the state of his marriage or about whether he would ever consider leaving his wife. Did I want him to? Although I'd always told myself that I didn't love him, I was now beginning to think what my friends could already see: that I did, but was too scared to admit it. So I did what I was good at: complete avoidance. I had been, if not happy, then certainly content to plod along as things were. Until Charlotte.

Back in the The Wee Pub, the voices in my ears sounded weird and quivery as if the conversation were taking place at the bottom of a swimming pool. I heard Christian say: 'And this is Charlotte. She's just joined our firm. She has her first jury trial next week. And I'm just giving her some advice. And . . .'

And. And. And. Trying to retain an element of poise, I forced myself to smile and say hello. She was not just slim, but a full-blown waif and looked about seventeen. She was sitting on a high stool. Small and petite, with auburn red hair tied into two cute little side bunches, bright green eyes and flawless, unmade-up skin, she was striking. And she knew it. She could hardly take her eyes off her own reflection in the window.

After an almost imperceptible nod towards us, she took up the conversation and steered it in a slightly different direction. 'I was just showing Christian my tattoo.' When she said his name, she flashed him a gorgeous smile. 'Look.' As she stood up on the footrest of the stool, she lifted her top, pulled down her skirt to reveal a concave stomach and, if you bent down and stuck your nose in her crotch, you could just about make out a Hello Kitty the size of a ten-pence piece above her right hipbone.

An awkward silent glance passed between me, Katy, Rachel and Emily. Even without saying a word, I knew that we were all thinking exactly the same thing: what kind of woman behaves like that? At least it comforted me to believe that's what they were thinking, so I wouldn't be alone in my bitterness.

Christian interrupted the silence by asking what everyone wanted to drink. When he came back, I could vaguely hear him talking about trials, giving Charlotte and Emily a disturbing lecture about how easy it is to dupe a jury.

But I could hardly concentrate. I felt as if I were having an out-of-body experience or just waking up from a dream. I nodded intermittently and put on a fake smile now and again. My mind was racing, falling over itself with things to say, but I don't think I managed to utter a word. I had been telling myself that I must leave before him, but, after about thirty minutes, and with half of his pint of Guinness remaining, he looked at his watch and said: 'Right, I better be off home. Early st—'

'I'll share a taxi,' Charlotte interrupted. She managed to finish her drink, jump off her stool, put on her very cool green leather coat, grab her bag and say goodbye all in one swift move.

I looked at Christian, but he avoided eye contact. The moment they left, the tears began to fall.

* * *

'This has little to do with Christian and Charlotte and everything to do with previous unresolved conflicts.' These were Dr J's first words, about fifteen minutes into the session the following evening. (For the first time, I'd wished my Wednesday session was in the morning like the other two, rather than at 6 pm.)

I'd hardly slept at all after seeing them. I lay awake oscillating between hating him and loving him, hating her and wishing her dead, and hating myself. Miraculously, I managed to stop myself calling him the next morning, but I was pretty sure that was only because I was telling myself I'd 'take it to therapy' first. I was equally certain that, as soon as I had my next glass of wine, no matter what had happened with Dr J, the willpower not to contact him would dissolve. I thought I'd been feeling better about the situation over the past few weeks, but when I saw the two of them together, I felt even worse than I had when I was first told about them last year.

As soon as I lay down on the couch, I asked Dr J, more in hope than expectation, to force me to delete Christian's number from my mobile, even though I knew it off by heart. 'If I phone him, you can refuse to see me or increase your fees or get a hit man to break my legs or something, anything,' I said, half in jest, half in dire desperation. 'I need to be stopped. All these horrible feelings are back and I'm terrified of what I'm going to do.'

I was convinced, based on nothing other than the intense and nauseous feeling in my gut, that Charlotte was going to 'get' Christian and spend the rest of her life with him. I was admonishing myself for never having told him how I felt, somehow believing that this would have prevented the soap opera I felt as if I were now playing a part in.

When Dr J suggested my feelings were misdirected, I immediately protested, even though I knew she had a point, of sorts. I assumed she meant Johnnie and I was aware of the irony. With him, I would have been perfectly entitled to throw a hissy fit, but didn't. Now, ten years later, with a man I had absolutely no right to, I was on the verge of losing my mind.

But apparently Dr J wasn't referring to events as recent as a decade ago. No, with her, the root of everything was much further back. To unresolved conflicts I wasn't even aware of.

So I ignored her, as I often did in areas of confusion or ambivalence, and continued to rant: 'Do you know the difference between me and Charlotte? She identifies something that she wants and she goes out and gets it. Nothing stands in her way. She's one of these super-confident, pushy types. She's probably never been rejected in her life. I, on the other hand, hold back and wait to be asked.'

'You sound like someone who is competing with her bigger and better sister for the exclusive unconditional love of her parents.'

'Charlotte is at least a decade younger than me,' I replied, gazing at the ceiling.

Dr J paused before speaking. I was beginning to realise this was to give me time to reflect on the many different reasons why what I'd just said was the wrong thing to say. 'Her age is irrelevant,' came the eventual reply from behind my head. 'In your mind, she's bigger and better.'

And so the sparring continued a bit longer. I told her that I'd never made any demands on any man I'd ever been with. I never contacted Christian when it wasn't safe or sat outside his house or phoned him at home. He called all the shots. I never asked for anything. Which I thought was something to be proud of. Until Dr J ripped it apart and said it was further evidence of my child-like passivity in relationships.

'You sound like a little girl who thinks it's wrong or bad to want something, which may be part of the reason you ended up in a situation like this in the first place. You sound as if you have no respect for your own rights and needs.'

In my mind, I said 'fuck you', but I found myself shaking my head in dismay, because I knew there was truth in her words.

She was unusually talkative, making more observations and interpretations than she ever had before. When she asked for more details about the relationship, I resisted the urge to rhapsodise about how much I loved him and instead admitted that I could now see that it was so dysfunctional it could hardly even be described as a relationship.

I told her that, for the last eight or nine months, I hadn't allowed myself to think too much about what I was actually doing or what my feelings were. I avoided it completely. I never discussed it with him. We just pretended it wasn't really happening. Whenever I saw something about infidelity in a magazine or newspaper, though, I'd read it much more avidly than I'd have done before. But I was like an alcoholic who was still in denial. I consoled myself with all sorts of excuses to try to convince myself that it wasn't a real affair – I struggled even to say that word – and to make myself feel morally superior. I had a long 'at least' list going: at least his wife's probably at it as well (I had no evidence of this whatsoever. It was simply an assumption I made based on the fact that she seemed to be at work until 9 pm most nights, and it comforted me enormously to believe it was true); at least I've never asked him to leave his wife; at least we don't steal whole weekends together; at least I don't sit outside his house like a maniac; at least I don't tell him I love him; at least I don't ask him if he loves me or where he thinks this is going. In short, I shuttled between soothing myself with the fiction that it wasn't a real affair and, when that failed, telling myself that at least I was behaving like the perfect bit on the side. I gave myself a nice pat on the back for that.

'These are the things I'm finding hardest to deal with and most embarrassing,' I admitted to Dr J. 'I thought, because I'd never made any demands on him, that it would all somehow work out in the end. And, even more humiliating is that I actually thought I meant something to him. I thought I was the only one. Or at least the only other one, which would still, in some warped way, have been good enough for me. I wouldn't have ended up here, in therapy, if he and Charlotte hadn't got together.'

'That is an assumption,' she said. 'A convenient assumption. When you find yourself having to make assumptions, it is worth asking yourself why.'

I knew where this was going. If I blamed them, I didn't need to take responsibility myself. I was slowly learning the size of the gulf between saying 'I'm being mature, I'm taking responsibility' and actually being mature and taking responsibility.

After a while, she continued: 'Christian and Charlotte may be the catalyst that brought you to therapy, but I don't think they are the root of your difficulties. If it wasn't them, I wonder whether it might have been someone else: different characters but a similar story. Blaming them stops you from having to look at why you got yourself into this situation – one that, at some level, you must have known was never going to have a happy ending – in the first place.'

I sighed and retreated into silence.

It was broken by more of the calm but cutting words of Dr J.

'What I'm also hearing today sounds like a little girl who thinks that just by being *good* she'll be rewarded. And this need of yours to feel special, to feel superior.' She let this land with a long pause before elaborating. 'Many people with a need to feel better than others have a deep-rooted fear of not being acceptable to others.'

I listened to the sound of the rain ticking against the window. Gradually other small noises became audible – the faraway hum of traffic, her clock, creaking floorboards from another part of the apartment. I was listening to them but I was also hatching a plan.

I reached down for a tissue. 'Do you know how I feel about all of this?' I didn't wait for an answer. 'Stupid, pathetic, humiliated, helpless, out of control. And, yes, I feel jealous. Insanely jealous of this young, super-confident woman who spots what she wants, goes for it and gets it. And, yes, I also feel anger. Intense anger like I've never felt, or, at least, never acknowledged, before.

And, for once in my life, I'm not going to turn it inwards. I'm not going to keep it to myself. Thanks to you, I'm going to be assertive and do something about it.'

I waited, hoping for some sign of approval. When it became obvious it would not be forthcoming, I continued.

'I'm going to write a letter to his wife. She deserves to know the truth about the jerk she's married to. And I'm going to get in touch with Charlotte. It's so obvious she has him on a pedestal, just like I did. She idolises him. I want to warn her not to fall for him, not to make the same stupid mistake as I did.'

There was a deafening silence from behind my head.

In my mind, I imagined her saying: 'Lorna, that's a great idea. Go ahead and just do it. Here, let's write the letter together. Come, join me at my desk. You can even sneak a look at my pictures. Let me help you get in touch with your inner bitch. You say this kind of behaviour is out of character, but it's good sometimes to act impulsively. To break out of your comfort zone. So go ahead. Rock the boat. Speak your mind. Get in touch with your anger. Tell his poor wife what her husband's really like and share the wisdom of your ways with this other poor, young, deluded woman. Great idea. Play at being everyone else's therapist rather than realising that this is not about them. This is about you.'

But I knew by now, from the books I'd read, from my experience with Dr J so far and from conversations with Louise and Katy, that good therapists don't give advice. They try not to infantilise their clients, but instead to treat them with the dignity of adults. They try to help them face difficult decisions, and to accept full responsibility for the consequences of their actions or inaction, all on their lonesome. And, most of all, they don't hand out permission slips to go ahead with mind-numbingly stupid plans of vengeance. The only trouble was that I wasn't ready or willing to be treated with the dignity of an adult. I wanted to be told, or at least strongly advised, what to do in a nightmare situation like this, so that I could blame someone else if it all ended in tears.

I knew it was wrong and childish, but then again, so is a large chunk of adult life.

Instead of backing my plan, Dr J, as expected, quietly reflected what I'd just said back to me so that we could thrust it under her microscope and explore the dark truth behind the words. 'You say his wife *deserves* to know about her husband's behaviour. And you say you want to *help* this other woman not to make the same mistake you made.'

She let this hang in the air for a while before continuing: 'It seems to be important for you to present yourself as selfless and altruistic. Since day one, you have tried to present to me a rather angelic facade. Even in this affair with a married man, you've told me how wonderfully you've behaved in it. And now you say you want to *help* these other two women. You seem to find it impossible to admit to doing something, anything, for selfish reasons, or ever to be motivated by baser instincts. Most ordinary mortals out there are motivated by self-interest. Yet you, for some reason, need to cling on to the belief, no the delusion, that you are somehow not like that.'

I was just about to launch into my defence, but I didn't. I thought very carefully about what she'd just said and I twitched. God, she was getting good at this. Several times in the last few sessions she had steered off at what seemed like an irrelevant tangent only to highlight some uncomfortable truth about myself I hadn't previously known.

I blinked rapidly and sighed. I pulled at the skin around my cuticles. Shook my head. Then I put my hands over my face.

'I guess you are probably right,' I said. 'This is very difficult to admit, but I suppose what I want to do is hurt him because he's hurt me.' There was something uniquely refreshing about being completely honest with someone about these deep and ugly motivations. 'Yes, that's it. I'm so angry with him. I want revenge. Because he let me, he even encouraged me, to fall in love with him. And then, when I did, he dropped me and moved on to someone new.'

She repeated my last sentence, perhaps so that I could hear again how infantile and pathetic it sounded.

'Blame other people and you never have to take responsibility for your own behaviour,' I imagined her saying.

For a while only silence emanated from behind me, until Dr J broke with convention and came as close as it is probably possible for a therapist to come to actually telling someone what to do. 'Please do not react with your potentially lethal impulsiveness,' she said, with what sounded like a tinge of alarm in her voice. 'Therapy is about learning to feel the full extent of all your feelings, including the very uncomfortable ones, like anger and jealousy and fear and regret and rage. It is about learning to acknowledge these emotions in all their intensity, to experience these feelings fully rather than avoid them or act impulsively to get rid of them or to pass them on to someone else. And it is about learning to express them cleanly and directly, only if and when that is appropriate, and without destroying or punishing yourself or anyone else in the process.'

I lay in silence and I thought about the absolute fucking mess I was in.

'You are angry with him and with yourself, but please don't take it out on another woman, whose circumstances you know nothing about. Please do not hurt someone else because of your own anger, self-hatred and guilt – all the things that got you into this situation in the first place. Let's get to the root of that. Now, I am sorry, but our time is up.'

I picked up my bag and walked to the door. I opened it, but, before I left, I turned round to look at Dr J. She was still in her chair, sitting forward and with what I thought seemed a slightly sad expression on her face.

'I wish for once you'd say something, anything, nice to me,' I said, tears streaming down my cheeks. 'Something that would make me feel a bit better about this monumental mess I'm in.'

'That is not my job,' she said.

As I turned and walked away, I thought about how much I wanted a hug.

I sat outside in my car for about half an hour until I was in a fit state to drive. It was early evening. The clocks had just gone forward and it was light outside. The rain had stopped, but it looked as if another shower wasn't far away. The inky clouds were racing along and were so low that it made me feel strangely claustrophobic. I watched the weather for a while to try to escape from the words of Dr J that were still swirling around my head.

Rationally, I knew that my plan was brainless, but I still had this overwhelming urge to do it. I even managed to put my own positive spin on it: about being assertive for once; about expressing my anger rather than turning it inwards and so forth.

As I drove home, I thought: you can't win with therapists. You do nothing and you're too passive. You take action and you're too aggressive. The only solution was possibly sheer bloody not listening. I was going to go with my instinct. My mind was almost made up. I just needed one person to reinforce my prejudices and I was all set for destruction. I dried my eyes, went home, had a shower and made a few calls.

* * *

Later that night, I met Katy, Rachel and Emily in Chinaski's. I told them about my plan to write to Christian's wife and to meet Charlotte. Katy shook her head in obvious exasperation. 'Can we remember the facts here, puleez! You were losing interest in this guy until he lost interest in you. If, before Charlotte came along, he'd suggested leaving his wife for you, you'd have run a mile. You wanted him because you couldn't have him. That was safe for you. But now, because he's moved on to someone new, you're suddenly totally obsessed with him again. He's become the great lost love of your life. You're not interested in anyone else, especially if they're interested in you. You've become some lovesick woman. And he has this hold over you. It's pathetic. And Lorna, stop going on about how stunning she is. She's absolutely not. She even looks like a wee girl – I mean she has no tits and no ass. She looks prepubescent. And any woman who doesn't have female friends has major psychological issues. Anyway, why are we spending so much time talking about her? Why do women always do this? What about him? He sounds like another angry adolescent masquerading as an adult. Which is probably why you were drawn to each other.' I held my head in my hands. Katy carried on: 'It's not even what you really want. It's just unconditional exclusive love, which is what children want.'

Rachel agreed that I shouldn't write the letter. 'It's not your job to shatter his wife's illusions about her husband. That is a private matter for the two of them,' she said. 'And, remember, people have a natural tendency to shoot the messenger when they don't want to hear what's being said. Although in this particular case, you would, of course, deserve to be shot.'

She recounted a cautionary tale about a woman who'd told her best friend that rumours circulating about the friend's husband's infidelity were true. 'Do you know what the wife did?' Rachel asked. 'She turned on her best friend, saying she was just jealous of their marriage because she was single and asking what kind of so-called friend would say something like that. She's never spoken to her since, but she still hero-worships her husband. Who is, of course, still shagging anything and everything that moves. People are fucking nuts, especially when it comes to relationships.'

As for sharing the wisdom of my ways with Charlotte, Rachel laughed dismissively. 'Come on. You simply want her to know that you've already had what she wants. It's about letting her see that she's not as special as she thinks she is. That she wouldn't be the first. Or the last. It has nothing to do with helping her not to repeat your stupid mistake. People, as we all know only too well, have to make their own mistakes.'

Damn. My hopes of recruiting reasoned, cold-blooded allies for my plan of destruction weren't going well. But thank goodness for Emily. I'd heard it said by many therapy sceptics (in fact, I used to use the line myself) that if you have great friends, you don't need therapy. I was figuring that this was because there will always be at least one who will tell you what you want to hear.

'Why should these guys have the best of both worlds?' she said. 'The words 'cake' and 'eating it' come to mind. They are stuck in loveless marriages that they're too weak and cowardly to leave. At first, they attempt to avoid the guilt by trying to manoeuvre the wife into making the decision for them. They withdraw, stop having sex, criticise. Make the wife feel like shit, basically. But when the wife doesn't bite, and she never does, because as everyone knows, when someone no longer wants you, even if the rational part knows it's not working, the irrational part wants them more than ever and—'

Shaking her head, Katy interrupted. 'This is so your own stuff.'

Emily sighed heavily. 'It just pisses me off that these guys can play at happy families and, to relieve the boredom, have the thrill and excitement of an illicit affair with a young stupid woman who boosts his fragile fucking ego. And he can trade her in for a younger model every few years so he's constantly idolised and adored and validated and worshipped. And his monstrous ego gets bigger by the day. And his adoring wife remains oblivious. To hell with that. Do his wife a favour, do his next dumb victim a favour – write the letter.'

We ordered another bottle of wine, while Emily continued: 'If you don't write that letter, it will be for no reason other than to protect him. Because you're still in love with him and under his control. Because you don't want to upset him and you don't want him to get angry with you or to hate you. Fuck that. What about you? He's hurt you. He's upset and humiliated you. A strong woman would do it. A strong woman wouldn't give a damn if he hated her for it.'

I nodded, glad to have finally received the permission I'd been hoping for. 'You're right. You're absolutely right. A strong woman would do it. Cheers.'

* * *

The next morning I woke up with that awful sinking feeling in the pit of my stomach. There was a notebook on the pillow next to me. Some people dial under the influence, I just scribble. At the time, it seems really profound. Deep thoughts, occasionally poems, about the human condition and the meaning of life.

When read in the cold light of day, however, it is, without exception, cringe-inducing drivel. And that is only the bits that actually make any sense.

Hesitantly, I opened the notebook. On the first page there was a barely-decipherable scrawl in what looked like an eight-year-old's handwriting. 'Blah, blah, blah. I'll never love anyone else. Blah, blah, mumble, mumble. How do I love thee? Let me count the ways. Mumble, mumble. What's the sense in sharing. Blah, blah, blah. This one and only life.'

For a moment, I felt pleasantly surprised. It was nowhere near as bad as usual. But then I remembered I'd stayed up until two, drinking wine, crying, listening to Candi Staton's 'Young Hearts Run Free' and The Magic Numbers on repeat and reciting, aloud, the love poems of Elizabeth Barrett Browning.

The tearstained scrawl was an unholy blend of the three, like the results of Jeff Goldblum's self-experimentation in *The Fly*.

I turned over the page and there it was. An illegible scribble which, on closer inspection, turned out to be a draft of 'the most difficult letter I will ever have to write'.

'Dear Mrs—, I'm v sorry to be the one to tell you. The truth is – your husbandistotalJERK. Love him. ILOVEHIM. HATE HIM. LOVEHIM. HATETHE FUCKINGJERK.'

* * *

Over the next few weeks, Dr J continued her relentless poking and probing at the inside of my head. Sometimes I ignored her. Sometimes I disagreed with her. But most of the time, as annoying and uncomfortable as it was, I had no option but to agree with her. She seemed to have a unique knack not only of seeing the ugly truth, but also of reflecting it back to me in a way that made it difficult to argue with. And this, I was beginning to realise, is the difference between having great friends and being in therapy. Outside, in the real world, if someone criticises or just disagrees with you, the first human instinct is to defend yourself, often without even being aware that you are doing it. In therapy, you slowly discover that, while no one can function without defence mechanisms, most of us rely excessively on them. Gradually I began to understand that this thing between Christian and I was not the great love affair of the century that I'd stupidly believed it was. We were two seriously fucked-up, totally selfish individuals. I also came to the very uncomfortable realisation that only someone with a pretty low opinion of themselves, someone who didn't like themselves very much, and who had major communication problems, would ever have got into a situation like that in the first place. Although I was beginning to understand this, I was still thinking about him at some point every morning, noon and night. As wrong as it was, I missed him. He was a very hard habit to break. I was feeling better about him but I wasn't cured of him.

* * *

I didn't particularly want to go to Louise and Scott's party, especially since they'd made it clear that they were going to try to fix me up with one of their socially inept nerdy doctor friends, men who conspicuously lacked the bedside manner of the gorgeous attendings, residents and interns (I didn't think of them as actors) on the medical dramas on American TV. They were at least all from the Accident and Emergency department where Scott worked. 'All the good ones are taken,' I moaned. 'The rest are single for a reason.' But I reluctantly forced myself to wash my greasy hair and put on a dress. At least meeting new people would distract me for a few hours from ruminating about Christian and Charlotte.

Louise and Scott live in a big detached house at the end of a sleepy cul-de-sac in Glasgow's answer to Wisteria Lane or Knots Landing. Their house is far too big for them. It has four bedrooms, a study, a massive dining kitchen, which, according to the estate agent, was its unique selling point, and it looks out across a grassy field where all the local children play 'kiss, cuddle or torture', if the youth of today still plays games like that. It is the kind of place where people wash their cars or mow the lawn on a Sunday afternoon. Sometimes, when I go there, it repulses me.

Other times, which are becoming more frequent, I long for nothing more than to live there with a family and do nothing more exciting than wash the car or mow the lawn on a Sunday afternoon.

The party got off to an unexpectedly good start when Louise opened the door with a tray of champagne and whispered: 'He's not bloody well here. He couldn't make it.'

For a second I didn't know who she was talking about, then it dawned on me. 'Great. I'm seriously not interested in anyone,' I said.

We went through to the kitchen, which opens onto a large patio. A few people were outside and another dozen or so were indoors. A sumptuous spread was laid out: meats, salads, salmon, pizzas and lots of snacks and nibbles.

'This is my sister, Lorna,' Louise announced proudly. 'She's a journalist with the *Observer*.'

'Oh Christ. I hate the press,' bellowed someone called Malcolm, making a sign of the cross in my direction. 'Evil. They make up lies and print what they like and ruin people's lives. Far too much bloody power.'

Shit. Everyone looked at me expectantly. 'Er, well, democracy can't exist without a free press, you know. We, well not me personally, but my colleagues, hold the people in power to account. And, er, someone once said if they had to choose between government without newspapers, or newspapers without government, they wouldn't hesitate to choose the former.'

'The latter,' someone corrected me.

'Yeah, whatever,' I muttered.

'Fucking savage beasts,' Malcolm yelled. He'd clearly made an early start on the liquid refreshments.

'That was Thomas Jefferson,' said a man with a lovely deep sexy voice.

'Huh?'

'It was Thomas Jefferson who said that about the press.'

'Oh right, very good,' I said, taking a gulp of my champagne.

'And he was a man who was savaged, even abused by the press. More than Clinton, more than Blair.'

'Yes, exactly,' I said, giving Malcolm a look which said *ha fucking ha, you prick,* and smiling appreciatively at the surprisingly well-informed individual who had just come to my rescue.

He smiled back, awkwardly extended his hand, then quickly withdrew it. 'Um, hi. David,' he said. If my mind hadn't been contaminated with someone else, I'd have found him good-looking, in a Roger Federer kind of way. He wasn't Christian, obviously, but had a similar tall, broad, physique and the same big warm brown eyes. He also had lovely Federer-like thick, dark, messy hair.

He leaned towards me and, as everyone else started chatting amongst themselves, whispered: 'Malcolm's dad was jailed for fraud. And it was reported in the local paper.'

I looked at him with a frown.

'It's easier for him to despise all journalists than to accept that his father is basically a criminal.'

I nodded. 'Everyone needs a scapegoat. Anyway, nice to meet you,' and I strode off outside. He may have been unusually attractive, but I was in no mood to end up stuck in a corner with him wittering on about misdirected anger – I got enough of that with Dr J – and press freedom all night.

I wandered out to the patio. It was a lovely April evening. The air was fresh and cool and clear. The garden was a blurry of buds and the lawn had turned a deep green colour, confirming that spring had arrived. The time for birds to tweet. The time for new beginnings.

My brother-in-law, Scott, and some of his friends were debating someone's decision to have a dry wedding.

'I'm taking a flask,' someone said. 'I'm going to get hammered beforehand.'

'Ohhh nooo you're not,' neighed some awful woman – the bride-to-be, it soon transpired – with a long ginger mane, which she tossed over her lily-white shoulder in the manner of Miss Piggy. 'Anyone suspected of being under the influence won't be allowed in.'

They must be recovering alcoholics or professional moral superioritists, I thought, just as she said: 'We're not recovering alcoholics and it's not a moral stand. We just hate alcohol. It's a dangerous shield that people hide behind.'

Alcohol is not a shield, I thought indignantly, polishing off my first flute of champers, just as someone replied: 'I don't agree. In fact, I think it is the reverse. It enables people to let their guard down. It removes inhibitions. You know the saying: In vino veritas.'

'But some people can't handle too much truth,' I mumbled to myself, paraphrasing Louise, Katy and Dr J, as I escaped back through to the buffet in case the situation on the patio became in any way confrontational.

After filling my plate modestly – I didn't want anyone to think I was a greedy heifer who couldn't control her appetite – I joined a group of five or six people, including David.

'So what kind of journalism is it you do, Lorna?' he asked.

'Ever interviewed anyone famous?' added a guy called Jerome.

I racked my brains. What kind of journalism do I do? Good question. I thought it might have been a bit of a conversation killer to tell them that the last memorable piece I wrote was about being in intensive psychotherapy because of my communication problems, difficulties in getting in touch with my feelings and my inability to form a healthy equal relationship with an adult member of the opposite sex. Had I ever interviewed anyone famous?

'Er, I've interviewed the First Minister of Scotland?' I said, almost apologetically.

'Oh, right,' Jerome said, clearly unimpressed. 'Anyone else? Any footballers or celebrities?'

My mind was blank, but then I remembered. 'Yes! I once interviewed that guy who plays Will in *Will and Grace*. I can't remember his name, but he was gorgeous. And straight. Happily married, though, unfortunately. I did ask.'

'So what was the last piece that you wrote about?' David persisted.

'I did a big investigation into the scandal of patients infected with HIV and hepatitis from contaminated blood. It's the worst medical disaster in the history of the NHS and successive governments have refused to hold an inquiry into it. It's an absolute disgrace,' I said, feeling rather proud of myself, despite the uncomfortable expressions I'd elicited among my audience.

'That was in Sunday's *Observer* just there, wasn't it?' David said, with a somewhat surprised smile. 'I read it. It was very good. And, unfortunately, accurate. A very sad story.'

A compliment – oh no, oh yes, oh no, oh yes. 'Oh right, cheers, very good, anyway, whatever. More champers anyone?' I said, quickly changing the subject, and looking around for Louise.

'How long have you been with the *Observer*?' David asked.

'A couple of years.'

'And where were you before that?'

I gave him a brief job history.

At this point, any normal, well-adjusted, socially-skilled person would, of course, have asked David, or someone else in the group of medics, a question about their lives, jobs, holiday plans, hobbies, thoughts about the Hippocratic Oath – meaningless relic or invaluable moral guide? – voting intentions or views on the war in Iraq.

But, being somewhat socially retarded, I decided to devote the next hour or so to telling stories about my inauspicious start in the world of journalism.

My first job was at a local paper in Oban, a small town on the west coast of Scotland, about a two-hour drive from Glasgow. It's known as the 'gateway to the isles' and is surrounded by jaw-droppingly beautiful scenery. The locals appeared to be a friendly bunch and in my first week there I was told by at least half a dozen people that their doors were always open and I could drop by anytime. It has, however, also been said that Oban is the sort of place that you could move to at two months old, remain for the next eighty years of your life, but still be looked down upon by some of the locals as an outsider.

On my first night there, I took a stroll along the promenade and was stopped by several strangers who said: 'Ah, you're the new girl at the paper. Up from Glasgow.' One man, a local councillor, winked and said: 'I know everything about you.' I smiled back, though I was beginning to feel mildly terrified. I later found out that when I was there, it had the highest number of CCTV cameras per head of population than any other place in Britain. Locals insisted it was about safety. 'Outsiders' said it was about paranoia. Either way, I found it troubling rather than impressive when the local police chief boastfully demonstrated how my every single move in Oban would be captured on camera.

I managed to survive my year there by sharing a house with a hilarious, outrageous gay guy, trying to become a connoisseur of fine malt whisky and presenting a late-night talk show for lonely hearts on the local radio station, Oban FM. The programme was called *The Love Train*. I used to say, in a husky late-night radio presenter voice: 'Hello, it's me, Rosie Lee, here,' (the editor of the paper said it would be a conflict of interests if I worked at the radio station, so I had to do it incognito), 'driving the Oban love train.' From there we'd go straight into The O'Jays track of that name. No one actually ever rang in, though, which was marvellous, as it enabled me to play all my favourite sad songs and dedicate them to a girl whose boyfriend, the singer in a band, had left her broken-hearted after ditching her in favour of a young blonde groupie.

'That was me – the broken-hearted one, not the blonde groupie,' I clarified. David smiled. Lovely teeth and smile, I remember thinking fleetingly, before quickly continuing.

There were three other reporters working at the paper: one who hardly said a word to me in the entire year but conversed constantly and genially with the other two; another who was okay; and a third who spoke to me only to tell me, repeatedly, that I didn't have what it takes to be a journalist and that she doubted I'd ever amount to anything. It was tough being a trainee reporter. Especially because I was twenty-eight at the time. The other juniors were seventeen.

On my first day I was put in a cupboard with a bundle of out of date press releases and told to practise writing news in briefs. Otherwise known as NIBS, these are the two-sentence non-stories that no one bothers to read. Things like: 'A fisherman was fined £20 at Oban Sheriff Court last week after being found guilty of stealing one bottle of vodka and one bottle of whisky from Tesco.' And: 'Two cars were involved in a collision on the A85 outside Oban last week. No one was injured.' The next day I was told to go away and not come back until I had six good stories.

During one of my first weekends on the job, I had to cover a Highland show on the island of Mull, then an agricultural event outside Oban, and two coffee mornings. The brief I'd been given was simply: 'words and pictures'.

Eager as ever, I tackled each job, including the coffee mornings, as if I were investigating for an award-winning current affairs or documentary programme like *Panorama* or *Dispatches*. With my notepad in hand, I interrogated a pensioner as if he were a terrorist suspect after he was announced winner of the two-headed cabbage competition for the eighth consecutive year: Do you have proof that this isn't the same two-headed cabbage that you entered last year? What's your motivation for this kind of behaviour? Have you always been interested in two-headed cabbages? Can you share your feelings about this incredible record-breaking win? How do you plan to spend the £1.50 prize money?

I felt a little bit stupid asking the winner of the Best Young Heifer whether his cow was a boy or a girl and whether it had any children. And I nearly got myself killed while running about a muddy enclosure with six angry Highland cows, in high heels (me, not the cows), trying to get a photograph of the champion. But all in all, I thought it was a job, or four jobs, well done. As I sipped a fifteen-year-old Glenmorangie in The Oban Inn on the Sunday night, I felt exhausted but quite chuffed with my first proper journalistic assignments. I'm a natural, I thought. But I was stripped of that idea first thing on Monday morning. As I was writing up my report from the Highland show, I heard a terrible commotion behind me.

'Look!' shrieked one of the three reporters. 'Look what she's done.'

'Oh no. What a nightmare,' snorted another. 'She's landed us all in it with this.'

I slowly turned round. They were gathered round a photograph that I had taken. I looked nervously from side to side. Now, I'd be the first to admit that photography isn't my strong point, but I was actually quite proud of the shot I'd managed to get of the winning Highland cow from the Bunessan show. It had taken a while and I'd only just managed to avoid a head-on collision with its horns. 'It's, er, Frances Dawn Beg the third,' I stuttered. 'A fine beast, I'm sure you will agree. A beauty of a beast, ha ha. She was the champion of champions. Not a bad snap, eh?'

'Look at it,' the woman who was supposed to have taken me under her wing snarled. 'We can't put this on the front page. Or on any page for that matter. Our readers will go mad. We'll get thousands of complaints.'

I studied the image closely. It was in focus. Through a gap in her long fringe, you could see her lovely big brown eyes staring straight at the camera. She seemed happy enough. In fact, from some angles, she even looked as if she was smiling. Her owner was standing proudly alongside, looking quite dashing, I thought, if you're into farmers. I really was at a complete loss to see what was wrong.

'Look. At. Her. Legs,' spat my lovely colleague.

Somehow, the way the stupid cow was standing, with one of her hind legs hidden behind the other, it looked as if she had only three legs. Hmm. 'It's not that big a deal. No one will notice,' I almost said, but since they were treating this as some kind of national disaster, I thought it might be best to keep quiet until they'd calmed down. So I just made a face that I hoped translated into: 'Oops.'

'Oh. My. God!' Another ear-piercing squeal. 'Look what she's done with this one. She's completely ruined it. The poor beautiful horse. How humiliating for him. She's got his ears pinned back. Look everyone. Look what she's done to the lovely horse's ears. Why didn't you make sure his ears were forward? He looks like a donkey.'

I looked at the photo and then at my colleagues and thought, who cares if it looks like a freaking donkey? Donkeys may be stupid, but at least they're cute. At least they don't take themselves too seriously. And anyway, I'm not a bloody wildlife photographer. I wasn't taught, in my postgraduate journalism course that I borrowed £3,500 to pay for, how to interview and photograph cows and horses and black-faced frigging ewes. I wanted to say all that, but what I actually said was: 'I'm really, really sorry and I promise I'll try harder next time.'

As I finished speaking, David was looking at me with a curious smile. The others were actually grinning. Which I interpreted as a cue to continue. Since the Lorna-as-hapless-fool angle seemed to be working, I went on to tell them all about my disastrous stint as a teacher at one of the poshest private schools in Scotland. I got this job just after Johnnie dumped me, before I became a journalist, and my excuse for everything was that I was 'emotionally fragile and vulnerable and not in a good place'.

Contrary to the usual standards of deportment expected of the teaching faculty, especially at such a prestigious school, I had got slightly tipsy (i.e. horribly drunk) at the senior pupils' Christmas party and gone on to what was supposed to be a pupil-only bash at one of their vast mansions afterwards. I left at about four in the morning, having spent much of the time discussing with a group of pupils why I couldn't accept their £100 bribe to snog one, or indeed all of them. I slept in for the final day of term and thought I was going to get sacked as it quickly circulated around the entire school that Miss Martin was at the after-dance. But instead of being dismissed or even getting the belt, my temporary one-year contract was made permanent because of, according to a letter from the headmaster, 'my extremely enthusiastic approach to all aspects of school life'. Which, although hugely relieved about, I also found slightly disconcerting.

Most of the pupils were lovely. But, at the end of my first year, two of the spoiled-brat ones, with unacceptably stupid names like Aphasia Veranda daddy's-a-millionaire Brocklehurst the third, sent me a card when they left which I still have. It says:

'Dear ~~Miss Martin~~ Lorna,
You were a very unusual teacher who likes to gossip too much
and who dwells too much on the past. We know your
experience at our wonderful school, particularly your first term,
had its ups and downs, but we leave feeling totally confident
that you have learnt your lesson. You are here to teach, not to
tell pupils that you have a broken heart and that you used to go
out with a singer in a band who wrote songs about you.'

They were seventeen. I was twenty-six.

David laughed gamely. I smiled back. 'Crazy,' I said, reflecting on that period of my life.

'You've been around then?' he asked.

'A bit,' I said.

'And are you happy where you are now?'

'Kind of. I work from home and I found the isolation very difficult at first. But I started seeing someone at the beginning of the year and, as utterly bizarre as it is, it seems to be helping.' The words were out before I realised that they probably shouldn't have been.

'Oh.' He frowned then looked a tiny bit disappointed.

'Is it serious?' he asked, with a little grin.

'Oh, you know, not serious serious. Just the usual crazy relationship stuff.'

His brow furrowed and the corners of his mouth turned down slightly. He looked confused, but he nodded and said, 'Oh well, it was very nice to meet you.'

I drained my glass and said, 'It was very nice to meet you too.'

It wasn't until I was in a taxi home and the conversation I'd had with David was on replay in my mind that I realised it probably sounded as if I were seeing someone in the romantic sense as opposed to in the head-examining sense. I don't know why this bothered me, but it did.

May

Exit Dr J (Temporarily). Enter Dr McDreamy

It is bizarre what happens to you when you're having this kind of therapy. Sometimes you feel as if you have two heads. Or at the least two voices inside your head. I hadn't noticed exactly when Dr J had taken up residence inside mine, but the result was that, even when I wasn't in her consulting room, there were periods almost every day that acquired the surreal, over-determined quality of a session with her. Even the most seemingly innocuous event could end up subjected to her ruthless, forensic dissection.

One warm and sunny morning at the beginning of May, I was shopping for a present for Lewis for his second birthday. I was heaping praise on myself for my uncharacteristic forward-planning. His birthday wasn't for a fortnight and normally I'd have left gift-hunting, like everything else, until the very last minute. But not only was I buying early, I'd also decided I was going to get him something extra special and lovingly thought-out. While wandering about, I got it into my head that it would be a good idea to knit him an intricate Aran jumper. It was an ambitious project, but as I examined the luxury wool and fancy patterns in the John Lewis department store, I knew it was perfect.

It was when I was at the check-out, waiting in a queue, that my internal Dr J made her appearance. She took apart, in an oleaginous, whiny, insinuating tone, which she didn't actually have in real life, my motives. Our imaginary conversation went as follows:

Me: Hey! Hi. Why do you keep following me around?

Dr J: Not only do you need me to, but you want me to. Otherwise you wouldn't have said hi, would you? You'd have avoided me the way you try to avoid all the uncomfortable things in your life.

Me: Ha ha.

Dr J: Did I say something amusing? Or are you, as usual, forcing yourself to laugh, even when there is nothing obviously funny, as a way of hiding your pain?

Me: Oh for God's sake.

Dr J: It hasn't escaped my notice that you have, in all the work we've done together, managed to avoid talking in any depth about the very painful matters that brought you to my door in the first place. I'm not talking about your little love triangle – it was inevitable that something like that was going to happen sooner or later with you – I'm talking about the real underlying fear and pain that drives all the self-destructive things that you do, including, for instance, that little suicide mission you went on in Thailand earlier this year.

Me: I don't know what you're talking about.

Dr J: Oh, I think you do. You just don't realise it yet. Those family matters that you've skimmed across, insisting that they're no big deal.

Me: They're not.

Dr J: Hmm. Anyway, as usual with you, you're trying to side-track us once again. Let's get to the point – the reason I popped up just now.

Me: Yes, quite. It's not as if I can get into any trouble here. All I'm doing is being a fabulous aunty to my adorable nephew. Even though the little rascal is partly to blame for my problems. Ha ha ha. That is all I'm doing.

Dr J: No, that – sadly – is never all.

Me: What do you mean?

Dr J: Well, why do you think you're going to such extreme lengths to get your nephew an extra-special lovingly thought-out, personalised gift this year that, by the looks of things, will require you to stay up knitting 24/7 for the next two weeks and

which he, being only a toddler, will be none the wiser?
Me: Because I love him so much?
Dr J: Try again.
Me: I like knitting and haven't done it for a while and I enjoy
setting myself a really tough challenge?
Dr J: Oh dear. We really haven't made that much progress at
all, have we? It is, of course, because last year Katy gave him a
beautiful, hand-made memory book which she'd obviously put
a great deal of thought into and which he and his parents will
treasure for the rest of his life. It was the most talked about
gift and it rather overshadowed the yellow plastic dumper
truck you got him at the last minute.
Me: Hmmm. I'd forgotten all about that.
Dr J: No you hadn't.

And, just like that, I was no longer buying simply wool and knitting
needles, I was participating in a keenly contested competition. I
was purchasing an opportunity to make sure that this year, unlike
last year, it was I who gave King Lewis the most impressive gift.
As I handed over my cash (I was not going to let her change my
mind), I expressed silent disbelief that therapy could transform even
a simple shopping trip to buy a birthday present into such a psychological goldmine.

* * *

By the beginning of May, I'd had around forty sessions and it was,
without doubt, the strangest relationship I'd ever experienced in
my life. I wasn't even sure how much, if any, improvement I'd
achieved in that time. It was hard to say what it was accomplish-
ing, other than helping me realise that I wasn't the person I
thought I was. I certainly felt much less anxious, though I did feel
rather dazed and confused a lot of the time.

* * *

One bright spring morning, Dr J asked what I was like at work.
'What do you mean?' I replied suspiciously. She didn't respond,

which I took to mean that I was to say whatever came into my mind. She was always haranguing me to do this.

I told her I thought I was conscientious. 'I have a pathological fear of making mistakes, of appearing stupid, so I'm very thorough. I'm plagued by self-doubt. Whenever I send a story I immediately think it's rubbish and start thinking of all the things I could and should have done to improve it. Because I work from home, I think people in the office are laughing at it and saying, why the hell did we employ her? It's paranoid, I know. And self-obsessed, I know that too. If my phone rings and it's my boss, I automatically think, shit, I've done something wrong.' I told Dr J this, I grudgingly admitted that it wasn't quite as acute as it had been before I'd come into therapy.

'I think a lot of journalists are a bit like that,' I added quickly, because I didn't want her thinking it was just me. 'I think a lot are driven by a deep-rooted insecurity and a fear of failure and inadequacy. And a lot are control freaks. Actually, I know one journalist who has to run three miles a day every day. If she misses one day, she'll do six miles the next. And she only has a small number of selected foods that she's allowed to eat. It's very weird. I think it's all about control. You know, it's as if, by having all these rituals and routines, she feels protected or something, as if nothing can get her. It's crazy. Why do you think she does all that?'

'Who cares?' came the voice from behind my head. 'What's far more interesting is why you want to use your time and money talking about someone else. We're not analysing anyone else. Focusing on other people's flaws and problems is a very convenient way of avoiding your own. Let's talk about you.'

'Grrr,' I growled under my breath, before going on to tell her about press awards, which are the Best Thing Ever when you win, but a shameless, excessive backslapping political stitch-up when you don't. Sounding apologetic, I told her I'd been in both camps. She asked if awards and other forms of external validation or recognition were important to me.

'Nope, of course not,' I barked, a little too quickly and aggressively.

In the ensuing silence, I was being plagued by an unpleasant flashback.

Over the years, I've done countless excruciatingly embarrassing things. But the worst has to be the day I phoned the chairman of the judges for the annual Scottish Press Awards, the Oscars of the country's journalism industry, to ask, in tears, why I wasn't on the shortlist.

He was, understandably, flabbergasted. He politely explained that the standard was exceptionally high and that the judges decided that my work simply wasn't good enough. I practically broke down. 'Not good enough?' I sobbed. 'Did you say not good enough? Did all the judges think I wasn't good enough? Did anyone go out on a limb and say they thought I was nearly good enough? Or showed potential to maybe one day, if I kept trying, be good enough?'

While he listened in stunned silence, I explained that I'd spent almost a year on a campaign to expose the long-term detention of child asylum-seekers. Sounding more desperate and deranged by the second, I told him that, until I'd been rejected by the judges, I had thought it was the best work I'd ever done as a journalist and that I'd been extremely proud of it.

'Well, that's the important thing. That's the only thing that really matters,' he said, and hung up.

'Either he was just saying that to get rid of me, or he'd been in therapy and actually meant it. Ha ha,' I said to Dr J. She wasn't amused. Or if she was, she was keeping it to herself.

In the silence that followed, I thought back to that year of my life during which I became completely obsessed with saving one particular family of asylum-seekers: a mother and her four beautiful and intelligent children. I shed so many tears for them and couldn't stop thinking about them locked up for over a year in a former prison. I raised money to buy them Christmas presents; I visited them when they were deported. I even made inquiries about adopting them. As I lay back, the sun from the window behind me dappling the floor and walls, I was now having to ask myself some very uncomfortable questions. Who was I actually doing that for? Who was I crying for? Who was I trying to save? Them or me?

* * *

In another session in early May, I proudly told her that I'd changed my mind about writing a letter to Christian's wife. As usual, I initially tried to make it sound as if pure altruism had motivated this spectacular volte-face. 'I tried many times to write it, but I could never find the correct words. I eventually realised it's not my place to interfere, any more than I already had, in the private matter of someone else's marriage. It's between the two of them.'

Dr J said nothing.

I then admitted that, after struggling to write the letter, I even considered hanging about outside his wife's office to tell her in person. 'I had this insane idea that we were both in the same situation – the man we loved was about to be stolen from us by this stunning, young, super-confident home-wrecker. I actually had visions of us hugging and comforting each other and becoming really good friends. It's insane. Utterly insane, I know.' I shook my head. 'Anyway, I decided that I wouldn't resort to childish playground tactics. I decided to deal with it like a grown-up.' We sat in silence for a while as I mulled over what I'd just said.

The therapy hour is intended to be a temple of complete honesty. The aim is to be entirely, brutally honest with yourself. At first I thought it was like confession, a safe and secure place where you can get things off your chest and get absolution. But it's nothing like that. In confession, you're not challenged, whereas in therapy, hardly anything is unchallenged. Almost everything you say is dismantled and examined to find out what's really going on and how honest you are being with yourself about your feelings and your motives. With Dr J, I found it impossible to hide from the full and absolute ugly truth for long. It often felt as if every single statement, every word, every pause, every silence, every bloody comma, was seized from the air between us, thrust under a powerful microscope and subjected to an in-depth forensic analysis in an attempt to eke out everything. It made me realise how easy it is to hide from yourself in the real world, without even being aware of it. In therapy, there's no escape. 'I didn't write the letter,' I eventually confessed, my face hidden partly behind my hands, 'but I did something else, maybe not quite as destructive, but still pretty awful, because although I had been feeling better about the whole situation, I still couldn't stand the thought of the two of them together.'

* * *

A few weeks after I'd bumped into Christian and Charlotte in The Wee Pub, my resolve never to speak to him ever again, and to walk away with my head held high, melted after someone else told me she'd seen the two of them together in The Rogano enjoying a cosy romantic meal. I called him, in tears of course, and told him what I'd heard. He was silent. I asked if he ever thought about what he was doing to his wife, but I had no right to ask that. I was doing whatever I could to try to make him feel guilty enough to stop philandering. I said I couldn't believe what I'd been planning to do; that it was so completely out of character and that I hated myself for it. There was a palpable air of fear and regret and disbelief in the silence between us. I told him about the letters I'd written and how close I'd come to sending them. The next time, I sobbed, I would. I could sense that he was stunned. And terrified. After a moment, he said, 'Do that and I will fucking destroy you.' I said sorry and hung up.

I found it difficult admitting this to Dr J because I didn't want her to think I was capable of emotionally blackmailing someone. I honestly didn't think I was.

* * *

At the end of May, Dr J was heading off on holiday. She had told me her vacation plans at our first session: one week now and the entire month of August. She said she wanted to give me plenty of time to 'prepare myself' for her absence, which I had thought was perhaps a tad self-aggrandising and over-dramatic. Therapy had become an important part of my life, but not *that* important. During the last few sessions before she left, she took a surprisingly more pro-active role, always trying to direct the course of our conversations. She told me she thought her going away would be a perfect opportunity to explore my 'abandonment and rejection issues'.

'But I don't have abandonment issues,' I protested. Perhaps I shouldn't have mentioned that the night before I'd dreamt that I had my arms wrapped tightly round her neck while crying and begging her not to leave me.

This dream made little sense to me. But it gave Dr J another excuse to return, like a sniffer dog to a suspect package, to my childhood. She was constantly trying to revisit that, and I was constantly telling her that: 'It was uneventfully normal. It was happy. Nothing terribly exciting happened to me and nothing tragic happened to me. It wasn't *The Waltons*, but nor was it misery memoir material either.'

I had previously given her the following version of my early life:

I told her I was well fed, watered, loved and nurtured. We started off in a one-bedroom tenement in Glasgow, but I wasn't starved, abused or neglected. My dummy wasn't dipped in methadone to 'soothe' me when I was crying. Nor, to my knowledge, was I raised on liquidised 'sausage supper' – Glaswegian for deep-fried sausage and chips, another local delicacy for newborns in some parts of this fair city, according to members of the medical community I'd spoken to. I wasn't left to cry (I checked with my mum), as advocated by some of today's parenting 'experts', who think babies should be subjected to the same strict training routines as puppies. Nor was I handed over to a substitute carer. My mum was there for us 24/7 until we started school, and, even then, she worked nights so that she was there when we came home from school. I was loved. I was wanted. My needs were met. So why on earth, how on earth, could I have abandonment issues?

My earliest school memory was from St Charles's Primary in Maryhill, one of Glasgow's less desirable areas. One morning during my first week, our lovely long-haired young teacher said we weren't allowed out to play during the interval because of the rain. Nor, she warned, were we to leave our seats. We were to sit silently, drinking our free milk. She asked if everyone understood and we all nodded and in unison said: 'Yes, Miss Doherty.' She slammed the door behind her. At first, no one spoke and no one moved. But it wasn't long before some of the more rebellious boys started whispering. It spread like an infection. A couple of the really brave pupils decided to go a step further: they left their desks and ran around the classroom. I don't know what possessed me other than, perhaps, the inability to resist the power of peer pressure, or the desire to follow bad boys, even at the age of five, but I decided to join them. A few minutes later, the bell sounded and we rushed back to our chairs. No harm done.

Miss Doherty returned to exactly the same picture of innocence she had left.

'Did anyone leave their seats?' she asked.

'No, Miss Doherty,' we chorused.

'Are you sure?'

'Yes, Miss Doherty.'

'Are you absolutely sure?'

'Yes, Miss Doherty.'

She stormed out of the room. When she came back with Sister Bernadette on one side and Sister Margaret on the other, I burst into tears. 'I'm sorry, I'm sorry, I'm sorry, I'm sorry,' I sobbed, as I ran towards them begging for forgiveness. Miss Doherty handed Sister Bernadette a piece of paper from which she slowly, gravely read out the names of the eight pupils who had been seen – from heaven, obviously, as opposed to the small panel of glass in the door – leaving their chairs. We were lined up in front of the class and whacked repeatedly on our knuckles with the edge of a ruler until they bled. The fear of God and a crippling guilt complex were duly instilled. Never, I vowed that day, never would I step out of line again. Not ever. And apart from the odd minor transgression here and there, I had largely stuck to my promise, until, of

course, recently, when I committed one of the most widely con-
demned sins. No wonder I ended up in therapy.

'Perhaps it's not Christian's fault or Charlotte's or Lewis's?
Perhaps it's that bloody Miss Doherty and those nuns who are
responsible for all my issues? Ha ha ha,' I said. To which Dr J
replied, 'I wonder why you always have to try to make a joke? I'd
have thought you'd have realised by now that there are no jokes
here.'

I ignored her and continued. The next vivid memory was from
the Shetland Islands, where I learned, as part of the curriculum,
how to do Fair Isle knitting, which, I discovered many years later,
is a very useful skill to have in times of heartache or for creating
extra special gifts for beloved nephews. I was nine when the
teacher wrote, in her ominous red ink, 'see me' on my arithmetic
jotter. I was terror-stricken. I feigned illness for a week to avoid
going to school while I racked my brain to see whether I'd done
anything wrong.

Eventually it dawned on me. It had to be the mild sexual fantasies I'd been having about snogging one of my classmates. I'd
recently seen *Grease* and was a bit obsessed with it. But I hadn't
told a soul that I'd been pretending to be Sandy and daydreaming
about kissing a fellow pupil, who was my young Danny. Holy
fuck, I thought, can the guy upstairs even see inside my head to
find out what I'm thinking? There was no doubt about it: I was on
my way to hell.

My mum eventually dragged me back to school and I nervously approached the teacher, Miss Adamson, with my jotter.
'Nothing to worry about,' she said sweetly. 'It just makes your
work even neater than it already is if you do a double underline
like this,' she demonstrated with a ruler, 'at the end of your
sums.' That was it. I'd spent a week lying on the sofa pretending
to be dying, missing important lessons, all to avoid a small piece
of ruler etiquette. I wasn't sure whether the tears I burst into
were of relief or rage.

'I suppose,' I informed Dr J, 'when I think about it now, looking
back, I must have been an anxious wreck from a very early age.'

'Hmmm,' she said.

Another memory came back to me. I must have seen something on the news about a high-profile miscarriage of justice case and suddenly became convinced, and terrified, that I or a member of my family was going to be jailed for a crime they didn't even commit. Childhood suddenly seemed a rather terrifying experience.

'I went to five different primary schools all over Scotland,' I said, in desperation. 'Maybe that's why I'm not good at sticking at things? I'd have just made new friends when we'd move and I'd have to try to make new ones again. We were always on the move, with my dad's job. I think he was searching for something, you know, a better life for his family or something crazy. I dunno.'

On other occasions, I tried to go further back. I'd read somewhere that Freudians, supported by an overwhelming number of scientific studies, believe that the way we are cared for in the first six years of life has a major influence on who we are and how we behave in relationships – whether we're controlling, manipulative, bullying, submissive, whether we fear authority or like to challenge it, and whether we play the parent or the child role. There is also evidence that position in the family, gender and number of siblings has a major impact on the kind of adult you become and how you behave in all future relationships.

I made a joke about the fact that my parents had captured every moment of Louise's early years, every developmental milestone, on camera. Because she was the firstborn, they had hundreds of photos of her as a baby, lovingly displayed in album after album. There were scores of her sleeping, being bathed in the kitchen sink, looking very cute with apple-red cheeks when she was teething. The golden locks from her first haircut have been treasured to this day and, although relatively poor at the time, my parents somehow managed to scrape together enough cash to get a professional photographer to come out to our flat to shoot her first holy communion. There were hundreds of prints of Louise looking all angelic in her mini wedding dress pledging her love to God, and of: Louise and my mum, Louise and my dad, Louise with Gran and Granda. I think there was one of me, crying of course, and Louise. I'm surprised there wasn't a snap of Louise with the Pope.

By the time I appeared on the scene, it was clearly a case of been there, done that. So your cheeks are bright red and you're in agony because you're cutting your first tooth? Big deal, who cares, here's a rusk, get over it. In contrast to the 300-odd images of Louise's early years, there were maybe a dozen or so of mine. No lovingly retained evidence of my first haircut, no inaugural potty moment or baby-in-the-kitchen sink shots. Aha, perhaps this is where my issues of inadequacy and jealousy stem from? It's not the fault of Christian and Charlotte or Lewis or those nuns. It's my own bloody mum and dad's.

We finally settled in Milngavie, a leafy suburb of Glasgow, when I was nine and Louise was eleven. The first significant memory I have from that period was of being teased relentlessly by a handful of boys about my nose, which they declared too big. Though I've grown to accept it for what it is, back then, during those confusing adolescent years, I hated it and resorted to extreme measures – trying to break it, going to bed with masking tape stretched over it and tearfully begging my mum to take me to a plastic surgeon.

'I was convinced any surgeon with a heart would take one look at me and perform reconstructive rhinoplasty immediately as a charitable gesture. Ha ha ha,' I said.

'It was funny?' came the stern voice from behind my head.

'Not at the time, obviously. But, looking back, yeah, I guess it was. Kind of.'

'If you're having to hazard a guess, then perhaps you might want to think again? Remember this is a place where you can be open and honest. The idea is to uncover the secrets you've been keeping from yourself and to reinterpret those early chapters of your childhood and adolescence.'

I sighed heavily.

'Kids can be cruel.' I shrugged. 'What can you do? You can't undo something that's already happened, so what's the point in getting hung up on it?'

'Who said anything about trying to undo the past? We can be hung up, as you say, on things that we're not even aware of. When we become aware of them, we paradoxically often stop being so affected by them.'

I lay in silence for a while. I remembered a few years ago hearing that the loudest, most relentless, most vociferous opponent of my nose had died of a heroin overdose. I expressed shock and sadness at the tragic waste of a young life, and I meant it, but another thought, a transient, unexpressed (until now) one, on learning the news, was: 'Good. Because you were a nasty little prick who made every day at school utter fucking hell for me.' And he had. I tried to make sure I sat in the back corner of every class so that he wouldn't catch my profile and start hurling abuse across the classroom.

'Maybe it wasn't so funny after all,' I admitted. 'But no point crying over spilt milk. What's done is done.'

And I moved swiftly on. Of all the things that shaped me in my childhood and adolescence, the most significant was when I was fifteen and my family had a 'little crisis'. First, my dad, a typical Scottish man, with repressed emotions, big dreams and a phenomenally high work ethic, was made redundant. He'd never not had a job since he was fifteen himself, when he was forced to leave school to earn money to give to his step-dad, who was a chronic and compulsive gambler. His pride was completely destroyed, but, typically, he said nothing about how he was feeling. On reflection, it was obvious that he was unable to cope with unemployment when his upbringing had taught him that idleness is a sin and that his role was to support his wife and children. As a result, he withdrew completely, disappearing inside himself for a long time. I think maybe this was his mid-life crisis.

It was a horrible time. I remembered that he would sit without the lights on, or without the TV or radio on, because he wasn't earning any money and didn't want to use electricity. He just sat in a chair, drinking black tea and speaking even less than usual. My dad's a passive man. I've never known him to raise his voice or lose his temper. Ever. Everything is kept in. I used to avoid going home from school because I couldn't bear to see him like that. I'd sometimes see tears in his eyes. But if anyone ever asked him if he was okay, he'd just say 'fine'.

Around the same time, my sister, who would have been seventeen, was diagnosed with a brain tumour.

There was a long silence. The first time I told Dr J about this, she sounded unusually compassionate and said: 'That must have been a very difficult time for your whole family.'

'Worse things happen to people,' I replied, in good old stoic fashion. 'It wasn't that big a deal. Nobody died. In my job, I've met parents who've lost children and children who've lost parents in the most horrendous circumstances. I didn't lose anyone. It really wasn't that big a deal. Anyway. Shit happens. You move on. So, there you have it. The story of my childhood. That's it.' And I wiped away some tears.

'In here, that, sadly, is never it,' came the voice from behind my head.

But that morning in May, the last session before she went on holiday, she returned to it and refused to relent. 'I wonder if you'd like to say any more about that period?'

I shook my head. 'I don't think there's anything else to say.'

Silence.

All of a sudden, I was fifteen years old again. It was just before Christmas and we were in the neurosurgical unit of the Southern General Hospital. A lovely man called Professor Teasdale was talking about Louise's pituitary gland. It should have been the size of a pea, but was the size of a golf ball. There had already been months and batteries of blood and eye tests, CT and MRI scans and X-rays. At the time, it was the biggest tumour of its type they had seen and she was the youngest person they'd known to have had it. The professor was talking about the operation, something called transsphenoidal surgery, which involved cutting under the upper lip and going in through her nose, drilling through the base of her skull to attack the tumour and then taking muscle from her hip to replace the removed part of her skull bone. He also mentioned radiation and some medication that she'd need to be on for the rest of her life, and possible complications if she were ever to become pregnant. Although the operation involved a relatively new technique at the time, it had a high success rate and the prognosis was excellent.

Louise, who later said her cocky arrogance was probably a mask for the terror she was too young to feel or understand, said no, she wasn't going to have the operation. She'd be fine without it, thank you very much. The professor said if she didn't have surgery, she would lose her sight within two years, be in a wheelchair in three and be dead before she was twenty-one.

I have no idea how my mum and dad reacted to this news. I can't remember. I imagine my mum would have tried not to cry for Louise's sake and I imagine my dad probably went into his own even deeper silent kind of shock that was hidden from the outside world and possibly even from himself.

Eventually, Louise was, of course, persuaded to have the operation. I remembered going up to see her the night before the surgery. She was crying because she had just found out that a procedure they'd carried out earlier that day hadn't been successful and they were going to have to do it again. It involved tying an elastic band underneath her nose and another across her forehead, pulling them as tightly as possible and then injecting a dye into the vein protruding from her forehead. She was crying because she said she had never felt pain like it in her life. She didn't want to talk to us, but she didn't want us to go home either.

My most vivid memory from this whole period was waving up to my sister – she was on the sixth or seventh floor of the unit – from the car park after we left her that night.

The next night we went up to see her. The operation had lasted about six hours. When I saw her lying on the hospital bed, I remember going cold and light-headed and slumping down on the floor in tears. Her face had swollen so much it looked grotesque. She looked like the victim of a brutal assault. Her nose, which was packed with bandages, was like a boxer's after eighteen rounds. She had a drain in her spine, and a nose bag, because of a cerebral fluid leak. She was also confused and exhausted and pretty groggy after the anaesthetic. She couldn't speak, but, at one point, she sat up and threw up dark red blood everywhere. I sat on the floor crying the entire time.

'Did I cause it?' I remembered asking my mum when we went home that night. Because I'd once sunk my teeth into Louise's head during a fight, I had begun to wonder if I was responsible for this crisis that had befallen my family.

That was the last time I went to see her until she was transferred to another hospital a few weeks later.

Sometime, during all of this, I went off the rails: drinking, smoking and staying out late. And then, just as suddenly, I stopped. I told my friends I didn't want friends anymore and I stayed in my room for a while. Looking back, I think I was copying my dad's way of dealing with things: withdrawing, avoiding, hiding, running away.

In the middle of remembering all this, and telling Dr J about it, I started to cry. Really cry. The tears which I kept mopping up kept on coming, running out of my eyes, as if from an infinity pool, and down the sides of my cheeks into my ears. I had never really thought back to that period in my life before. I'd told people, matter-of-factly, that my family had had 'a little crisis' when I was a teenager and it was 'tough', but I had never gone back and taken time to think about how everyone must have felt.

I'd recently been clearing through some old stuff and found a note Louise had written to me a few nights after her operation. It said: 'Hi, pal. How are you? I am sorry you felt tired tonight and could not make it up to see me. But never mind. Thanks very very much for the wee rabbit, Lorna. It was very thoughtful of you. Hope to see you soon. All my love, Louise x.'

I'd bought her a little blue cuddly rabbit and made up some feeble excuse so that I didn't have to visit her. I shook my head. I didn't know why I hadn't wanted to go back up to the hospital to see her. I was a hormonally deranged adolescent, but that was hardly an excuse.

'I can't imagine how my mum must have felt. How she coped with all that,' I said as I lay gazing at the ceiling. 'Or my dad. Or

Louise. It must have been a nightmare for everyone. And I cannot imagine how people cope with actual loss, especially of a child. I'm just thinking that so many of the stories I've been drawn to as a journalist are about unimaginable losses, as if I want to find out how people deal with it.'

Eventually the voice from behind my head said: 'And what about you? I wonder how you must have felt during that time? You were still very young at fifteen.'

I shrugged. 'Who cares? My dad was redundant – such a horrible word. He disappeared. My sister nearly died. My mum was trying to hold it all together. I honestly don't have a clue how I felt.'

'Maybe you felt abandoned by the three people you loved and angry with them for having no attention left for you . . .'

I shook my head. 'No. No. No. That's absurd. Ridiculous.'

'This is not about finding fault or about apportioning blame; it's about understanding who you are. Why you are the way you are. Maybe you felt angry with them, without even being aware of it? Children are often angry with their parents but don't know how to express it, so they keep it in. And feelings, remember, can seem completely irrational. They don't always follow rational rules. In fact, usually they don't. So perhaps you felt angry, but you also felt guilty for having such thoughts?'

As selfish and irrational and unpalatable as it sounded, it also began to make some sense to me.

For the rest of the session, I lay back and, through tears and in silence, watched a series of flashbacks from my adult life through the prism of what she'd just said.

* * *

The plan, while in therapy, was not to get involved with anyone new until I'd sorted myself out. But, out of the blue, I was asked on a blind date. I'd never been on one before and, under normal circumstances, I'd have politely declined. But, as my friends kept telling me, there is nothing like a new romantic obsession to take the mind off an old one. Or, in cruder terms, the best way to get over one man is to get under another. I had no intention of jumping into anyone else's bed, but I quite liked the idea of going on a date. Generally speaking, Scottish people don't do dating. They have a couple of drunken snogs with someone then, before they know it, twenty years have passed and they're married with children. So there was a certain novelty factor involved.

The thing with Adrian wasn't strictly a blind date. We'd met a month ago at a party. At least, that's what he said. The slight problem was, I had no recollection of the encounter, which suggested I had been either: a) very drunk b) very unimpressed or c) both.

But he went to the trouble of getting my email address from a colleague, which I thought was rather sweet of him and very flattering for me, though one of my friends saw it as a sure sign that the guy was a weirdo or potential stalker.

His email said: 'Hey Lori, it was lovely chatting to you at Lisa's party. I get back from my month-long dry stint in the desert tmrw. Fancy a glass of wine to help me quench my thirst? Adrian x'

Initially, I thought it was a case of mistaken identity. Not only had I no memory of meeting a guy called Adrian or telling anyone my name was Lori, but I didn't know any Lisas. And, while I liked the image of being such a voracious party animal that I'd lost track of where I'd been and the people I'd met, the truth was duller. The only party I'd been to in the previous month was Louise and Scott's.

I called Katy and Rachel, who were as baffled as I was. Then I rang Emily, who, after consulting her scrupulously detailed diary, managed to pin down the event. Six weeks ago, I'd gone with her to a birthday night out for one of her friends – not a party, just drinks after work. But while she was quite clear on the friend's name being Lisa, Emily was as bamboozled as I was about the identity of Adrian.

Out of curiosity, I replied to his message with: 'Hi Adrian. I'm intrigued. But I feel I have to be honest and the truth is I can't remember ever meeting you. I don't have a clue who you are! This may be because at Lisa's birthday drinks thing I had a terrible cold and had taken lots of medication [a downright lie]. Can you please tell me a little more about yourself? What do you do etc? I can't imagine myself ever going out with a man who is into yoga or a vegetarian. Apart from that, I guess it's just about whether there's a spark, isn't it? Rather than, you know, going through a check-list or something. In saying that, he would have to be funny and I do find myself attracted to men who have big strong, sexy forearms and big hands. Spk soon. Lori x.'

In his reply, he said that his friends would describe him as handsome, witty, of above average IQ and looking 'a bit like Richard Gere'.

Bloody hell. Although more of a George Clooney fan myself, all of a sudden my mind was flooded with scenes from the end of *An Officer and a Gentleman* in which Gere, dressed in his starched white military uniform, strode purposefully through the factory where a very fragile and vulnerable-looking Debra Winger worked, and swept her off her feet. He carried her in his big strong arms off into the sunset while Joe Cocker and Jennifer Warnes were belting out 'Up Where We Belong', and all Debra Winger's colleagues were on their feet, clapping and wiping away tears of joy and happiness.

'Cool,' I replied, trying to sound casual rather than ecstatic. 'Where and when?' While I waited for his reply, I downloaded 'Up Where We Belong' and listened to it on repeat for the rest of the day.

Adrian was forty-two, an engineer, well read and well travelled, according to his last email. He lived alone in G12, Glasgow's answer to Notting Hill. Hurrah, I thought. He wasn't married, but nor did he appear still to be dependent on his mummy and daddy, physically, at any rate. He said he had forearms as thick as tree branches and hands like garden spades. 'Not literally, of course, but I can assure you, you won't be disappointed,' he added, flirtatiously.

We arranged to meet at The Wee Pub at 7 pm on Friday.

* * *

There are few things in life sweeter than telling someone who rejected you, and broke your fragile heart that you'd been trying so hard to protect, that you've met someone else and moved on. Strictly speaking, I hadn't. But I was going on a date with a Richard Gere lookalike and that was close enough for me.

So, when Christian called me on the Thursday – the first time we'd spoken since I'd emotionally blackmailed him weeks ago – I was thrilled.

'How are you doing?' he asked, sounding uncharacteristically sombre.

'Absolutely fantastic,' I replied. 'You?'

'Yeah, okay. I've had better episodes in my life.' He hesitated for a moment before saying: 'Look, do you fancy a drink?' Not just the two of us, he qualified immediately. That would be too dangerous. He said a crowd of people were going out after work the following night. I could join them. 'It would be nice if we could put the past behind us and try to be friends again, don't you think?'

'Aw, I'd really love to,' I said, trying to allow just the right level of mournful sarcasm to creep into my voice. 'But I'm going out with my new boyfriend.' I smiled as I said the last three lovely words.

He stuttered: 'Oh, right, cool. Well, have a—'

I interrupted him. 'My new boyfriend's a paediatrician (sexier than an engineer) and he's the double of George Clooney (sexier and younger, I think, than Richard Gere). He lives in G12. He's a pretty amazing guy, actually. He's not at all self-obsessed or egotistical or insecure like, you know, like some other guys. He's totally amazing.'

Ugh. As I said this, an uncomfortable image of Dr J appeared in my mind. This was happening with increasing frequency. She might have been on holiday, but I couldn't seem to escape her. She was wearing an icy glare and shaking her head in disgust and disappointment. 'Piss off and leave me alone,' I said silently to her.

'That's great,' Christian said, sounding annoyingly, offensively genuine. 'Have a lovely night. Maybe catch up with you some-time?'

'Maybe,' I said. 'But I'm really busy these days. Anyway, enjoy your night out tomorrow. Where are you going, by the way?' *How great would it be*, I was thinking, *if he said The Wee Pub and, when he walked in, me and Adrian were snogging away passionately in the corner?*

'Babbity's,' he said. Damn. Babbity Bowster's was a pub in the Merchant City, on the other side of town, a favourite haunt of lawyers.

'Oh well. Very good. Have fun. Byeee,' I said, and went to hang up.

'Take care,' he said.

Grrr.

* * *

The next night I was so nervous about my partially-sighted date, as my friends and I had taken to calling it, that I had to take 20mgs of propranolol (a beta-blocker often used by musicians and other performers to prevent stage fright. My lovely GP had prescribed this a couple of years earlier when I was in an anxious frenzy about something or other and I kept a stash for emergencies). And then, while trying on loads of different outfits and working myself up into a heightened state of indecision, I developed a blotchy anxiety-related rash on my neck. Eventually I opted for a black and white tartan wrap mini skirt from Hobbs, a black polo neck and high-heeled black boots. When I walked into The Wee Pub only five minutes late, I glanced around and my first thought was: 'Oh my God, I've been stood up.' There was no Richard Gere lookalike, nor anyone remotely answering to that description, in sight.

There was only one man who was alone. He was sitting on a high stool at the edge of the bar drinking a pint of heavy. He looked a bit like John Prescott, but with white hair and a redder, ruddier complexion. He was grinning at me. I smiled politely back then looked around again for my date. 'Yoo-hoo,' he bellowed, then extended his arms as if we were long-lost lovers. 'Lorna. It's me. It's Adrian.'

Why? Why? Why do things like this happen to me? I'd told everyone I was meeting a guy who was the double of Richard fecking Gere. 'Oh, um, gosh, right, er, hi,' I stuttered. 'You said you, er, looked like, er, well, never mind, anyway. Very good. Have you been here long?'

Ignoring the question, he shouted so that everyone could hear him: 'Come on over, lass, pull up a pew. What you having to drink then, eh? You can have whatever you want. It doesn't matter how much.' I assumed he was referring to the cost as opposed to the quantity. 'Here . . .' he barked at the woman behind the bar who was busy serving someone else. 'Get this lovely young lass anything she wants. It doesn't matter how much. Pronto.'

It should be refreshing that, in this image-obsessed age, some people remain blissfully unaware of their own appearance and physical imperfections. But, in this case, it wasn't. Because poor Adrian lacked the wit or personality to make up for it. Call me shallow, but I was devastated. While I worked my way through the first glass of wine, he told me and the rest of the pub, in far too much detail, all about his most recent ex-wife, whom he said was a model, as were the two before. When he reached for his wallet to show me a picture of her, I felt a moment of both horror and empathy. *Oh my God*, I thought, cringing, *is this what I was like with Johnnie? Needing to inform people ad nauseam that someone once loved me. I'm loveable – look, I can prove it. Yikes!*

'She,' Adrian said, looking proudly at the picture in his hand, 'said I was the best lover she'd ever had in her life. When we decided to have kids, I hit the target on the first night.'

Oh God Almighty. 'Really?' I replied, because, really, what else can you say sometimes?

As he began to drone on about the vast fortune he had amassed from his 'hobby' of buying and selling property, all I could think about was the drink I could be having with Christian.

Eventually, when my head was practically slumped on the bar,

Adrian said: 'What about you then, eh? What's your story?' I would normally find it hard to turn down an invitation to talk about myself, but instead I made a snide comment about Britain's (i.e. his) sad obsession with home ownership and property prices, then said I'd like to leave, if it was okay with him, as I didn't think there was a spark. He disagreed, told me he felt 'amazing sexual chemistry' between us and tried to persuade me to stay for another drink. 'No,' I said, feeling rather proud of myself. In pre-Dr J times, I'm thoroughly ashamed to admit, I probably would have stayed, got drunk and, by the end of the night, started to see shades of Richard Gere in him. And it doesn't take much imagination to see where that would almost certainly have led . . .

Instead, I jumped in a taxi, muttering, 'Babbity's and Richard fecking Gere, my fecking arse' to the driver. When I arrived, there he was. The gorgeous. The sexy. The funny. The entertaining. The perfect Christian. He was surrounded, as always, by a group of wide-eyed young women, but at least Charlotte was nowhere to be seen. When he spotted me, he came over, gave me a little peck on the cheek and asked where my wonderful new boyfriend was. I told him a sanitised version of the truth and we laughed about it, both forgetting about the emotional blackmail and threats handed out to each other the previous month.

At the end of the night, both drunk, I suggested, a little hesitantly, that he could, if he wanted, come back to mine. He closed his eyes and sighed heavily. Oh no! Instant regretification. I felt awful. I wished I'd never asked. If only I could turn the clock back, just one minute. Shaking his head and staring at the ground, he said: 'No. We can't do this anymore. It's so wrong. I'm trying to fix things.'

I turned and got into a taxi so that I could pretend to myself that I was the one who had walked away.

* * *

I woke up the next morning with a terrible dose of The Fear. Naturally, I blamed alcohol. I hated the demon poison. I hated myself for drinking it and the horrible person it turned me into. I hated Christian. I hated Dr J. I hated Louise. I hated everyone. I hated incompetent people and the blissfully happy and everyone who lacks the ability to laugh at themselves. I hated the couple who live in the flat opposite for no reason other than that they were cooking breakfast and I could smell the lovely food and I wanted someone to make *me* a bacon sandwich. And I hated the people who live in the flat above me for no reason other than that I could hear them walking about and laughing.

If I hadn't been drinking, I'd have remained poised, dignified and in control. I'd never have asked Christian to come back to mine. He'd never have been able to take the moral high ground. And I'd never have woken up so full of self-loathing and self-recrimination. The physical symptoms – the nausea and pounding headache – were actually a welcome distraction from the much more uncomfortable emotional ones: the humiliation and anxiety. Why was there no immediate over-the-counter cure for these? I reached for one of the notebooks beside my bed and wrote: 'I am never going to drink again. Ever. I know I've said it before, but this is a new low. I am now officially a non-drinker.'

* * *

Towards the end of Dr J's holiday, I actually found myself missing her. It is strange how you can miss someone even if you don't think you like them very much. I was longing to get back to her. But, in a weird way, she was still making an impression. Sometimes I found myself thinking or acting like her.

One night I was out with Katy, Rachel and Emily – they were drinking wine and I was feeling very smug and superior because I'd managed to stick to mineral water.

A friend of a friend of Katy's strode into the bar looking supremely confident, if slightly aloof. The woman, Victoria, joined us while she waited for someone and immediately revealed that she'd just given her boyfriend of two years an ultimatum. Either they move in together (she's in her late twenties, he's thirty-five) or she would 'have to think about' where the relationship was going. Unsurprisingly, he said he needed to think about her demand. His response seemed to have taken her by complete surprise.

'I love him so much,' she said dreamily, apparently oblivious to the fact that this was the first time three of us had met her. So inappropriate, I thought, steamrollering in like that.

She continued, almost in a monologue: 'But things just weren't moving forward. He's the most laid-back guy in the world, which, in some ways, is what I love so much about him. I've already moved most of my stuff in and he hasn't even noticed, but, you know, I want him to actually ask me to move in. I do love him. And we never argue. We get on so well. We're soulmates. I know he really loves me too. We just click. But, if it were up to him, we'd just plod along like this forever. It's just the way he is, I know that. Anyway, I had a chat with my mum and we decided it was time I gave him a little nudge. I'm glad I did, but I just didn't expect that response. I'm not sure what to do now.'

She looked at us expectantly.

I had to bite my tongue and stop myself from smashing my forehead repeatedly against the table. Katy had mentioned this girl before, telling us that she had heard she was so desperate to move in with her boyfriend that she had considered 'accidentally' getting pregnant – all her friends were – to move her relationship to 'the next level'.

Katy gently said: 'It sounds like you have some stuff to sort out. Some relationship issues. I mean, it's not actually healthy never to argue with your partner. Or try to coerce someone into making a lifelong commitment. You know it's these passive, easily coerced ones that end up straying further down the line. Anyway, enough about him. About you. Have you ever thought about therapy?'

She looked at Katy as if she'd just suggested sawing off her beloved's limbs and eating them for dinner.

'Therapy?' she shrieked. 'Are you joking? I don't need therapy. I mean, it's not that I'm against it or anything. I know some people need that kind of thing. But definitely not me. I don't need anyone's help—'

Katy interrupted. 'We all need a little help from time to time. There's no shame in it.'

Victoria shook her head. 'I don't need anyone's help. It's just my boyfriend. It's just the way he is. He's too laid-back. I definitely don't need to pay someone to listen to me or tell me what to do with my life. And anyway, I go to the gym five days a week. That keeps me sane.'

There was a slightly awkward silence, during which Rachel and Emily looked nervously at me.

I wanted to say: 'Sweetheart, you are one frighteningly dysfunctional lunatic with major co-dependency issues. How sad. It is blindingly obvious to everyone, apart from you, of course, that this guy simply isn't into it and that you have a major problem forming functional adult relationships. If you need to give someone an ultimatum, or if a guy's dragging his heels, there's only one reason for it. He's not that into it.'

Fortunately, I didn't say it. I just thought about how much easier it is to dispense advice than to receive it, or even adhere to your own. Instead, I smiled politely at her and said: 'Men, huh? Completely off their heads.'

* * *

One Sunday morning, more than a month after Louise and Scott's party, my sister called me in a frenzy of excitement.

'Guess what?' she gasped.

'Mmm?' I moaned.

'David likes you. He told Scott.'

'Who? What? Why? I'm still asleep. It's Sunday – the start of my weekend.'

'They were out last night for a few beers and David told Scott that he really liked you. This was after it was established that you were single. He seemed to think you were seeing someone and he asked Scott if it was serious. Scott told him you weren't in a relationship and he said he liked you. In fact, his exact words were . . .' She shouted to Scott: 'Scott, what did he say again?' In the background, I could hear my brother-in-law say wearily: 'She's everything he'd look for in a woman.'

'Did you hear that?' Louise asked excitedly. Before waiting for a reply, she added: 'He did also say that you were a bit self-obsessed, but he thought it was quite funny and he could see through—'

Fully awake now, I interrupted: 'What? He said I was self-obsessed?'

'Yeah. I think he said it kind of jokingly. You know, she likes talking about herself, ha ha . . .'

'He actually said that? He said I like talking about myself?' I said, utter disbelief in my voice.

'Er, yeah. But, well, you do.'

'No, I do not,' I protested.

'Yes, you do.'

'No, I don't.'

'Yes, you do. Scott, does Lorna like talking about herself?'

There was no reply. 'He's giving me that look. That, you know, *Is the Pope a Catholic?* look,' Louise explained. 'Anyway, Lorna, who cares? There's no such thing as a human being who isn't self-obsessed, though there are degrees, of course. So you are self-obsessed, but he thought it was quite funny and he really likes you.'

'I'm not as self-obsessed as . . .' I listed a couple of people.

'Lorna, not only are you self-obsessed, but you are a complete and utter nightmare,' Louise sighed. 'I'll speak to you later.'

Two minutes later I called her back. 'So what did he actually say about me?' I asked, a little sheepishly.

She laughed. 'Here, Scott, tell her what he said.' She passed the phone over.

I heard Scott groan in the background. 'Oh God, how many times am I going to have to go over this?' Then he told me everything.

'Hmmm,' I said. 'He actually said those things?' But then I thought, something's not right. 'Hold on a minute,' I said. 'If he likes me, why did he wait for so long before telling you? Why didn't he contact you immediately?'

'Lorna, he's a guy,' Scott explained. 'There isn't the same desperate urgency. Plus, he thought you were seeing someone.'

'Yes, well, I meant . . . Oh never mind. Anyways, I'm not interested in men just now, but tell me, what does he do? He's a doctor, yeah?'

Scott, with a hint of sarcasm, said: 'Didn't you ask him? You were talking to him for most of the night. Or were you too busy talking about, er—'

I interrupted. 'We were chatting about hundreds of things – politics, the importance of freedom of speech and expression, the Iraq war, art, literature, poetry, the Hippocratic Oath. So, tell me, what does he do?'

Scott told me that David was a doctor who had recently moved to Glasgow from London. He was about to start training in paediatrics (at which point I nearly passed out), but was currently working in Accident and Emergency.

'He's a lovely guy,' Scott said. 'He's very bright, very funny, a very good doctor. An all-round top bloke. All the nurses fancy him. They call him Glasgow's own Dr McDreamy.'

Ohmigod.

'Right, tell me just one more time, and I promise I'll never ask again, what exactly did he say about me again? Exact words?'

'You're totally self-obsessed.'

'No. The other bit.'

In a weary monotone, Scott repeated it.

'He seriously said that?'

'Seriously.'

'Totally seriously?'

'Bye, Lorna. I'm hanging up now.'

Hmm. Such a shame I'd vowed to steer clear of all men.

June

Who Knows where the Time Goes?

It was a brilliant sunny Monday morning at the beginning of June; warm and bright, with only a couple of cotton wool clouds in an otherwise perfect blue sky. There were flowers everywhere. Even Dr J's waiting room, which had always felt quite gloomy, seemed less drab.

I was anxious about seeing her again after her week's holiday and felt as if I'd been on a break from school, running around unsupervised, getting into all sorts of mischief. Now, it was the first day of the new term. Time to get back to the grindstone, atone for my most recent sins and discover a bit more about my screwed-up self. But I wasn't just feeling a sense of duty, I was also genuinely looking forward to getting back to the routine and the new normality that had been established in my life. It was just a sense of inevitable foreboding about how much facing up to the truth I was going to have to do that had had me tossing, turning and conducting imaginary conversations in my head with Dr J since 5 am.

As she walked towards me in the waiting room, she looked different. She'd always looked healthy, but now she had a very obvious post-holiday glow about her. She looked refreshed. Her batteries had been recharged. She had a light, healthy suntan, and she'd done something different to her hair: a cut and, I think, a soft perm.

Even her clothes were different. Gone was the dark formal business suit and in its place was a light blue, linen shift dress and a pair of low, wedge sling-back sandals. I could see her toes, which, for some inexplicable reason, mildly freaked me out. They were painted! Not scarlet – that would have been too much – but a light pearly colour. It was summer outside, but still the transformation came as a surprise. It made me realise how accustomed I'd become to the conservative, authoritarian, grey but reliable Dr J, despite her strange ways.

I imagined that she'd gone to Italy for her holidays, probably Venice. I have no idea why I thought this. She hadn't told me and I hadn't dared ask. Nor had I spotted an airline ticket, city guidebook or any other give-away signs or clues in her office. I had simply created this picture of her wandering through cobbled streets hand in hand with her tall, bespectacled and distinguished-looking husband (naturally, another figment of my imagination). I had visualised them drinking coffee, laughing and people-watching in Piazza San Marco. I could see them eating in fine restaurants and going to the opera. Again, despite the absence of any supporting evidence, I had a feeling she was an opera lover.

Although I knew nothing whatsoever about her personal life, I had convinced myself that she had two daughters, one of whom was married with a baby son. I wasn't sure yet what the other one was up to. The image I had of her was more abstract. She might have been a writer of some kind, or drifting, having a bit of a premature mid-life crisis. I assumed the married one lived in Italy.

Dr J had already told me that she would be taking all of August off. I imagined she would be spending the entire month in Italy with her older daughter and her beloved grandson. All of which was totally daft. I didn't need a substitute mother, especially not in the dubious form of Dr J.

We had another of our special long silences at the beginning of the session. Dr J was probably mentally humming the overture from *La Traviata* . . . I was trying not to think about her toes, but I was finding it tricky. During many of the silences in therapy, I would conduct bizarre conversations in my head. A phrase or sentence would reach the tip of my tongue, but I'd catch it before it was allowed to escape and then I'd mull over all the possible lunatic ways it might be interpreted.

Me: Did you have a nice holiday?
Dr J: Why do you ask?
Me: Because it is normal and polite.
Dr J: Surely you must realise by now that there is nothing normal and polite about what we do in here? It's what's underneath the normal and polite that I am interested in. The question behind the question. What lies beneath the facade. So, come on, what's really on your mind? Are you angry with me for abandoning you? In the same way that you're angry with your mother, father and sister for abandoning you?
Me: For fuck's sake, no. Of course I'm not fucking angry with you for, as you put it, abandoning me. And, for the umpteenth time, my family did not abandon me. As for you, I didn't even miss you. I didn't even notice you were gone. I had a ball. I even went on a blind date.
Dr J: As I thought, you're still extremely hostile and antagonistic. You're furious with me for abandoning you. This is completely understandable. Don't worry. We can work through these difficult emotions together and hopefully get you genuinely involved again with your feelings and with your life. Now, come on, what's really on your mind? Huh? My toenails, by any chance?

I had to mention them.

'If there is something big, you avoid talking about it, then nothing else of importance gets talked about either,' Louise and Katy often said, not just about therapy but about any close relationship.

I took a deep breath. 'I know this is utterly ridiculous,' I ventured, 'but, well . . .' I rolled over onto my right side and glanced behind me to her feet. 'It's just that you've, er, you just seem different today and it's kind of taken me by surprise.'

'Would you like to continue?' she said, in a warm voice, which freaked me out even more. 'Don't censor yourself or try to prejudge. Just say whatever comes to your mind. Just think out loud.'

She'd tried, unsuccessfully, to get me to do this before – 'free

association' – which involves expressing without reserve everything and anything that comes into your mind, regardless of
whether it appears trivial, random, irrational, tactless, humiliating, offensive, embarrassing or indiscreet. Or all of the above.
Now, talking gibberish when you're drunk and no one under-
stands what you're going on about because they're all drunk too,
and you can't remember what you were saying the next morning
anyway, is one thing. But doing it in company, in the cold light of
day, knowing that all sorts of things are going to be read into it, is
quite another and much, much more difficult than it sounds. In
fact, it was virtually impossible.

I made a couple of false starts, then unleashed a stream of
incoherent thoughts involving Italian ice cream, mothers, the
opera, painted toenails, love affairs and people not being who you
think they are.

'That's good,' she said. I could tell by the tone of her voice
that she was smiling. 'That's excellent.'

* * *

The most important date of the month was the big surprise party
for my mum to celebrate her sixty-fifth birthday and retirement.
I love my mum enormously, and think she's an amazing woman,
so it might seem a bit odd that I did nothing to help prepare for
the celebration. My dad and Louise organised everything – the
venue, the drinks and buffet, the DJ, the decorations, the cake, and
they contacted all my mum's family and even friends she hadn't
seen since her nurse training days. It was impressive. But I'd been
really busy at work – I was currently obsessed with trying to
single-handedly force the government to hold an inquiry into
Britain's contaminated blood scandal, oblivious to the fact that
bona fide top-notch investigative journalists had been on the case
for two decades before me – and as planning, organising and getting results weren't my strengths, I had rationalised that I'd do
better to leave all the work to others. All I did was contribute to the
cost. But when I stepped into the yellow and gold balloon-filled
function suite at Milngavie's Clober Golf Club and saw all the time

and effort Louise and my dad had put in, it made me feel a bit selfish and inadequate.

'God, you and Dad have done an amazing job. I wish I hadn't
been so busy at work and I could've done more to help,' I said,
secretly hoping that my words would make it past the censors.

Not a chance. Louise gave me one of her sceptical, raised-eye-
brow looks. 'Don't make this about you, Lorna. Tonight is all
about Mum.'

'Grrr,' I mumbled.

My mum, who thought she was going out for dinner, walked
into the golf club with my dad and their lifelong friends, Dorothy
and Jimmy. (Louise and I still call them aunty and uncle, even
though we're not related, and their children do the same with our
parents. Their daughter, Gail – my 'cousin' – is married to Stefan
Dennis, who plays Paul Robinson in the long-running Australian
soap series, *Neighbours*. My mum, a woman of many unsung tal-
ents, made their wedding cake, which appeared in a spread in
Hello! The picture caption even said it was made by 'Aunty Rose'.
This is my family's greatest claim to fame, and is mentioned whenever the opportunity arises. Which is surprisingly often, because
people are always talking about what was on TV last night, or
Kylie Minogue, and it's very easy to steer all such conversations
towards a certain street in Erinsborough and a cake-based anecdote.)

It was clear from the look on my mum's face that she was genuinely flabbergasted. It took several minutes for everything to sink
in. She was frowning and saying 'Oh my God, Pauline' and 'Oh
my God, Julie', as all the faces from her past began to register. She
was nearly in tears. I pushed through everyone to get to the front
to hug her as it finally hit home for me how important and special
this occasion really was.

Since the moment I'd stepped into the hall, my brain had been
percolating the hazy notion of doing something to compensate for
my lack of involvement in organising things over the previous
months. I thought I spotted an opportunity halfway through the
night when the party was in full swing.

I asked the DJ to play a track from the CD I had in my bag, 'Who Knows Where the Time Goes' by Fairport Convention, which is quite possibly my favourite song of all time. Even thinking about it makes my eyes moisten and sends a shiver through me. I have to admit, it probably doesn't scream 'we're having a party' like, say, 'Agadoo' – that classic which practically begs you to grab a strawberry daiquiri and let the good times roll.

The DJ looked a bit mutinous, but when I explained that I was the birthday girl's daughter – i.e. not to be disobeyed – he obligingly put on my CD. As soon as the moody masterpiece began, revellers began to look at each other in confusion, trying to figure out whether they knew the tune. Some made ominous shrugging gestures with their hands and shoulders. Before Sandy Denny's wistful voice had completed the first line about the evening sky and the fact that all the birds were leaving, everyone had followed suit and fled the dance floor. Even Lewis, who normally 'dances', or at least bends his knees and claps his chubby little hands to anything, including every street busker he passes, toddled off in disgust. And Louise went nuts. 'What the hell are you doing? It's a party, not a bloody wake,' she shrieked at me.

'Ah, but,' I protested, 'I thought Mum would like it. It's a beautiful song. It will remind everyone about how precious time is and about the fragility and preciousness of life. People need to be reminded—'

'Not at a fucking party,' she snapped, before storming up to the DJ and asking him to play something upbeat. The next thing I knew, The Nolan Sisters were belting out 'I'm in the Mood For Dancing', which had everyone back on their feet immediately.

Defeated, I went back to sit next to Katy at the back of the room, strategically near the buffet. 'It's avoidance, you know,' I said to Katy, while scoffing a sausage roll. 'No one wants to face the harsh truth: you're born, you die. That's it. End of story.'

'It *is* a party,' she said. 'Probably not the best place to dwell on such matters.' I changed the subject. Slightly. 'I can't believe my mum's sixty-five. Sixty-five! It sounds so old. It's, like, a pensioner.

My mum is now officially an old-age pensioner. She's entitled to free bus travel anywhere in Scotland.'

'I can't believe I'm thirty-six,' Katy said, shaking her head. 'Everyone wants more time, but what would they do with it? Piss it away, probably. Have you ever considered whether you would be willing to repeat the precise life you have lived again throughout eternity?'

I frowned. 'What?'

'I think it was Nietzsche. I think it's about asking yourself whether you're living your life in such a way that you would be willing to repeat it eternally. We've all made wrong choices. Made mistakes. But to recognise that and then live the rest of your life in a way that eliminates any future regrets.'

'Hmmm. No one likes to admit to having regrets. It's too sore. You put a positive spin on it because you have to. The other day I was watching this programme on TV about the changing face of families. They interviewed two couples. One had four kids. The other had none. They both said they'd made the right choice, but of course they're going to say that. Who's going to say, no, I wish I'd done it differently. And the ones with kids said they thought people who didn't have kids were selfish. It was as if they really believed that they were doing everything for the sake of their children. Never thinking that they might actually have made a self-interested decision. And the childless couple said the others were selfish because of over-population. It's nuts. Everyone accuses everyone else of being selfish, but no one likes ever to admit to doing anything themselves for selfish reasons.'

'You've changed your tune.'

'It's my crazy therapist. I'm starting to see everything differently.'

Katy nodded and laughed. 'At work, we sometimes ask patients to think about what they'd like their epitaph to be or to imagine how they'd like their life to be summed up, or to write their own obituary. It's kind of shock therapy. Everyone tries to ignore the passing of time, then you wake up one day and it just kind of hits you that you're no longer on the ascent, not everything's possible.'

'Yeah, I know what you mean,' I said. 'But at the same time, it's not until you realise this – like, really realise it – that you start to live. You don't just know, you *know* that it's just a short lease we've got on life.'

'Do you know why lots of people have crises around the forty-year mark?' Katy asked. I shook my head. 'It's when people become aware that the choices they've made haven't been truly free ones. They are consequences of their culture, time and more than anything, their families.'

As if on cue, the DJ played the theme from *Fame*, 'I'm Gonna Live Forever', and the people on the dance floor went manic with excitement.

All of a sudden, I came to a resolution. 'I think I'll make a wee speech,' I said to Katy, and stood up, weaving towards the DJ again.

The next thing I knew I had the microphone in my hands. That was okay, but the problem was I was talking into it.

'I don't often get the opportunity to be the centre of attention these days,' I said, through a squall of feedback, 'so I couldn't resist this chance to be in the limelight for a few minutes tonight, hee hee.' I heard Katy and my dad laugh. I saw a few other people look at each other with raised eyebrows.

'Well, who knows where the time goes, eh? It's a good question, isn't it? I can't believe my mum is sixty-five. It sounds so old. And I can't believe I'm thirty-five. Thirty-five whole years old,' I said, shaking my head. 'It's unbelievable. I'm closer to forty than thirty! Forty! Imagine being forty!' (Most of the guests were well past forty, but I didn't let that stop me.) 'I'm struggling to get my head around this. When I was young I used to think by the time I was thirty, never mind thirty-five, that I'd be married with children, living out here in the leafy suburbs. Instead, I still live in a dingy little rented flat and I've been involved in . . . well, no, ignore that last bit. Anyway, I'm still trying to work out what I want to do when I grow up.'

There were a few giggles, mainly from my dad, Scott and Katy. I caught Louise's eye. She was shaking her head despairingly.

'Anyway,' I said, winding things up like a skilful public speaker. 'I just wanted to say I think my mum and dad are amazing. Not flawless, of course. Because I've just recently discovered that no one is. In fact, I just read somewhere that underneath this lovely facade we're all wearing, there is lust, rage and repression all battling for supremacy. Apparently. Anyway, as I was saying, everyone makes mistakes, but as long as you learn from them and don't repeat them, well, that is the important thing. So, anyway, no one is perfect, but they're probably as close as it's possible to get. So here's to my mum and dad. Amazing but flawed. Like all the rest of us.'

Miraculously everyone dutifully raised a glass. As I came down from my podium and the DJ started up again, I heard the unmistakable sounds of Black Lace, and those unforgettable lyrics from 'Agadoo', pursuing me like a malevolent clown.

***

The next time I saw Dr J, I hardly noticed the sunlight pouring in her window. Nor did I pay any attention to what she had on or whether her toes were painted or even visible, because, as soon as I lay back on the couch, I couldn't stop crying. 'My mum is sixty-five! How can she be sixty-five? She doesn't look sixty-five. And she says she doesn't feel it, especially since she started going to dancing three times a week and looking after King Lewis two days a week. It just made me think about mums. About how utterly amazing they are.'

One of my most vivid early memories, I announced through the sniffles, was when I was about five. I was unable to sleep because it had just dawned on me that my mum and dad were going to die one day. It was, I suppose, my first existential crisis.

I started wailing. My parents, who had sprinted into our room, tried to console me, but they couldn't give me the answer I wanted, which was basically for them to tell me that they were going to live forever.

They tried to comfort me by saying they were both only in their mid-thirties and were unlikely to pass away for a very, very long time. But it wasn't working. Eventually, my mum, presumably in an act of desperation, mentioned the fact that my gran and granda, who at that time would've been around sixty-five, were still alive and well. 'I mean, Granny and Granda will probably die long before we do,' she said, stroking my head. Although I'm sure she meant well, it wasn't the most soothing statement she's ever made. It set me off again. 'Oh no. My granny and granda are going to die. Wah! And then you and Dad are going to die and then I'm going to die. We're all going to die. Wah! Wah! Wah!'

I'm not sure, at that time, whether I managed to fully articulate what I was thinking: 'What's the point of living, if all we're all going to do is die?' But my parents were certainly a bit concerned by the whole episode. Being neither devout believers nor professors of philosophy, and, since it was long before the days when parenting manuals offered conflicting advice on just about everything, they were ill-equipped to deal with this kind of situation. So they did what any good parent would do. They used all their savings to buy us the entire twenty-nine-volume set of the adult *Encyclopaedia Britannica*. Even though we couldn't actually read yet.

Thirty years may have passed since that little wobble, but I still seemed to be worrying about the same things.

Several months before my mum's birthday bash, we'd had a different kind of party to celebrate my gran's ninety-fourth. Six of her nine children were there, lots of her sixteen grandchildren, and some of her twenty-three great grandchildren. She even has a brood of great-great grandchildren. Which completely blows my mind. She has so many birthdays to remember – more than fifty – and, although everyone tells her not to bother anymore, she never forgets one. She's still independent, living alone in her high-rise in Glasgow, and is mentally as sharp as a tack. But she needs a stick to help her walk and sometimes seems quite lonely.

When I arrived at her party, she said she hadn't seen me for a long time. I made up some flimsy excuse about being really busy at work.

Whenever I said I was 'really busy at work', which was often, Louise would raise her eyebrow. She said I prioritised and was 'over-invested' in work. She often accused me of thinking my job was more important than other people's. 'No I bloody well do not,' I used to retort, even though I did. I was only now realising that being immersed in work 24/7, which I was, was a distraction from the more important things in life.

Work was also a convenient excuse because I couldn't possibly tell my gran the truth: I'd been avoiding her. I had become too scared to visit her because she reminded me too much of life's transience and my fear of what's round the corner.

My gran loved talking about her life and telling stories. She often reminisced about how, when the war started, she refused to allow her children to be evacuated because she didn't want to split them up. So they stayed in their tenement in Possilpark and, whenever they heard the wail of the air-raid siren, she would pull a mattress into the hall, turn the lights out and get all her children to huddle down. She alone would try to protect them. And somehow she managed. Her whole life was about taking care of other people.

'How can someone be nearly a hundred years old? How can someone have had nine children? All bar one at home. Without pain relief. How can one woman have looked after six of those nine children on her own for four years while her husband fought in a world war? How can someone have been married to one man for more than half a century? And then been all alone since he died seventeen years ago? I cannot get my head around this.'

As well as thinking about my mum's and my gran's lives, I had been pondering my dad's of late. My dad had always seemed to me to have had lots of unfulfilled goals and dreams. I remember, when I was young, I'd see him start all sorts of projects, things which were perhaps intended to improve himself. He always wanted to be a writer, for example. He read constantly. And he was a big fan of that crazy 70s string art craze. Most of the plans never came to any fruition; his existing obligations always got in the way. I was thinking about what he might have been if he hadn't been forced, when he was still only a boy of fifteen, to go out to work and hand over all his earnings to a man who hated him.

Years ago, I interviewed Michael Martin, the Speaker of the House of Commons – otherwise known, at least by some sections of the press, as Gorbals Mick. He is my dad's cousin and they grew up together in one of the most deprived parts of Glasgow. I used the interview as an opportunity to find out about my dad's childhood.

Whenever I had tried to ask my dad directly about it, he'd shaken his head dismissively or said, 'I've told you all you need to know: I was in my twenties before I discovered that Spam wasn't sirloin steak.' I didn't understand what he meant until my mum explained that the first time they went out for dinner together, he ordered steak. When it arrived, my dad apparently said to the waiter: 'What's that? I ordered steak.' He really thought, so the story goes, that the infamous pink luncheon pork he'd eaten every night, or at least on the nights they could afford to eat, was what his mother had always told him it was: a cut of fine Scottish beef.

When I interviewed Michael Martin, he told me that all the local women said my paternal grandfather, who died in the war when my dad was three, was the best-looking man in Anderston. When I asked my dad about this, he said: 'Pass me the remote control.' I asked him if he had a photo of his dad and he shook his head. Then I asked if he would write down his life story, not worrying about the grammar or all the 'rules' of writing, and he said: 'Lorna, please. Stop being so stupid.'

It wasn't until Lewis came along that my dad, suddenly, seemed to cherish the moment. He seemed content at last and began to really savour life.

I found myself sobbing again. 'All these sacrifices people have made. I can't stop thinking about them. Wondering how we could ever repay them. My gran's not going to be around for too much longer, is she? And then when she's gone, we'll all wish we'd spent more time with her, asked her more about her life. Why do we wait until it's too late to make the most of what we've got?'

Eventually, the voice behind my head said: 'It sounds to me as if you are worrying about your own life, about what you've done and where you're going. Because you still cannot bear to acknowledge your own pain, you prefer to feel other people's. But I wonder if you are actually worried about your own time running out.'

***

There were few things that embarrassed me more than when we were in a pub and Katy would bellow at the top of her voice: 'Another reason you're so fucked up is because you refuse to acknowledge that you might never have a baby and you might never meet Mr Right.' And then she would be off on one. 'I mean, does it ever cross the minds of women like you that you might not even want to have children? You're conditioned by society to *think* you want them and you're looked down on as, at best, a self-ish tragic freak, or at worst, a second-class citizen – or maybe that should be the other way around – if you dare to even think about exercising your right to choose not to. This is what I mean when I say we're the modern day suffragettes.'

Katy truly believed this. The first time she said it, I felt, even though I tend to avoid confrontation if at all possible, that I had to challenge her. 'Come on. Didn't the suffragettes get trampled to death by horses and go to prison and go on hunger strikes and stuff? What exactly is it that we are doing? What are we fighting for?'

She looked at me with wild anger in her eyes. 'What are we doing?' she repeated, her voice dripping with condescension. 'We are saying no, women won't be bullied and nagged and coerced into doing something that they don't want to do. We are saying fuck off to control-freak politicians who try to bribe people with fucking tax incentives to get married. We are saying fuck off to people who call women selfish because they have careers but not children. Are men ever called selfish because they have a fucking job? What exactly is it they want us to do? Go on the dole until the right guy comes along and impregnates us? It's utterly fucking offensive and sexist. So we are saying no to anyone who tries to tell us how to live our lives. What we are fighting for is a society that allows women to make an informed adult choice between moth-erhood and childlessness, remaining single or getting married, and that has equal regard for all those choices. That is what we are doing. We are fighting for women to be treated equally to men.'

'Oh, righto,' I said, not quite sure whether I thought she was making great sense and should consider going into politics or whether she was talking complete drivel.

I normally tried to avoid these kinds of discussions with Katy, unless we were in a really noisy bar or the middle of the countryside, because I could not imagine anything more unappealing to anyone who would have been able to overhear, which was usually most of the pub. I'd never known anyone with such a loud voice or such a blatant disregard for what other people thought of her. Generally, I preferred to pretend that my biological clock wasn't an issue, because I knew that even thinking about, never mind mentioning, your internal egg timer was deeply unattractive and a sign of desperation. So, whenever that topic came up, I would normally reply to Katy, in a barely audible voice: 'I'm totally chilled about all that kind of stuff.'

But the last time we had this conversation, she roared: 'So why the fuck did you get your ovaries scanned last year to find out when your sell-by date is?' I saw half a dozen heads in the bar swivel round at this, followed by the gentle slopping sound of a pint of beer being discreetly spilt.

Ah, yes. I'd forgotten about that. 'Er, well, er, for journalistic purposes,' I shouted towards the bar.

This was one of the things I really loved about journalism. You could get up to all sorts of nonsense under the all-concealing auspices of 'journalistic research'. Once, when a few 'upmarket' swingers' clubs had opened in London, I rushed excitedly into my editor's office and said I would like to go along to 'expose what goes on in this kind of establishment'. I was, of course, only trying to find a semi-legitimate, non-sleazy way to satisfy my own curiosity. The editor was delighted, but, when I told some other people, they expressed shock and horror. Someone, pulling a 'how totally gross' face, said they were full of fat, middle-aged people in overcrowded jacuzzis. But the deal-breaker was when Rachel said she'd heard about a friend of a friend of a friend who'd gone to a swingers' club in Sheffield and bumped into her own mum and dad. I have no idea whether this story is apocryphal, but it had the effect of immediately draining the colour from my face and rendering me slightly light-headed. Can you imagine anything worse? I'm pretty sure my parents never have and never would go to one of these places, but the thought alone was enough to force me to invent some feeble excuse and pull out of that assignment.

So I didn't get to a swingers' club in the name of journalistic research, but I did get my ovaries scanned. It was when Lewis was about one year old and, although I wasn't fully aware of it at the time, I can see now that I must have been in a state of shock about his arrival and the impact this had had on my entire family. One day I asked my mum what age she was when she went through the menopause and she casually said: 'Thirty-nine.'

I felt as if I'd just received two sharp blows to the ovaries. Thirty-freaking-nine! Like most twenty- and thirty-somethings, I'd always thought the menopause was an ugly but unavoidable metamorphosis that afflicted old ladies with white hair and varicose veins. I'd heard the experts talk about an average age of fifty-one, but when you're in your thirties that seemed not just a decade, but half a lifetime away. It had never crossed my mind that it might happen to me before I'd found The One, married him and had three, but preferably four, children who were perfect and beautiful enough to be on TV.

Now, there I was, wondering whether it was genetic and, assuming it was, trying not to get myself into a fit of panic. At first, I did what all educated adults do when confronted with some unpalatable truth: nothing, except pour myself a large glass of wine. But I couldn't ignore it for long. The internal tick-tock, which had been a constant but distant sound since I started playing 'houses' and 'mums and dads' when I was around five, was erupting into a deafening alarm clock whose snooze button no longer worked. I started to think about my options. I typed 'single woman' and 'adoption' into Google and discovered that I was far from alone. But then came a warning: 'If you are only looking to adopt a child to prevent loneliness, to keep you company, or because you think it

might be a good idea because celebrities have done it, think again.'
So I thought again and contemplated asking a male friend to
donate sperm; or getting drunk and propositioning the first okay-
seeming guy I could find. Or doing the lonely hearts. Or asking my
ex, who will make a truly wonderful father, to take me back. Or
stealing Lewis. Or getting my eggs frozen.

Then I had another, marginally saner, thought. The previous
year, two Scottish scientists had published research suggesting it
might be possible to predict the onset of the menopause by meas-
uring the volume of a woman's ovaries. It had sparked the usual
frenzied debate in the media about 'selfish' career women and
whether they should have access to the world's first reliable
'menopause test'. In an act of desperation, I contacted them and
practically begged to be their first guinea pig. They were, understandably, reluctant. They had turned down similar requests from
hundreds of women because, they stressed, they were working
purely with a hypothesis and had yet to secure funding for a large-
scale, long-term research project.

But I promised to highlight this in the article and assured them
I would take their word only as a guide. A few weeks later, I was
sitting in a flowery gown, waiting to get a three-dimensional scan
of my ovaries. And a few weeks after that, I had written an article
about being the first person in the world to have taken this con-
troversial new test. It predicted a normal menopausal onset
between the ages of fifty and fifty-one. Never in my life had I felt
so elated at being told I was average, only average. Or at least that
my ovaries were.

'That article you wrote was really quite embarrassing, from
a psychoanalytic point of view,' Katy reminded me now, as the
conversation in the bar returned to a relatively normal level.

'Looking back, maybe it was a bit. But no one ever died from
embarrassment, did they?' I'd read this somewhere and knew that
it must be true because I've embarrassed myself hundreds of times
and am still here to tell the tale.

***

By mid-June, I was nearly at the end of my second alcohol-free week following the latest Christian debacle, and was thoroughly enjoying being back in control of my life and feeling superior to those sorry, weak-willed individuals who needed to drink to have a good time. There had been no contact between Christian and I since I'd drunkenly invited him back to mine. After that night-mare, I tried to draw a final double yellow line under the whole sordid affair. After months of haranguing Emily to tell me any little morsel of news she caught wind of through mutual work acquaintances, I asked her not to tell me anything, no matter how juicy (I could hear my onboard Dr J tut-tutting, saying something about avoidance or going from one extreme to another, but I didn't care).

My first night out on the wagon was much easier than I imag-ined, because I didn't tell anyone and no one noticed. I just wandered around with a three-quarters filled flute of champagne all night, occasionally making small fishlike movements with my mouth, but resisting the urge to dip right in. The second, at a dinner with friends, was much more difficult. It was a very un-Scottish type of drinking: in moderation, to accompany good food. Someone said I must be very strong because abstinence required superhuman willpower, which fed nicely into my superiority complex.

My skin had been looking clearer, I'd been feeling much more alert in the mornings and I was eating more healthily. 'Alcohol is evil,' I announced one night to Louise and Katy. 'I love being a non-drinker.'

As I sipped my mineral water, they laughed. 'You are basking in an illusion,' said Katy.

'You're just jealous,' I replied haughtily, 'because you lack my self-control and self-discipline.'

'You sound like our patients,' Louise said. My sister helped set up the Glasgow Priory's increasingly busy eating disorders unit. 'They get a sense of achievement out of depriving themselves. It deludes them into thinking they are in control. But black and white, all-or-nothing thinking isn't healthy. Life is about doing things in moderation, Lorna.'

Anyway, my abstinence came to an abrupt end at a leaving do, when I was one day shy of my two-week anniversary. I knew Christian would be there, so I spent the day agonising over the pros and cons of going along. The main pro was: I'd see Christian. The main con was: ditto.

Eventually, I managed to get the pluses to outweigh the minuses, by including things like: it will be a good test of my feelings for him; I can't avoid him forever; I can leave before he does, thereby reclaiming the power; it will be character-building to put myself into such an anxiety-provoking situation, and other such woolly incentives.

It was a beautiful summer evening, with the after-work crowd out enjoying the alfresco cafe culture. I met Katy, Rachel and Emily in Bar Gandolfi at 7 pm, before going to Arta, where the party was being held. I spotted Christian immediately. He was looking sexy and gorgeous as usual. Then I saw Charlotte, who, though it pains me to say it, was also looking annoyingly attractive. She was wearing a little black halter-neck dress. Not the sort of thing a lawyer could wear to work. She must have changed for the occasion. Despite what Katy said, she oozed the confidence of a homecoming queen. A good-looking guy, who might have been her boyfriend or just a hapless suitor, was loitering obediently behind her, carrying her jacket and bag.

At first, still on the mineral water, I was calm and dignified. I had a brief, civilised conversation with Christian, but I can't remember what it was about. The weather or something equally superficial. At one point, Charlotte skipped gaily across the room towards us. 'Hey girls. Mwah mwah! Mwah mwah!' she said, making two exaggerated air kisses for the four of us to share or perhaps fight over. I groaned silently but forced a smile. 'You're looking great,' she said to me. 'I like your, er, hair and your outfit.' I was just about to rebuff her compliment – my hair was, after all, tied back in a ponytail, and I had on a pair of jeans – and comment on her undeniably lovely dress, when she turned to Emily and said: 'You're looking great too. I really like your dress.' She then admired Katy's hair and Rachel's overall appearance.

A couple of people had told me, way back last year when I first started going crazy about the whole thing, that Charlotte was lacking in the personality department. 'She's never had to develop either the art of being an interesting person or that of taking an interest in others. And it's mind-numbingly obvious after two minutes in her company,' someone had said about her. Although hearing other people bitch about her had given me a moment's pleasure, at the time I'd put the remark down to jealousy.

Now, as I listened to Charlotte spouting her bland and repetitive niceties, I wasn't sure whether I felt secretly delighted or thoroughly depressed. After all, from what I'd observed so far that evening, Christian still appeared to be enchanted, despite what he said.

Rachel, always excellent in awkward social situations, had moved the conversation on and asked Charlotte how her jury trial went. A wrinkle creased her brow, then she said: 'Eh, what? Oh, great, thanks. Dying for a fag. Catch you later,' and she practically sprinted towards the door.

Seconds earlier, I had noticed Christian in my peripheral vision, heading outside, presumably for a cigarette. The guy, who'd been carrying Charlotte's bag and jacket all night, dutifully followed her as she scampered out the door.

When they returned, she was gazing up adoringly at Christian, while the human coat rack was a step or two behind.

'Look at her,' I shrieked as quietly as it's possible to shriek. 'The way she's gazing up at him. She idolises him. He goes to the bar – she appears at his side. He goes outside for a cigarette – she disappears a second later. She's giggling at everything he says. God, what a pathetic human being she is,' I concluded, with a masterly hypocritical flourish.

Katy brought me back to the real world. 'That used to be you. You are enraged because you can see what you were like in her. And you know what they say, the things we dislike most in others are the characteristics we like least in ourselves.'

In the past I'd have at least attempted to defend myself, but I knew she was absolutely right. I wanted a drink. I ditched the mineral water and swapped it for a large glass of wine. It was my first drink in almost a fortnight and, after just a few sips, it went straight to my head.

We were joined by a friend of Christian's who nudged me into a corner.

'I know what's been going on,' he said darkly.

'Oh,' I replied.

'I know you loved him and, who knows, maybe he loved you a little bit. But I doubt it.' God Almighty. I was all for honesty, but this was a little too brutal. I had still secretly been clinging onto my illusion that I had been the first, that what we had was special, that it actually meant something to him.

'What a fucking idiot I've been,' I said, more to myself than to him.

'Women are always falling in love with him,' he continued. 'And he encourages it. But he's having his own difficulties just now. So if there's even a tiny part of you wondering, here's the 411: it's never going to happen. He's like a lot of people – a kid who needs to be adored. And if it's not you or what's-her-name,' he nodded over to where Christian and Charlotte were huddled together, 'it'll be one of the hundreds of other stupid women like you who will always fall for guys like that.'

I nodded and gritted my teeth as I digested his perceptive remarks. 'Thank you,' I mumbled. I looked over at Christian and Charlotte. He was obviously telling a story. His face was animated and he was gesticulating with his hands. She was gazing up at him. When it was clear he had delivered the punch line, there was a moment's hesitation, then Charlotte burst into thunderous laughter.

Pausing only to down a black Sambuca, I jumped into a taxi and left them to it. I didn't shed a tear on the way home or when I got into my flat.

'This is the end of that shameful affair,' I said to myself, as I lay in my bed. I'd uttered these words before. Hundreds of times. But this time I knew I wasn't just saying it. This time I really meant it.

'And for that it is high time,' I heard my indwelling Dr J say.

self-acceptance (nearly)

July

Tell Me what You Want,
what You Really, Really Want

On a Sunday morning a few weeks later, I woke up to another excited phone call from my sister.

'What are you doing next Saturday night?' she said, as soon as I answered.

After six months on the couch, I was better at making plans and sticking to them than I used to be, but that didn't mean I'd become a total idiot. Especially in situations like this, when there was a very high risk of being tricked into committing to something before I even knew what it was.

'Louise, you know I don't like to be tied down to anything,' I warned. I thought about what I'd just said and quickly qualified it: 'Apart from therapy, of course, which shows I can commit, and work, obviously, which is unavoidable. But, aside from that, I like to be free. As free as a bird. To do whatever I want – to go anywhere, to do anything, at the drop of a hat.' Okay, so we might have to revisit that idiot evaluation.

I heard a sigh. 'Are you on something? When was the last time you did anything other than go to The Wee Pub or stay at home watching DVDs on a Saturday night?'

'Probably your party in April, actually,' I reluctantly conceded, seething at having to admit to leading such a mundane life, and being little more than a wine-swilling film and box-set addict.

'Exactly. So why not do something spontaneous by agreeing to commit to something?'

'Hmm, when you put it like that, it certainly does make it sound more appealing. So, what is it you want me to commit to?'

I heard the excitement return to Louise's voice. 'Remember David? The lovely doctor who likes you?'

Oh God, not him again. Yes, he was rather attractive and seemed, on limited acquaintance, to be smart, interesting and good company, but the plan was to steer clear of all men. 'Yes, what about him?'

'Well, he's going to Malawi to work in some remote Aids hospital. He's having a little farewell night out on Saturday. He asked Scott to mention it to you and said you're welcome to come along.'

There was an unmistakable, inexplicable lurch in the pit of my stomach. It wasn't excitement but mild panic.

'But I thought you said this guy really liked me?' I said.

'Yeah, he does,' Louise replied, with confusion in her voice. 'Why?'

'He can't like me that much, otherwise he wouldn't be moving to Malawi, would he?'

Louise laughed and was about to say something, but I started talking over her. 'Oh well. I'm sure he'll meet some stunning young junior doctor over there whose parents work for the foreign office or diplomatic services or something, and she'll have travelled all over the world and gone to a private all-girls' boarding school and speak loads of languages, and she'll be all tall and skinny and gorgeous. With perfect hair and perfect teeth and all the rest of it and he'll fall head over heels in love with her, and they'll get married and live happily ever after. Well, good luck to him. Good luck to both of them.'

Louise sighed. 'He's not *moving* to Malawi. He's going for one month.'

'Anyway,' I continued, oblivious, 'why are we even having this conversation? I'm not interested in this guy. I'm not interested in any men. I'm celibate. Didn't I tell you?'

'No, you didn't mention that, Lorna, but that's fantastic news. Avoiding what you really long for will, I'm sure, bring you true happiness and contentment.'

'Grrr,' I growled. 'I'm not avoiding anything. I don't *long for* a relationship. I hate relationships. They're too much hassle, too complicated. They cause me far too much anxiety. Should I text? Should I not? He hasn't texted back immediately, does that mean he's not into it etc, etc. I can't be bothered with all that anymore. I love being single. I can do as I please. I love going to my big double bed all by myself, with a cup of tea, some biscuits and my favourite DVDs. There's no room for another person. I love my life just as it is, thank you very much. Now goodbye.'

After I put the phone down, I could hear Louise's words in my mind's ear: 'He's not *moving* to Malawi. He's going for one month.' And felt strangely relieved.

* * *

Before that conversation with my sister, I had been thinking about how much progress I'd made since Dr J entered my life and started her bizarre emotional vivisection. I hadn't exactly undergone a phoenix-like transformation, but I'd definitely changed. In some unexpected ways.

By July, I noticed that I was no longer driving recklessly. In fact, I was driving like a ninety-year-old member of the Institute of Advanced Motorists. I obeyed the speed limit at all times and didn't use my mobile phone anymore while at the wheel. These days, I shook my head in disgust at those who did. Previously, I was able to speed, send a text message, crack open a can of Diet Coke and eat a packet of crisps all at the same time. Because I'd always assumed nothing bad would ever happen to me, I did this without giving much thought to my own or anyone else's safety. Appalling, I know, but sadly true.

But, despite the good news for my fellow citizens, I was aware that I hadn't come to therapy to learn to be a more considerate driver. I'm not sure if that alone would have been worth the £3,500 I'd spent so far, the early rises and the boxes of Kleenex I'd gone through, but, still, it was an undeniable sign of progress. Baby steps towards conducting myself in a more mature and responsible fashion. We spent a lot of sessions talking again about those family matters and I began to see how much that had affected me, without really realising it.

I slowly noticed other signs of improvement, too. I was no longer preoccupied with thoughts of Christian. If he did enter my head, even if accompanied by Charlotte, the primary feeling was one of sadness, shame and regret, rather than rage or envy or bitterness. Something had definitely changed – I wasn't calling him. Granted, he wasn't calling me either. Perhaps the real test would be how I reacted if he ever did? But I was no longer going places where I thought I might bump into him.

I also felt generally more contained. Although I quite often wept during and after therapy sessions, I'd stopped crying in front of friends, colleagues and complete strangers. If I bumped into someone I vaguely knew – a former colleague or someone I'd been introduced to once or twice before – I no longer responded to a simple conversational 'hey, how's life?' or 'how you doin'?' with a long, rambling and far too detailed account of precisely how I *was* doing. It seemed paradoxical that, while I was in therapy to 'get in touch with my emotions', I seemed to be much less inappropriately open and emotional outside of Dr J's strange sanctuary.

Then there was the 'S' word. I noticed that I was apologising far less for things that I should never have been taking the blame for in the first place. It was so deeply ingrained that it was a hard habit to break, but whenever I was on the verge of saying sorry to someone who'd just bumped into me I would immediately hear Dr J from her perch inside my head, asking: 'What is this compulsive modesty of yours all about?' Or: 'Why do you constantly want to take, or at least be seen to be taking, the blame and responsibility for everything?'

My attitude to work also altered. I hadn't really realised the extent to which my whole identity was tied up in my job. It defined who I was. I didn't think of myself primarily as a daughter, sister, friend or aunt, I thought of myself first and foremost as a journalist, and it had dawned on me that I'd had a rather unhealthy dependence on seeing my byline in a newspaper in order to feel like a worthwhile member of the human race.

So, instead of starting every week telling myself that I *must* find phenomenal stories and try to write them up as fantastically as I could, I took the self-inflicted pressure off. I stopped setting myself up to fail. I realised that, on the off chance that I ever managed to find these sensational stories that I was looking for and express them in black and white the way I imagined I could in my head, it wouldn't change a thing. It wouldn't make the world a better place and nor would it suddenly make me feel happy or successful or content. In short, I gave up striving for perfection and accepted my limitations. I made a pact with myself that I would do the best I could and, if that was 'only' average, then that would just have to do. As a result, I'd become more relaxed yet at the same time more productive at work. I also began to enjoy it much more. I am average, no more, no less. Once upon a time not so long ago this thought would have appalled me. Now it made me smile.

I felt as if I was living life at a much slower pace. I stopped running and going to the gym. If I went for a swim, I no longer hogged the fast lane and set myself a target of fifty lengths. I now took the slow lane and plodded up and down, doing a maximum of twenty lengths in the same time I used to do fifty, but enjoying every minute of it. One friend commented that I no longer had a Shrek-like look of permanent anxiety on my face. Basically, I chilled out. I sometimes felt as if I'd lost two stone, but it was the weight of worry that had gone.

Another change was that I'd come off Prozac. I'd started taking it again the previous year, and intermittently before then since I turned thirty.

I had initially been very reluctant to start taking anti-depressants. My reservations were due largely to the stigma and the feeling of weakness that I couldn't pull my own socks up, but I also had my suspicions of the multi-billion-pound drug industry. I remembered reading a story in an American newspaper about a woman who didn't like the way her husband was handling the family finances. She wanted to start looking after the books herself but didn't want to 'insult' her husband. Her doctor suggested an anti-depressant to make her feel better. Which, I thought, was completely insane.

Before I started taking Prozac, I completed a depression check-list that I found on the Internet. It asked: 'Have you been feeling sad or down in the dumps during the past week?' I nodded and ticked the box that said 'A lot' and was awarded three points. Another asked: 'Does the future look hopeless?' Does the person who created this read the newspapers? I wondered. Escalating crime, environmental cataclysm, a widening gap between the world's rich and poor, so much death and destruction, al-Qaeda, a different health scare story every day – of course the future looked hopeless. It's a wonder any of us get out of bed in the morning. I ticked 'A lot' again and received another three points. Next: 'Do you feel worthless or think of yourself as a failure?' Through the haze of my misery, I was able to emit a wry laugh. I have rambling notebooks from when I was seventeen saying: 'Dear diary, I am such a failure. I feel as if I have wasted my whole life and disappointed everyone.' Another three points. 'Do you have trouble making up your mind about things?' Christ Almighty. Of course I do. Who wouldn't when faced with a life involving so many choices? My local supermarket stocks 107 varieties of pasta and thirty-eight different types of milk. Decision-making is difficult. It involves renunciation and elimi-nating or killing other options. The root of the word decide means 'slay', for God's sake. For every yes there is a no. I nodded my unhappy head again. And so on it went, until I tallied up my scores and discovered that I had severe clinical depression. This came as a terrible shock, so I did it again, finessing my answers. Mild depression. Which was, obviously, slightly easier to come to terms with.

Next, I completed an anxiety check-list. The first question was: 'How much have you been bothered by anxiety, nervous-ness, worry or fear in the last week?' There wasn't a box for constantly, but I created one and awarded myself a bonus of six points. 'Do you have concerns about looking foolish or inade-quate in front of others?' I was beginning to quite enjoy this. I created another new heading: from the moment I wake up in the morning until I switch the light out at night, and gave myself another bonus. I added up my total score. It was off the scale for severe anxiety. Oh well, I thought, looking on the bright side, it's always good to have a diagnosis: chronic anxiety.

Finally, I completed a dysfunctional attitude scale. As expected, I had severely dysfunctional attitudes. I 'agreed strongly' with just about all of the thirty-five statements, the first five of which were:

> I cannot find happiness without being loved by another
> person.
> If I am to be a worthwhile person, I must be truly outstanding
> in at least one major respect.
> I must be a useful, productive, creative person or life has no
> purpose.
> If you cannot do something well, there is little point in doing it
> at all.
> I should be able to please everybody.

And so on . . .

I went to my GP and gave him my diagnosis. He was fantastic and very thorough and carried out his own tests. He prescribed Prozac. I protested, saying I'd never had a day off work and wasn't suicidal or unable to get out of my bed, like I imagined really 'depressed' people would be. I was 'high-functioning', he said, but still clinically depressed.

I stared at the green and white capsules for a week and read everything I could find about them.

I discovered that, in the prosperous western world, the last ten years of rising wealth have been accompanied by a massive explosion in the number of people taking anti-depressants. In Britain, the most recent figures showed that 31 million prescriptions for happy pills are written each year and a third of GP consultations are for depression. In America, the figure is 118 million, making anti-depressants the most prescribed drugs in the country.

Surely, all these people can't be clinically depressed? I thought. But on the ancient principle that if you can't understand 'em, join 'em, I decided to start popping.

After four weeks, I noticed that it had taken the edge off my anxiety. I also lost a little weight without even trying and felt as if I was wrapped in a warm blanket. In fact, after overcoming my initial reluctance to start taking them, what I became most nervous about was having to give them up at some point, since I had quickly grown to regard those little happy pills not just as a temporary crutch, but as vital life support.

Just before I started seeing Dr J, I began to think maybe I would be dependent on them forever. I got my head around this by believing what the drug company marketing told me: that I had a chemical problem that required a chemical solution. There was, they said, something wrong with my neurotransmitters, which affected my brain's ability to absorb serotonin, which in turn affected my ability to feel good. Selective serotonin reuptake inhibitors (SSRIs), like Prozac, were what I needed to fix it. I tried to convince myself that it was no different from a diabetic who required insulin to survive, which was basically the conclusion of the drug companies' advertising.

Some people have physical problems. I figured I was more of a head case.

But, like many people, there was something I inherently didn't like about being dependent on a chemical to get me through the day so, after a few months of Dr J's treatment, I decided to stop. I didn't consult my GP about this, but discussed it briefly in therapy. I felt nervous about giving up, but I had no negative side effects. In fact, I noticed no difference in the way I felt after it was out of my system. And, although Prozac did help me as I recognise it helps countless others, I realise now that, in my case (and I suspect many others), it was nothing more than a sticking plaster. It numbed the symptoms of constant anxiety, inadequacy and low mood but did nothing to explore why I had those feelings in the first place.

In addition to giving up Prozac, the Dr J effect had also transformed my attitude to timekeeping. Instead of being late for just about everything, I was pathologically early. Especially for flights and for my sessions with her.

On the two mornings that I had a 'commitment', my euphemism for being in therapy (she described it as 'our work'), I automatically woke around an hour before my alarm went off, and I always gave myself plenty of time to get to her office. So, even though two of my sessions with her were obscenely early, I'd never been as much as a heartbeat late. Until . . .

A suffocatingly hot July day when I was stuck in a traffic jam. I'd been in Edinburgh on a story, was stuck in gridlock on the M8, and knew I wasn't going to make my 6 pm appointment. Which was putting me in danger of losing my new and peaceful vibe.

I had, of course, dutifully mirror-signal-manoeuvred my way into the left-hand lane as soon as instructed to do so by the flashing overhead signs. Other drivers were whizzing past, ignoring the warnings that the lane they were in would close 800 yards ahead. They were cutting in at the last minute, in front of considerate motorists (like me) who'd been patiently waiting in line for ages. At first, I managed to keep calm by ignoring them and doing some yoga breathing. I discreetly closed one nostril and inhaled deeply through the other. I retained it for a count of ten then I exhaled through the other. I repeated this wonderfully relaxing exercise until I nearly lost consciousness.

When I came to, it didn't take long for my calm state of mind to be usurped by my old but ever faithful friends: impatience, intolerance and anxiety. It is, sadly, a Buddhist myth that one cannot be disturbed by another, that it is only oneself who can disturb one's equanimity. Unless you spend your life in isolation, meditating, living only with cats, anaesthetised from your own feelings or simply in denial, then the truth is that other people will try to spoil your new found inner peace. As one car after another snaked past me, I started to feel less like the Dalai Lama and more like Michael Douglas in the film *Falling Down*. I was sweating – a lot – and gripping the steering wheel so tightly that my neck and shoulders ached. By the time my therapy session was due to start, and I was still stuck in what might as well have been a massive car park on the outskirts of the city centre, I was in the grip of a full-blown attack of road rage. I added the sound of my horn to the irate honking around me and joined in the abuse. 'You bunch of mother-freaking-fuckers,' I hurled out my window to the passing stream of vehicles. 'I've got a commitment! A commitment with Dr J. That I can't be freaking well late for.'

With my head back in my car, I explained the urgency to myself: 'Because she'll read all sorts of crazy stuff into it. She'll think I'm being passive-aggressive. And I'm not being passive-freaking-aggressive.'

I eventually arrived at Dr J's fifteen minutes late. Wiping the sweat from my forehead with my clammy palms, I apologised profusely – momentarily forgetting that I was supposed to have stopped apologising profusely for things that weren't my fault – and launched into an over-elaborate and tediously detailed explanation of the nation's congestion problems.

Somewhere in there was my ground-breaking suggestion that all road-building and maintenance projects should be carried out only between 10 pm and 6 am.

When I noticed the deathly silence behind me, I shut up.

'These things happen,' came the calm response.

'These things happen,' I repeated, in a high-pitched screech, to myself. All that worrying, all that perspiring, all that road rage, all that agonising about ruining my perfect record for nothing.

I let out a long, slow exhalation of breath and smiled. Dr J never failed to surprise me. Just as I was getting used to the way she looked for hidden answers in everything, she appeared, just as suddenly, to have changed her approach.

'So,' I grinned knowingly at the ceiling, 'I guess sometimes a cigar is just a cigar. As Freud famously said. I suppose some things should just be taken at face value. Maybe you don't always have to look deeply into everything for hidden meanings?' I lay back, satisfied and relieved.

Dr J was silent. Like a customer pondering the lobster tank in an exclusive restaurant, she often seemed to take an inordinate amount of time to select her words. It was as if she were doing it with great care and precision and as if there were many, many more words inside her that she wanted to use, but had to work hard to hold back.

After a while, she said, to my utter astonishment: 'Still guessing, still supposing, still having to hedge your bets.' She let this hang heavily in the air – souring the warm and soothing aroma of coffee.

And, all of a sudden, the cigar wasn't just a cigar. Because I had *guessed* that it was, *supposed* something should have been taken at face value, *suggested* there was no need always to look for a hidden meaning, the cigar became instead a potential goldmine, a glint of something in the dark and mysterious sea of my unconscious. Something worth Dr J getting her drill into.

I was stunned into speechlessness because I'd never heard her use this kind of direct and challenging language before. And there was more. 'Yet again we have this passivity, this subservience, this immature deference to those who you think are in positions of authority or whose opinions and views you think are more important, more valid than your own. You have never directly challenged anything I have said in here. You cry and you sometimes slam the door, but you still seem to struggle to express directly your honest thoughts and feelings. In fact, you seem to apologise for your own thoughts and opinions before they've even left your lips. I wonder why you are so eager to hand your power over to anyone – to me, to the men in your life, to your sister, to anyone, to everyone – rather than hold on to it yourself,' she said.

Her uncharacteristically aggressive comments made me feel like a naughty schoolgirl being scolded. I concentrated for a moment on the small sounds of her office – the dull ticking of the clock, the birds outside. I noticed that the heat in the room felt oppressive, even with the window behind her open. I thought about what she'd just said. There was only one thing I could think of to say under the circumstances.

'Hmm,' I sighed.

'Hmm?' she repeated, adding a question mark. 'Hmm, what? Hmm, you agree with my interpretation or, hmm, you think I've got it wrong and am out of order? It is important to try to express yourself more clearly. As I have said, in therapy, as a practice for real life, it is important to acknowledge exactly what you are feeling instead of hiding behind froth.'

I was utterly stunned at how forthright she was being. Where was the old Dr J, the one who sat silently listening to everything I had to say?

I came incredibly close to saying fuck you or getting up and walking out or bursting into tears and begging her not to shout at me. Instead I held my hands up and said: 'Hmm, yeah, sorry, I guess . . .' I stopped myself from saying 'sorry for saying sorry for saying hmm and I guess', and continued, still in an apologetic tone of voice, 'Yeah, I probably agree with the observation.'

Oh God. I corrected myself, before Dr J got the chance. 'I mean, I agree. I agree, okay. I agree. I don't probably agree and I don't largely agree. And I don't think I might agree. I just agree. I agree.' By this point, I'd almost forgotten what it was I was agreeing with.

'That's much better,' Dr J said, with the faintest hint of a smile in her voice.

Emboldened by her approval, I decided to state what was on my mind, as she was so often encouraging me to do. And to challenge her. 'I don't want to sound accusing, but do you know that you, er, say hmm quite a lot yourself?' I felt incredibly daring.

There was the briefest pause before she said: 'It is disappointing that you have prefaced your question – which is reasonable and legitimate – with an apology. It is also disappointing that you are being insincere with me. At least, I hope you are being insincere. Because why on earth would you *not* want to feel and sound accusing in the face of such apparent hypocrisy?'

My already frazzled brain began to ache even more. I shook my head and shrugged. Just when I thought I was mastering therapy, had learned everything there was to learn, understood her tricks, she threw me completely.

She continued: 'I am, therefore, going to disregard the first part of your question and answer the second. Which, by the way,

I am pleased that you asked. Yes, I am fully aware that in our work together I often say hmm. And I am going to make a comment that I hope will help you understand why: this is your therapy, not mine. It would seem to me to be a terrible waste of all your time and money if you took the easy option of trying to analyse me as a way of avoiding the much more difficult and painful one of fully confronting yourself, and facing all of these difficult things we spoke about earlier.'

Ouch fucking squared. This time it was, once again, me rather than Dr J who was rendered completely speechless.

* * *

At 6 pm on Saturday, when it became clear that no one was going to knock on my door and ask me to hop on board some ship heading into outer space or any other exciting spontaneous activity, I called my sister and, rather sheepishly, asked if I was still in time to redeem my voucher to attend David's soiree.

Louise, Scott and Katy came round to mine for a quick drink. 'Should I wear my map of Africa necklace as a mark of respect?' I asked them. They looked at each other in confusion before Louise spoke. 'What, exactly, is a map of Africa necklace?'

'This.' I showed them my cheap but sentimental necklace, made of the rubber from a tyre and wood from a tree. 'Map of Africa?' Scott said. 'It's horrible. It looks more like a piece of dried-up chewing gum.'

'Yeah, whatever, wear it if it makes you happy,' Louise said, frowning. After G&Ts, we wandered along to a bar called The Goat, a cool pub in the West End which manages to look trendy at the same time as feeling a bit like an old traditional drinking hole. I wore my favourite black and pink polka dot halter-neck top with jeans and flip-flops. And, of course, my map of Africa necklace. It was a beautiful warm summer evening. Every table on the pub's large outdoor patio was taken.

I spotted David straightaway, even from the other side of the road. He was carrying bottles of beer towards a group of guys. He was, at least from this distance, much better looking than I remembered him from Louise's party, not that he'd been a slouch in the looks department then. But my mind had been elsewhere at that time. As we got closer, I thought he looked even more like Roger Federer – the same quite deeply-set dark eyes, similar unruly hair and the same strong features. He looked relaxed in his Levi's and a plain white cotton T-shirt, comfortable in his own skin. Most attractively of all, he didn't appear to need to surround himself with a posse of adoring young girls.

'Hey,' David grinned when he saw me. Lovely smile. He quickly distributed the beers, pushed a curl away from his face and gave me a little kiss on the cheek. 'Nice to see you again.' He had a voice too, an amazingly sexy one. He gave Louise and Katy a peck too, while Scott got a manly handshake and simultaneous affectionate pat on the back. He introduced us to his friends: Joe, Faisal, Daryl, Christopher and Martin, then asked what we wanted to drink.

When he looked at me and said 'Lorna?' I felt, despite my declaration of spinsterhood, an unmistakable tingle. This was not a good development. I stuttered: 'Eh, what? Me? Oh, Miller, please. Thank you.' Oh shit. 'Very much.'

When he went to the bar, Louise gave me a sideways smile, while Katy said, in an unusually quiet voice: 'He is fucking gorgeous.' I looked at them, dazed and confused, and said: 'Eh? What?'

'He is fucking gorgeous,' Katy repeated, as if she too had been knocked off balance. 'Shush,' Louise said, after a few minutes. 'He's coming back,' she whispered, managing hardly to move her lips.

'So,' he said, giving us our drinks and fixing his smile on me, 'have you been interviewing any Highland cows recently?'

'Eh? What?' I replied, wearing that slightly bewildered expression that Louise says makes me look as if I've been allowed out for an hour from my care in the community programme.

'Frances Dawn Beg the third?' he said, with a slightly raised eyebrow. 'I think that's what her name was. From your days as a rookie reporter? You were telling me . . .'

'Ah yes.' The penny dropped. He remembered my lovely prize cow's name! 'And, er, no.'

'No?'

'No,' I repeated, in a serious, matter-of-fact tone, which, contrary to the intended impression, made me sound demented. 'You asked if I'd interviewed any Highland cows recently. No. I haven't.'

'Oh, right,' he said, taking a swig from his bottle of Miller. He pushed another curl away from his face.

Oh shit. Why? Why does this always happen to me? Why, whenever I start to like a man, even just a tiny little smidgen, do I feel the need to try to impress and, in doing so, instantly lose my sense of humour and start taking everything so literally? Why does it become impossible to follow the advice – that is not only common sense but reinforced in all the articles I've read in over two decades of women's magazines – to be charming and witty; keep it light and airy; don't talk about yourself too much; ask him a question or two. Why do I seem to be able to function in only one of two ways: as a brain-dead monosyllabic witless moron or, once the alcohol starts taking effect, a verbally incontinent fool? Why? Why? Why does it happen? And, more importantly, why the fuck hasn't Dr J cured it? The incompetent fool.

Louise, noticing the startled expression on my face, tried to come to the rescue and lighten the tone of the conversation.

'She might not have interviewed any Highland cows of late, ha ha ha ha,' she glared at me as if to say, *laugh or at least smile, you stupid cow, it was meant to be a joke*, 'but she's going to Jamaica next month,' she said brightly, looking at David. 'Aren't you, Lorna?'

'Mmm hmm,' I nodded, and managed to curl my lips into a weak smile. 'I am. I am indeed going to Jamaica next month. Yes I am indeed. I changed my mind about never doing another foreign assignment and accepted my boss's offer to go to the Caribbean.'

'Nice one,' David said. 'What's the story?'

'What's the story?' I repeated à la Dr J, only I wasn't wanting him to reflect carefully on what he'd just said to look for hidden meanings, I was simply buying time as I tried, desperately, to think of something funny to say. 'What's the story? What's the story? Morning glory. Ha ha ha ha ha.'

Repeating Oasis album titles for comic effect, however rhymey, clearly was not the way to go. This time it was David, Louise, Katy and Scott who had to force the weak smiles. As I glanced from face to face, I was sure I caught Louise and Scott looking at each other with expressions of dismay mixed with disbelief.

I took a large swig from my bottle whose label, I'd just noticed, I'd completely peeled off. Aha. 'Sex,' I shouted. 'It's sex. Sex. Sex.'

David's smile broadened into a grin. 'Sorry?'

'Sex. The story in Jamaica is sex.' I then managed to explain, without too much meandering, that my editor wanted a feature about the growing trend for female sex tourism: thousands of lonely, single middle-aged women from Europe and America flocking to the Caribbean to have casual flings with young black men. 'Sex, sand and sugar mummies. That's the story,' I said.

'Sounds like a tough assignment,' he said.

I was about to get defensive and explain that, like all journalism, it would be extremely taxing work, actually, but thankfully I stopped myself. Because of the Miller, however – all it takes is a few swigs – I was becoming more loquacious. 'I don't know whether my editor is being cruel to me or kind to me,' I said instead. 'Because, you see, he offered me the assignment just after I told him that I'd taken a vow of celibacy. I had to take this vow of celibacy because . . .' Ouch!

I glared at Louise who was staring across the road at the splendour of Kelvingrove Art Gallery and Museum, trying very hard not to look like she'd just surreptitiously kicked my ankle.

She gave me a look imploring me not to talk with compulsive honesty about the wreckage of recent relationship car crashes. Then, knowing me too well, and realising this probably wasn't possible, she decided to seize the conversation herself and steer it in what she presumed would be a safer direction by asking David if he was looking forward to his trip to Malawi.

All eyes turned to him but, before he had a chance to impress us with stories about saving people's lives, I piped up: 'I've been to Malawi.' I said this in the sort of tone that would have been more appropriate for someone like Neil Armstrong to say: 'I've been to the moon.'

At the end of a largely one-sided commentary about the country, during which I managed to make myself sound as if I'd been a high commissioner or a tour guide or something, and spent years there rather than one week, David said he'd already been. Twice. 'Oh, very good,' I said, then quickly drew everyone's attention to my necklace: 'Anyway, I wore this necklace tonight as a, er, as a kind of mark of respect, I suppose.'

Suddenly my internal Dr J appeared. 'I mean, I wore this necklace tonight as a mark of respect. I must learn to express myself clearly and not hide behind froth.'

There was more nervous glancing among Louise, Scott and Katy.

David laughed before looking at my necklace with a frown. 'What is it?'

'It's a map of Africa, of course. I got it in Malawi,' I said, before going into minute detail about the manufacturing and distribution process. 'A little five-year-old boy made it. His name was Chinsinsi, which means secret, and he lived in a village called Whisky,' I finished breathlessly.

David looked at me with that curious smile again and started talking to Scott about saving people's lives.

'That,' I explained to Louise quietly, 'is exactly why I've taken a vow of celibacy. I need to steer clear of relationships. They're a complete and utter freaking nightmare. The only thing harder than trying to get into one – at least with someone you've decided you like, even if just a smidgen – is getting out of one. I hate them. They're best avoided at all costs.'

Louise shook her head. 'Desire may indeed make teenage

idiots of us all,' she said wearily, 'but you don't half manage to make it a hundred times more complicated than it needs to be.'

A while later, when I'd recovered my poise and equilibrium, I was talking to David's friend Joe, who had packed in medicine to follow his dream of trying to become a journalist. He asked if I had any tips. I racked my brains to see if I could find any advice. Eventually, I remembered a brilliant man at the *Herald*. He had offered me the job at the paper and, in doing so, rescued me from the hell of local newspaper reporting in Oban. During one of my first (of many) crises of confidence triggered by being asked to write a front-page news story with a 'colourful' intro, he took me to The Press Bar and, after a couple of lunchtime vodkas, said: 'Some people are basically tossing themselves off onto the page. Their primary goal is to impress with fancy words and so many clever metaphors that no one has a clue what they're actually trying to say. Fuck trying to impress. Just tell the goddamn story.'

Joe laughed. So did I at the memory, which seemed so long ago and now, looking back, made me wonder whether that editor was in analysis, given his disturbing masturbation analogy.

'I guess, though,' I was thinking out loud, 'that some people enjoy watching others tossing themselves off.' I laughed. 'So I don't know, I guess there are no rules. I mean, there are no rules. I've got to stop guessing. I've got to stop hiding behind bloody froth.'

We chatted a bit more until, after a lull in the conversation, he nodded towards David. 'He's a one-off, you know. A fantastic friend. A little bit shy with women. But one of the really, really good guys.'

'Oh,' I said, because I didn't know what else to say.

A few hours, a few beers and a lot of laughing and talking later, David asked if everyone fancied 'one for the road' back at his place, which is Glaswegian for an all-night drinking, singing and talking about the meaning of life session.

I found myself looking to him for guidance – did he really want us to go or was he just being polite? 'Come,' he said, presumably sensing my uncertainty, 'even just to see the amazing views.' I didn't bother asking what the amazing views were of, but looked to Katy, who was up for it. Louise and Scott reluctantly declined, saying they had to go home to relieve my mum and dad of babysitting duties.

During the taxi ride to his flat – Katy, Joe, David and me in one cab, and Faisal, Daryl, Christopher and Martin in another – I gazed out of the window in a state of silent shock while the voice in my head said in an endless loop: 'He is absolutely gorgeous.' Not that this was going to sway me. I could objectively appreciate his handsomeness, of course, but that didn't mean I would be having anything to do with him.

'Ohmigod,' Katy squealed, the moment she entered his twelfth-floor riverside apartment. It had floor-to-ceiling windows in the lounge/dining/kitchen area with stunning views to the north and west of the city. Thankfully, it wasn't obsessively tidy: there was a pile of unwashed dishes; newspapers scattered all over a table; DVDs, some in their boxes, others not, strewn on the floor next to the TV; a few pairs of trainers lying around; an acoustic guitar propped in a corner. I stole a glance at the DVDs – always a good indicator of personality – *The Sopranos*, *The West Wing*, *Lost*, *The Wire*, *Six Feet Under* and *Curb Your Enthusiasm*. Fabulous. There was a huge abstract canvas hanging on one wall. I thought it was almost as stunning as the view but, just in case it was by someone famous that everyone should recognise, and not wanting to appear stupid, I didn't say a word about it.

David asked Joe to dish out beers from the fridge and put on some music, while he asked Katy and I if we wanted to see the view from the other side. Normally, I'd struggle to get excited about the obligatory tour of someone's new house – I usually find property so boring – but this was spectacular. It dawned on me that my entire dark and dingy ground-floor flat could fit into his living room.

'Wow. Wow. Wow,' I repeated, probably about forty times, after he slid open the door of his bedroom onto a balcony which looked out over the River Clyde.

'When did Glasgow become New York?' Katy asked. She was exaggerating, of course, but that's exactly what it felt like. Straight ahead was the city's new 'squinty bridge'. It was illuminated atmospherically in, of all the colours of the rainbow, a bright dazzling purple. Its shimmering reflection, along with all the other city lights in the murky black water rolling by underneath, looked stunning. Further along was the silvery Glasgow Tower, part of the titanium-clad Science Centre, and the city's new media village where the BBC and Sky had their Scottish headquarters. To the west, it was just possible to make out the dark silhouettes of six massive cranes, a reminder of the city's world-famous shipyards, dominating the night skyline.

'Wow. Wow. Wow,' I said, again. 'Glasgow looks absolutely amazing.'

'It's a great city,' David said. 'I love it.'

'So is this yours?' Katy asked. Which was what I had just been wondering.

'No,' he laughed. 'It's my brother's—'

'Is your brother a famous tennis player?' I interrupted, excitedly.

'Er, no,' David frowned. 'He works in the City. In London. He bought this place as an investment and was going to rent it out. But I needed a place to stay after, em . . .' He hesitated. 'So I moved in about a year ago. I was only meant to stay for a month, until I bought my own place, but I've not quite got round to it yet.'

We went back through to the living room. Joe was strumming the guitar, playing along to The Dubliners song that was on, and everyone was singing along to 'The Wild Rover'.

One for the road, indeed. An hour or so later, on my way back from the bathroom, I bumped into David in the hall.

We held each other's eyes for a minute until he said: 'I'm going for some fresh air.'

'Oh, right. Very good,' I said.

He smiled.

'You coming?'

'Eh? Well, yes, maybe. I don't know. Um, okay.'

I scanned his bedroom (which was en suite with the bathroom) a little more closely than I had when he'd shown us the view earlier. It was quite untidy, a good sign – not that I cared, of course. Lots of books – by his bedside there was a pile of around four (the only ones I could make out were *The Sportswriter* by Richard Ford and Norman Mailer's *The Executioner's Song*) and several of Sebastião Salgado's photo essay books and artefacts from what appeared to be worldwide travels. I stopped when I noticed a framed cartoon from the *New Yorker* on the wall.

'Oh my God, I love the *New Yorker*,' I gushed. 'It's my favourite. I love the film reviews and, oh, the cartoons. They are so good.'

The one on his wall was of a doctor trying to reassure an anxious-looking couple before surgery. The caption said: 'No, I haven't performed the procedure myself, but I've seen it done successfully on *ER* and *Chicago Hope*.'

'Brilliant,' I said, then volunteered my own favourite: 'It's of a woman writing in her diary. The caption is low self-esteem and she has written: "Dear diary, I'm so sorry to bother you today . . ."'

He laughed. Encouraged, I said, 'I have another. It's of a dog, a very cute dog, who is seeing a psychiatrist. Also a dog. The patient dog is lying on the couch and the shrink dog is sitting behind his head scribbling in his notebook. The reason the patient is so traumatised and in therapy is because, as the caption says: "They moved my bowl."'

David laughed again. 'No, wait. One more,' I said, before I realised I should just have left it at two, 'is of a father kneeling down to give his little boy, who is about to play a game of baseball, a pep talk, saying: "Just remember, son. It doesn't matter whether you win or lose – unless you want daddy's love."'

We went outside and leaned on the balcony, looking out towards the river, enjoying the view and the fresh air. There was silence, apart from the distant, vaguely trafficky sounds of city life.

For some reason I felt the need to clarify what I'd said at Louise and Scott's party.

'You know how I said I was seeing someone?'

He nodded.

'Well, I meant for my head as opposed to my heart.'

He laughed. 'What's wrong with it?'

'Well, initially, I thought there was nothing really wrong with it. But now, after seven months of analysis, I'm beginning to realise there was nothing really right with it.'

He smiled again. 'Does it help?'

'It's strange, but it does. You find out all these crazy things about yourself that you didn't have a clue about.'

He smiled. 'I guess the Russians have vodka, the Americans have shrinks. I suppose everybody needs something.'

'You guess? You suppose?' I said.

'Sorry?'

'No, I'm sorry, it's me. She's always saying that to me – no guesswork about your feelings, no assumptions about other people, don't hide behind froth.'

He laughed again.

'The other crazy thing is that I write a column about it,' I said. 'At first I thought I did it simply because I love to write. And I thought it would help other people. But thanks to my crazy therapist, I've realised that nothing is quite so straight-forward. There are so many different layers to everything. So I'm kind of getting my head around the fact that it might also have something to do with attention-seeking, avoiding intimacy by having a relationship with a large anonymous audience rather than a one-to-one relationship, power and control, observing myself rather than simply being myself and God knows what else. When I told my editor all of this, he insisted it would help other people as well, but still, it's bizarre. I remember reading somewhere that you go into this kind of therapy with one problem and discover you've actually got a hundred. I'm kind of in the middle of that bizarre journey at the moment.'

Good work, Lorna, I thought, wondering if I had perhaps volunteered too much information.

'So,' he said after a while, turning around so that his back was against the balcony, 'you're off to Jamaica.'

'Mmm hmm. But just for a week. And you're off to Malawi.'

He nodded. 'But just for a month.'

We looked at each other and smiled.

After a long silence, he said: 'So, how strictly are you adhering to your vow of celibacy?'

Oh dear God. I tried to stay calm. 'Pretty seriously.'

'Hmm. Is kissing included?'

'It depends.' Goodbye principles. Goodbye vow of anything I ever stupidly promised not to do.

'On . . . ?'

We gazed at each other. After what felt like forever, he gently placed his right hand on my left cheek, very slowly brought his face towards mine and kissed me.

Holy Mother of God. How amazing is snogging? I stumbled against the balcony for support. I hate that over-used expression about your legs turning to jelly, so let's ring the changes and say my legs turned to aspic. My entire body was tingling and numb. If I hadn't had something to lean against, I think my knees would have buckled under me. I was so weak, my muscles so relaxed, that I had to concentrate to stop my head lolling about from one side to the other. Which probably wouldn't have been very attractive. I think I was having what tennis fans call a Federer Moment. These happen after one of his impossibly perfect and beautiful shots. The jaw drops, the eyes protrude like novelty-shop eyeballs and strange uncontrollable gurgling sounds are made. It is apparently the closest non-believers have ever come to having a religious experience.

'Mmm,' I said again. He was a fabulous kisser.

He looked at me and smiled. Then he started all over again.

Four amazing snogs later, I said I would have to go home because it was inevitable that one thing was going to lead to another and I didn't want there to be any 'nonsense' or 'carrying on'.

Wearing an expression of suppressed amusement, he said: 'You do make me want to laugh.' I must have looked alarmed, because he immediately added: 'I mean, in a nice way.'

I smiled and said I was thinking I might give him my necklace to take to Malawi.

'That would be lovely,' he said seriously.

I tried to untie it but couldn't. He said: 'Let me try.' There was a moment while I felt the exhilarating sensation of his hands and breath on my neck. He managed to unravel the knot and handed it to me. I wrapped the string around the pendant, gave it a little kiss (which I know is weird and I have no idea why I did it) and pressed it into his palm.

He looked at it then quickly but gently closed his fist around it.

'Please bring my necklace back to me,' I said, before giving him a peck on the cheek and running away into the early morning air. It wasn't until I was halfway home that I realised I'd forgotten all about Katy. I called her and she said she was having a great time and not to worry.

In the background, I heard another chorus of: 'And it's no, nay, never . . .' ringing out as I pressed the end button on my mobile.

* * *

'Has your mind ever been completely free of a romantic fantasy?' Dr J asked, about fifteen minutes into our final session before her summer holiday, which was to last the whole of August.

'Of course,' I replied quickly. Too quickly. It didn't need a therapist to notice that I hadn't really considered the question. I'd simply responded with a defensive denial to what I had interpreted as an accusation. Dr J had reassured me many times before that this was only human. Slightly disappointing, though, after more than eighty hours of therapy.

I'd been telling her about David, but had made a concentrated effort not to get carried away. I'd kept it very factual: 'I've met this absolutely amazing guy – a doctor, paediatrician, a life-saver just like on an American medical drama. He even gets called Dr

McDreamy by the nursing staff. Thirty-four. Lives at Glasgow Harbour in a stunning apartment. He's going to Malawi to save lives.' But then I blew it by saying: 'We had the best kiss I've ever had in my life out on his balcony. The light breeze was gently blowing in my hair and I felt as if I was in a Hollywood movie. His lips were dead soft, like pillows, and I had that lovely snog rash thing on my chin. And he has those big man's hands that I just love. I thought I was going to faint after the snogging. And I gave him my necklace and said bring it back to me, you know, kind of like Cinderella. I think he might even turn out to be The One because, honest to God, I just can't stop thinking about him. It's like that Kylie song – I just can't get him out of my head.'

I felt so high on love I wanted to dance around her consulting room.

Which was when she said she thought I might have a tendency to go from one all-consuming love obsession to another.

'No, no, not me,' I protested. 'I know people who jump from one relationship straight to another. It's almost like they can't bear to be single. They're like chain-smokers, they haven't extinguished one passion before lighting up again. Pathetic. Whereas I love being on my own. I've been single for . . .' I calculated that, between the ages of seventeen, when I started going out with Johnnie, and thirty-five, I had not been properly going out with anyone for eight of those eighteen years. 'Johnnie for eight years and my ex for two. Christian doesn't count, obviously, because it wasn't a proper relationship. So I've been single for a total of eight years. I'm not afraid to be on my own.'

After her customary pause and, I presumed, consultation either with the ceiling or the rug, she said: 'First of all, you have told me that it took you six years to get over Johnnie. You said you saw him regularly and that there wasn't a day that passed when you didn't think of him or dream of getting back together with him – so you were still emotionally involved with him. And, secondly, with Christian, although it wasn't a 'proper' relationship, you were so heavily emotionally invested that you ended up here, in therapy, when it began to fall apart.'

I blinked rapidly but didn't say anything. I was still finding it hard to get used to the new Dr J. At that particular moment I wasn't sure I liked her better than the silent or at most monosyllabic model.

She continued: 'There is a difference between being physically single and emotionally on your own. Do you think you've ever been emotionally single?'

There was a bit of a weird role reversal going on in Dr J's office. At the beginning, it was Dr J who often said nothing. These days it was me who seemed to be retreating into silence all the time.

Dr J didn't conclude with: 'Because it's pretty obvious to me that you haven't,' but she didn't need to say it. It was hanging, unspoken, but obvious and unavoidable, in the hot air between us.

I don't know why, but for the first time in a while, I felt my eyes sting with tears. This was another of those unpleasant moments when I felt separated from myself. I suddenly saw myself from a distance and was shocked once again to find that I still wasn't the person I thought I was. Everything I thought I knew was wrong. After a while, Dr J asked me how I was feeling.

'Okay, I suppose.' Before she could ask me if that was how I really felt, I provided a more honest answer. 'Confused, actually. And sad. And disappointed. And, I know this will probably sound crazy to you, but this all comes as a bit of a shock to me. I actually looked down on the kind of women who I thought had a compulsive dependency on men. And prided myself on my independence. And yet, you know . . .' I shook my head and sighed heavily. 'I'm just thinking back over my adult life and all the crazy crushes I've had on guys. I think I've had a serious unconsummated crush on someone in every major newsroom in the country. And some politicians. And, of course, Roger Federer. When I think carefully about it, I don't think I have ever been completely free of a crush or a romantic fantasy. Which seems completely unbelievable.'

There was a short silence, after which I continued: 'I also feel disappointed and annoyed, because, and I'm sure this will sound weird to you as well, it feels as if you've ruined my fantasy about David. I was actually enjoying daydreaming about him. In fact, I was loving it. Dreaming about . . .'

At the last second, I decided to keep this next bit to myself, but I had the feeling that somehow she knew exactly what I'd been doing. Since the night on the balcony, when I wasn't replaying the kisses and conversations, my head had been filled with day-dreams: about our wedding; how gorgeous he'd look in a kilt; where we'd go on honeymoon and running along the beach hand in hand as the sun set; how adorable our children would look; their names – I was thinking maybe Daisy or Lola or Molly for a girl and probably Joseph or Patrick for a boy.

I'd been daydreaming about how wonderful it would be for King Lewis to have wee cousins to play with and look after. And thinking maybe we'd move to Africa for a year or two, where he could save dying children's lives and I could do a little bit of jour-nalism, or maybe just stay at home all day playing with hundreds of children. And, of course, I'd been thinking about whether to take his surname: Lorna Martin-Mackenzie or just Lorna Mackenzie. Nice.

And this was all after just one night of snogging. Dear God. What the hell's wrong with me?

There was another silence, during which I thought about what Dr J had said to me in previous sessions: about my readiness to think everyone else's thoughts and opinions, including hers, were more valid than my own. I decided to challenge her. 'All my friends do this as well, you know. We laugh about it. I don't think it's really that big a deal. Everyone does it. Everyone has fan-tasies. I mean, for God's sake, God's a fantasy, is he not? The idea that if you're good you'll go to heaven and bad you'll go to hell – that's another fantasy, a powerful one, to keep people in line. Fantasy is the hundred or so symphonies that Mozart once told a friend he had written in his head for his own pleasure. Everyone needs a fantasy. Fantasy is the mother of thought, the source of creativity.'

Dr J pondered this for a while, then said: 'Your friends are not here to defend themselves, so I must ignore that. Perhaps it is just another of your assumptions, a generalisation you have made to make yourself feel better?'

I slumped on the couch, feeling like a teenager being reprimanded by her mother and thinking I can't wait to have a month off from this.

She continued. 'As for your claim that everyone needs a fantasy, I simply do not accept this. There are some people out there who are in good psychological shape. Of course, *some* may indeed live a life of fantasy, but certainly not *everyone*. As I've said before, word choice is important. And as I've also said before, this isn't anyone else's therapy. We're not here to analyse your friends or people who believe in God. It's your therapy and yours alone. If people daydream or fantasise and it doesn't interfere with their lives, then we don't need to waste your time and money giving it another thought. But that is not the case for you. It is interfering with your life. I think you find it easier to embrace intimacy in fantasy but tend to avoid it in real life.'

I thought about this for a long time, then said noncommitally, 'Why would anyone do this?'

'What stops you from directly asking me the real question?' she said. 'The personal one: Why do I think *you* do this?'

'Dunno,' I mumbled, feeling once again beaten, clueless and incompetent.

'I think it is a way of trying to push me away. It is easier for you to talk in generalisations, perhaps even to try to solve the problems of other people, than to get in touch with your own true feelings and start solving your own problems.'

It freaked me out when she did this, when she hit on some flaw or personality trait. It suddenly seemed so obvious, blindingly obvious, and yet until she'd raised it, in her usual circuitous way, I had been blissfully unaware of it. It made me feel as if I'd been walking about with my skirt tucked into my knickers. Everyone could see it but me. I remembered something Louise and Katy often said about people having blind spots to their own flaws for a reason, but that they shield us from things that should-n't be ignored. They protect us until we're ready to handle the truth, they used to say, and until then, we focus on other people's faults and flaws and dramas so that we can avoid our own.

When these moments happened in therapy, I felt a strange mix-ture of emotions towards the woman sitting behind my head. I felt a strange love-hate thing towards her. And I often felt a jolt of tremendous affection for her, because, as painful, bizarre and uncomfortable as it was, I had a feeling she was helping me. At the same time, because it always seemed to be hidden flaws rather than virtues we were discovering, there were times when I hated her for drawing them to my attention.

'Okay,' I said. 'So why do you think I do this? Why do you think I avoid intimacy in real life but embrace it in fantasy?'

I wasn't expecting an answer to this. But I was oh so wrong.

'I think there are several factors that you might want to con-sider. I think you may be scared to make a deep attachment, to avoid the pain of another loss. I think the fear of abandonment strikes at an unconscious level for you whenever intimacy is on the horizon. I think there is a bit of you that feels unworthy of true love and feels that if anyone gets close enough to see and know the real you, they won't like it.'

She paused and I thought that was it, but there was more to come. 'I think you want someone to love you totally and uncon-ditionally, yet only your parents and your children, before they have grown up, should love you like that. So you make it impossible for anyone to be good enough. I think part of having a fantasy acts as a shield against isolation and loneliness. I think settling for one man means giving up the possibility of any other men and I think you are loath to relinquish possibilities. And I think you elevate these men into superhuman positions. You give them all the power so that it becomes their responsibility, not your own, to save your life and make you happy. Finally, I think you are in love with the idea of being in love, but are a little too scared to try the reality.'

I was lying back with my arms folded across my chest, tears in my eyes once again, and feeling as if the happy bubble I'd come in with had all but deflated.

But Dr J wasn't finished. She had one more card up her sleeve. 'It's nearly time for us to stop,' she said. 'But I want to say a couple more things before we say goodbye for the summer. You said I ruined your fantasy about David. I wonder whether this might be a good thing, because, no matter who he is, he could never have lived up to your great expectations. He's only human. He can't save your life. And finally, before you wake up one day and realise it is too late, you have to think carefully about whether you want the lonely life of daydreams and fantasies or the less enchanting but far more rewarding and fulfilling, though at the same time challenging and frustrating, reality.'

She paused for a few minutes. 'You have to think about what you want from life. What you really, really want. Otherwise, you are in danger of drifting along, daydreaming the rest of your life away.'

On the way home, I sat on a bench in Kelvingrove Park. I had started walking to and from sessions. It was a beautiful summer morning. I sat in silence and in shock, thinking about everything she'd just said to me and realising that it was all horribly true.

August

Sex, Sand and Cold Turkey

'Good morning, beautiful lady. Welcome to Jamaica,' a stunning young man called Leroy said. He extended his clenched fist for me to 'bump', this being the island's traditional expression of good wishes, friendship and respect. I bumped back, but felt a bit stupid, so said: 'Oh, er, hello there, boys,' at the same time.

His equally cute friend Denzel looked slowly, very, very slowly, from my head to toes and back, taking in every inch of my sun-starved, undetoxed bikini-clad body and lingering on certain bits longer than my most ardent boyfriend ever did. He sighed: 'You are the most beautiful lady I have ever seen here.' I giggled feebly. 'No, you must believe me. I'm not just saying this. You are a truly beautiful lady. Are you a supermodel?' 'Er, no,' I said, while thinking, how fab, now I can tell people I've been mistaken for one.

Despite my vow earlier in the year never to venture on another foreign assignment, I had gratefully accepted Kamal's offer to come here to investigate the growing trend for what had been euphemistically called 'romance tourism'. The less deluded referred to it as sex tourism or simply prostitution.

I was taking a stroll along a stretch of the seven-mile long Negril beach. With its bleached white sand, warm turquoise water and fringe of swaying palms, I felt as if I was in paradise. To complete the effect, I had Bob Marley playing on my iPod.

Despite my best efforts not to, and with all of Dr J's warnings still ringing in my ears, I had been daydreaming about the lovely David. But before I got carried away, a text message from Kamal jolted me back to reality. He was asking how the story was shaping up, which reminded me that it wasn't my own romantic affairs I should be dwelling on. I dutifully kept an eye peeled for middle-aged white women and their young Jamaican boy lovers.

Which was when I met Leroy and Denzel. They were both twenty-two.

When I told them I was Scottish, they said that *Braveheart* was their favourite film. 'Freedom, man,' they said, extending their fists again. I was about to launch into a staunch defence of the union – I love being British as much as I love being Scottish – but I remembered it was somewhat off the track of the topic I was meant to be discussing, so I said: 'Freedom, man,' and bumped back.

They offered to show me the Blue Mountains and caves with the persistent refrain: 'Beautiful lady, you need someone to look after you. Some of the other men you will meet will try to hassle you and rip you off. Especially if you are here all alone. We will take care of you.'

They also, as an afterthought, mentioned that they had the best coke and ganja anywhere in Jamaica. I politely declined, saying I wasn't at all offended – each to their own and all that, and explained about my terrifying near-death experience the time I tried, in a spirit of pure but mistaken hedonism, a sixteenth of an E, a dab of coke on my gum and three puffs of a joint. After having what I think in drug parlance is called a whitey, during which the world started spinning and I thought I was going to die, I was consumed with guilt and spoiled everyone else's night by repeatedly threatening to report myself (and, as a result, everyone else at the party) to the police. They dismissed my experience, saying their gear was pure and wonderful, unlike the 'Sshcottish schtuff'. Oh yes. In addition to being Jamaica's premier drug dealers, they also did a fine line in Sean Connery-esque accents.

When they realised nothing could persuade me to get high with them, Denzel changed the subject away from drugs and asked if I was related to Elle Macpherson, her sister perhaps? Then he tried a different approach. 'You are not like the other ladies who come here. You are different. I don't know what it is, but there is something different about you. I can feel it, from talking to you and looking into your beautiful eyes. There is something special about you. Something very special.'

Now, I was no longer completely delusional. I knew it was a well-rehearsed line and, just in case I was in any doubt, I could hear my onboard Dr J reminding me that there is, in fact, absolutely nothing special about me whatsoever. But still I'm embarrassed to admit that I felt ever so slightly flattered. Just a teeny weeny bit.

An hour or so later, I was sitting under a palm tree trying the traditional breakfast of ackee fruit and salt fish – strangely delicious, a bit like scrambled eggs – when I saw Leroy and Denzel again just a few footsteps away on the beach. They didn't notice me and were busy eyeing up two voluptuous British women who looked as if they were in their fifties or maybe even sixties. One had bleached curly white hair like Dolly Parton or Barbara Cartland. She even had on theatrical pink lipstick, a bikini to match and was dripping in gold jewellery. The other looked like Princess Diana's mother.

I heard Leroy saying: 'Good morning, beautiful, beautiful ladies. Welcome to Jamaica.' They all bumped fists. 'You are the most beautiful lady I have ever seen here,' Leroy said. 'What part of heaven did you fall from?'

'And you,' Denzel said to the other, 'are you a supermodel?' The woman laughed. He continued: 'You remind me of Claudia Schiffer. You have the most beautiful eyes I have ever seen. They sparkle like the stars in the sky. Ahh. So beautiful. When I look into those eyes, I can see into your soul and I can see that you are not like the other ladies who come here. You are different. I can feel it. You are a deep person. There is something special about you. Something very special.'

The women grinned and said they thought they might be too old for Leroy and Denzel. I, meanwhile, nearly choked from laughter on my breakfast. 'No, no. You ageless,' Leroy said. 'We are not like those men of yours back home. We have heard all about those cold and selfish, mechanical and uncomplimentary men. We know those men back home are intimidated by you strong-minded, feisty ladies. But not us. We are real men. We know how to make a lady feel good. In Jamaica, real men like real women. Mature and intelligent and big, beautiful women, like you.'

And that was pretty much the story in this peculiar part of paradise. I spoke to a local police officer who told me that an estimated 80,000 single women, mainly from their late thirties through to their sixties, and mostly Americans, Germans and Brits, flock to this island every year to use the services of about 200 men, known as 'rent a dreads', 'rastitutes' or 'the Foreign Service', though they openly call themselves gigolos or hustlers, who have made this beach – or at least a mile-long section of it – their headquarters. The cop said most guys go for the 'grand-mother types' first because they have more money, rather than the younger ones who are just looking for some fun. Some of the women just want sex; others are looking for true love, but seem to have had no luck finding it back home.

I went into a supermarket in the town centre and saw some of the oddest-matched couples I'd ever seen. There were scores of very young, good-looking Jamaican men, holding hands with women who from behind looked like Jerry Hall, but from the front looked more like something snatched from the Valley of the Kings. And they were probably the prize catches. There were also lots of huge, matronly types. But looks really didn't seem to matter. It didn't take a sex siren to draw men like moths to a light. If you came here and weren't hit on within half an hour, you could feel pretty certain you'd never be having sex again for the rest of your life.

On the way back to the hotel, I was talking to a guy called Elton. He explained that there is no welfare state in Jamaica and said men had a choice between working in a hotel and earning around £40 a week or 'romancing' a tourist – most of whom, he said, were high-earning, hard-working but lonely western women who, to the locals, seemed like millionaires. All the men, he said, ultimately wanted a ticket out of Jamaica to America or Britain, where they dreamed of finding a better life.

We had a coffee and chatted more. I didn't think he was a gigolo, because he was talking so frankly about the whole scene, but as I was leaving he said he would pick me up at 7 pm to take me to Alfred's, which seemed to be where everyone in Negril was going that night for a beach party. I said I'd make my own way. Which made him visibly angry. 'You are going to cause a war,' he said. 'I have seen you talking to lots of men. What's your game? You have told around fifteen men here that you are going to see them at Alfred's tonight. Don't you know what that means? They all think you want them to be your boyfriend. You cannot do that. It is dangerous. There is going to be war in Alfred's tonight because of you.'

I've seen men fighting over women in rom-coms and at drunken wedding receptions, but no one had ever shown any inclination to get into fisticuffs over me! Until now. I thought about texting Katy to tell her that, in the middle of a chilled-out reggae party on a beach in Jamaica, fifteen men were going to be rolling around in the sand in a bare-knuckle brawl to be my boyfriend. How exciting! If only my fifteen would-be suitors realised I had no money. That I had, in fact, gone into debt to pay for therapy because I was incapable of forming a functional relationship with a responsible adult male. I fleetingly entertained a fantasy about quitting therapy and paying Denzel, Leroy, Elton and others and practising with them, which would probably be much more fun and would definitely produce fewer tears. And there'd be the added bonus of getting to practice the physical part, too, instead of just focusing on the emotional.

Sadly, there was no brawl to win my heart. Or my (empty) bank account. It wasn't just that everyone was far too stoned (which they were), but by the time I got there, all the guys I'd been speaking to had hooked up with other 'milk bottles', as they call the 'sex tourists'. Denzel and Leroy, for instance, were grinding their skinny young hips against two women who looked old enough to be their grandmothers. I actually felt a bit insulted. I had been quite looking forward to seeing men scramble about in the sand over me! But it was not to be. A live reggae band was on stage playing Bob Marley songs all night. The Jamaicans were very good dancers, unlike their partners, who looked clumsy and ridiculous next to them. Although there wasn't a battle for my affection, I did manage to get lots of work done. I spoke to two British women, both in their late thirties, which made them babies on the scene, who had been coming to Negril two or three times a year for the last few years. Each had had several Jamaican lovers and said they thought it was just a bit of fun. They said the stupid ones were the older women who were looking for love and who genuinely believed that these beautiful eighteen-year-old guys had fallen in love with them. They thought it was all very delusional and agreed that it was quite depressing that women were basically paying for sex and compliments, however hollow. I thought these two women were relatively smart until one told me that she had timed this trip to maximise her chances of getting pregnant, as she'd always wanted a little 'brown baby'! I was speechless.

I chatted to another woman, a forty-eight-year-old from Miami, who had returned to spend a week with her Jamaican lover, after meeting him last year during a holiday with friends. She said she'd heard about these guys who trawled the beach and wondered what kind of dumb woman would fall for it. But she said her boyfriend, Winston, had persisted, wooing and charming her and showering her with compliments. She submitted in the spirit of oh-what-the-hell-you-only-live-once, but she still regarded it as a temporary love affair. He told her the things she wanted to hear and, in return, she paid for everything – meals, hotel, transport, tours and endless gifts. She also sent him money every month. I asked her if she thought it was a form of prostitution (girl reporter goes for heart of story) and she conceded that that was one way of looking at it.

Finally, I spoke to this guy, Rodney, who was nineteen. When his English girlfriend went to the bar, I asked him if he loved her. He smiled and said he had lots of 'special friends', then he pulled out his wallet and showed me photos of five women: his special friends from Britain, America, Germany and two from Canada. I asked who his favourite was and why. He pointed to Connie, a white-haired but attractive woman in her early fifties. 'She's got a lot of money,' he said. 'She pays for me to go to college and, when I'm finished, she's going to take me to live in America with her.'

I, rather naively, asked how he could have sex with a woman he didn't love or find physically attractive. 'I close my eyes,' he said, 'and I pretend she's someone else. A supermodel or something.'

The story I was doing looked at the rights and wrongs of female sex tourism. Is it harmless fun or is it exploitation and, if so, who's the victim and who's the perpetrator – the women who fall for declarations of true love or the poor, unemployed men who make them in the hope of getting money or a passport to a better life? Newspapers like strong conclusions: they like black and white; right or wrong; pro or anti. But the more I had of the Dr J treatment, the more I thought carefully about things, and I was realising that life is rarely like that. There is this massive grey area in the middle. Life is often messy, unpredictable, complicated, contradictory and unresolved. I was finding it harder to judge and was instead thinking, each to their own, as long as no one's breaking the law or abusing the vulnerable. I wasn't exactly sure what I thought about sex tourism in Jamaica other than it's not just me, it is indeed a mad, mad, mad, mad world.

* * *

I wrote the story quickly, sent it to Kamal and spent the next four days until my flight home trying not to daydream too much about David, because of what Dr J had said to me before she left. I found this virtually impossible: I was lying on a beach surrounded not only by sun, sea and sand, but also by honeymooning couples. I'd ditched Bob Marley and was now alternating between the decidedly untropical songs 'The Wild Rover', 'You Are My Joy' by the Reindeer Section and '500 Miles' by The Proclaimers, all of which had the effect of transporting me from my sun-lounger in Jamaica to a balcony overlooking the River Clyde.

And Dr J had gone on holiday, leaving me with her biggest bombshell yet. What *do* I want from life? What do I really, really want? A good question, but one that I was finding difficult to answer – out loud or even in writing – with total honesty. So I tried to generalise, even though I could hear Dr J deploring my evasiveness. What does anyone want? To be loved. To make their mum and dad proud. To say the important things before it's too late. To be healthy. To live a life that means something. To do a job that's rewarding and fulfilling. To not have too many regrets. To accomplish something memorable. To matter. To share your life and not be lonely. To not end up one of those bitter, angry, unfulfilled, judgmental types.

When my brain was beginning to ache, I escaped into the books I had borrowed from Katy at the beginning of the year. Most holidaymakers were enjoying light, entertaining beach reads. I, on the other hand, was making notes on *The Neurotic Personality of Our Time* and *Civilization and Its Discontents*, among others. Every so often, when I came across something thought-provoking or which freaked me out, while the sun shone outside, I would find a cool, dark nook and email Katy.

TO: katy2000@hotmail.com
FROM: lormarmartin@yahoo.com
SUBJECT: Did you know . . .

. . . that if you spend your life married to the wrong person – i.e. not The One – then the bereavement and detachment process tends to be much more prolonged, painful and complicated? This is because of regret – you end up grieving not just for your spouse but for yourself as well – for all those squandered years, and for what might have been. The thought of this terrifies me. In contrast, those who had the best, most loving, equal and supportive marriages went through the bereavement and detachment process more easily. This is based on a long in-depth study of widows and widowers by the master American psychotherapist Irvin D. Yalom. Katy, it is better to be alone, even if we do sometimes feel lonely and stay home alone, watching DVD box sets and crying, than to be with someone who you know in your gut isn't Mr Right. It is better to be lonely alone that lonely in a relationship, isn't it?

Lor

x

FROM: katy2000@hotmail.com
TO: lormarmartin@yahoo.com
SUBJECT: RE: Did you know . . .

You're in Jamaica, sweetheart. Go get yourself a Pina Colada. Or get high. Or get laid. You can work on your thesis, or play Dr Freud, when you get back home.

K

TO: katy2000@hotmail.com
FROM: lormarmartin@yahoo.com
SUBJECT: Did you know . . .

. . . that in our culture there are four main ways of escaping anxiety/fear: rationalise it; deny it; narcotise it – not just with alcohol or drugs, you can drown yourself in work, exercise or sex; or avoid thoughts, feelings, impulses and situations that might arouse it.

And, of course, you'll probably already know the most common neurotic trends, according to Karen Horney. They are the neurotic need for:

affection and approval;

power;

a partner who will 'save' your life;

self-sufficiency and independence;

social recognition or prestige;
perfection and unassailability;
personal achievement (i.e. relentless driving of self to greater
achievements);
personal admiration (i.e. having inflated image of self);
a life restricted within narrow borders for fear of making
demands.
Hope all's well
Lor
x

PS Is anyone completely not neurotic?
PPS What exactly does neurotic mean anyway?

On my last day in Jamaica, when I was about to send Katy an email to ask her if she thought I should move to a flat with a view of a cemetery (first advised, I'd just discovered, in one of the books I'd borrowed from her, by the French essayist Michel de Montaigne. His reasoning was that such proximity to death helped people to keep life in perspective: to trivialise the trivial and value what is truly precious), I clicked on my inbox. My heart flip-flopped. I had an email from David. It began: Hey Lady. The sexiest email opening ever! I read it through. It was quite brief. He said things were going well in Malawi, though the work was quite harrowing, and he asked about Jamaica. But it wasn't overly flirtatious. There was no mention of The Necklace or The Balcony Scene. He ended with D and an x underneath.

I read it again. And again. And again. And again. Probably about one hundred times. Hey Lady. Ohmigod. And D, with an x underneath. Wow. I had to stop myself from putting my lips to the screen and snogging the x. But he hadn't come right out and declared his undying love for me. Maybe he was just being chatty? As the doubts began to take root, I heard the insinuating voice of Dr J in my head, saying, *Good Lord, what on earth does this poor man have to do? He got your email address, didn't he? Isn't that a start, a good enough sign for you that he is interested?*

Especially for a Scottish man. What would be good enough for you – for the poor guy to have jumped on a flight from Malawi to Jamaica? To have taken out a full-page advert in the press? But then, of course, he'd have been far too keen. The man can never win with you. I wonder if anyone could?

Ignoring her, I considered phoning Katy or Louise or Rachel or Emily for their thoughts and to get their advice on how long I should wait before replying. I knew I mustn't respond immediately, obviously, as that would make me seem too eager. So I went for breakfast, during which I listened to The Spinners song 'Could It Be I'm Falling In Love' on my iPod on repeat and recited, word-perfect, his message in my head. Judging by the strange looks a couple of the waiters were giving me, I think my lips must have been moving, giving me that demented talking-to-myself look.

At the end of my breakfast, I had an epiphany. Because I'd been given such highly contradictory advice from my girlfriends in the past, I decided not to solicit their views on how I should respond to David's email. Nor did I heed Dr J's suggested 'strike when the iron's cold' approach. She had suggested that, whenever emotions are running high, you should try not to respond impulsively, but should instead sit with it for a while and thoroughly analyse your possible motives and consider the potential consequences of any action or inaction.

Clearly, this can take a couple of days, depending on the issue being contemplated. The only problem is that, the last time I tried it, not only did I squander a morning (when I should have been working) gazing out of the window deep in thought, but I ended up so confused by the afternoon that I had to lie down with a damp towel on my forehead. (And this was when The Issue was whether or not I should call Kamal to confess about a tiny mistake I'd made in an earlier story.)

Where matters of the heart are concerned, I decided that life's too short and precious to wait until the temperature has cooled. Besides, what if, while I sat around contemplating, he is swept off his feet by a stunning young junior doctor whose parents work for the foreign office or the diplomatic service and who looks like Angelina Jolie? I decided I wasn't going to risk it.

So, I left the breakfast room and strode purposefully towards my room to get my laptop, mumbling *carpe diem* to myself. I was going to respond instinctively. Well, almost. I spent a few minutes agonising over whether to start with 'Hey there', 'Hiya', 'Howdy!', 'Helloooo!' or 'Hi David'. In the end, I opted for simply 'Hi' and then I let it all out. I just wrote. I unleashed onto the page the sort of stream of consciousness stuff that Dr J is often encouraging me to do in the safe and secure confines of her room. Which may have been okay, except that, after I'd finished and clicked 'send', it dawned on me that, in replying to David's light and flirtatious five-paragraph email, I'd tapped out a 5,000-word novella. Actually, I might be exaggerating. It may have only been 4,000.

Because I'd read somewhere (no doubt a bestselling self-help manual) that men find driven and ambitious women attractive, I ramped up my credentials as a focused, ambitious individual who is dedicated to truth, justice and generally making the world a better place.

I do care deeply about those things, of course. I'm a journalist. But perhaps he didn't need to hear at this juncture and in excruciating detail that I'd been down sewers with street children in Romania, then covered the saddest story of my life from Bosnia and followed the heartbreaking journey of sex slaves in Albania. I conveniently glossed over the fact that I had worked on all these projects several years ago and, in more recent times, my most extensive trips had been inside my own troubled little head, via Dr J's consulting room three times a week. Instead, I ended that section with the following profundity: 'Isn't this one short life we've got an amazing, action-packed adventure? I like to think of it as a short holiday between, you know, what we were before – i.e. nothing – and where we're going after – i.e. back to what we were before, i.e. nothing.'

Because I knew, from being an avid reader of newspapers – ten a day, every day – that all men find single women, especially ones my age, who show any interest or desire to be in a relationship, deeply unattractive, I informed him that my life was so jam-packed, what with work, friends, family etc, that I wasn't at all interested in having a boyfriend just now. 'It would just get in the way of this amazing action-packed adventure that I'm having. God, I love my life and am so happy without a man in it,' I wrote before signing off: 'Anyways, hope all's well with you. Spk soon, Lor x.'

I smiled with satisfaction as I pressed 'send'. I felt really good about myself. For about half an hour. Then I started to panic as the cold light of realisation began to seep in. Still, I consoled myself, at least I hadn't actually attached my CV.

* * *

I checked to see if he'd replied. He hadn't. Half an hour later, I checked again. Still nothing. After another thirty minutes, I logged in again. Shit. I decided to distract myself by going for my first ever ride on a jet-ski. The driver, Vincent, asked if I wanted to see the nude beach at the world-famous Hedonism resort on the tip of Negril beach. 'Oh, yes please,' I said, knowing that if anything would take my mind off my own petty romantic worries, that would. Having learned my lesson about going away with strange men in Thailand, I made sure he was a bona fide member of the hotel staff and water sports department. First, we went tearing along to Rick's Cafe, an amazing clifftop, open-air restaurant and bar. Scores of locals, including children who looked as young as ten, were diving off thirty-three-foot cliffs into the ocean. Tourists were queuing up to jump as well. Before Dr J entered my life, and found a permanent perch somewhere in my brain, I'd probably have done it too. But I heard her say: 'Please, Lorna. Just observe. Don't turn this trip into a suicide mission as well.'

We headed further along, past all the couples-only resorts. I had my arms wrapped tightly around Vincent's tiny waist. 'This is amazing,' I shouted into his ears. 'I love the wind blowing in my hair and the warm sun on my back. This is fab. I feel as if I'm in a Holly . . .' I drifted off when I heard Dr J drifting in.

A few miles along the coast, Vincent slowed down and switched off the engine. He nodded towards the beach. I turned towards it and screamed in horror. Now, I am no prude. I knew I would be seeing a smorgasbord of nakedness and wobbling body parts. And that was fine. That wasn't the problem. The problem was:

'OHMIGODALMIGHTY, THEY'RE SHAGGING!' I screamed, piercing the surrounding peace and serenity, and pointing at a tight knot of limbs, which turned out to be three people. It was a Barbara Cartland double naked other than for her floppy hat, standing knee-deep in the water, with one glistening young Jamaican behind her, very clearly, you know, doing *it*, and another in front of her. He was also, very clearly doing some variation of *it*. 'I can't believe they're actually, you know, doing *it* . . .' I said, still aghast, but at least a bit quieter this time. Vincent looked at me as if I were a quaint Victorian relic, and laughed. 'Er, yes, *it* – as you call it – *is* what a lot of people do here.'

'But I'm . . . I'm Scottish,' I proclaimed, as if that would explain everything. 'We don't like to . . . well . . . I don't know . . . never mind. Maybe it's the weather or something?'

I got back to the safety of my hotel without any further outbreak of wobbly bits, though with my fragile nerves shattered even more, and immediately checked my email. No new messages, so I lay on a sun-lounger and tried to find solace in *Self-Analysis* by Karen Horney. I scribbled notes as if I were a student again, studying for my finals: We must not forget that in every neurosis the ability to love is greatly impaired. All neurotic persons are markedly unstable in their self-evaluation, wavering between an inflated and a deflated image of themselves. It is much easier to recognise other people's neuroses than to recognise our own. I doubled-underlined that last point.

As soon as the sun was up in the UK, I called Katy and told her first about the shenanigans at Hedonism, then about the email from David.

'Ooh, fab,' she said, referring to the message. 'Have you replied?'

'Yup, earlier this morning,' I said, trying to sound light and airy.

'What did you say?'

'Och, you know, I kept it kind of light and airy. And brief.' If only, I thought, feeling just a little guilty about not yet being able to tell her the truth.

'Ooh, fab,' she said again. 'Let me know as soon as you hear.'

'Yup, will do.'

* * *

When I returned from Jamaica, freckled and disturbed (about sex tourism and the fact that five days had passed since I'd released that crazy email into the ether without any response), my first assignment was at the Court of Session in Edinburgh. Sex was everywhere that summer, not that I was having any. I was as chaste as a Carmelite. It was one of the hottest summers on record and I spent a large part of it in the fiercely air-conditioned court six, covering one of the most sensational cases in Scottish legal history. Tommy Sheridan, the sunbed-loving politician, was suing the *News of the World*, the biggest-selling Sunday newspaper in Britain, after it published stories alleging he was a swinger, adulterer and cocaine-snorting hypocrite.

One good thing about being in court all day, every day, was that it meant I couldn't obsessively check my emails. The other was that I had hardly any time to think about Dr J's absence. And, of course, there was the sheer entertainment value. This time of year is known as the silly season because of the news drought. Stories about the weather, travel chaos and meaninglessly biased and subjective surveys, which would normally be lucky to make 200 words on page fourteen, end up getting two 1,000-word double-page spreads accompanied by in-depth analyses about what it all means for the future of western civilisation. So the Sheridan story came like manna from heaven.

The case had everything: a charismatic married political party leader, claims of three-, four- and even five-in-a-bed sex, visits to swingers' clubs, call girls, a sex columnist, and allegations of cocaine-snorting thrown in for good measure. There was also wildly conflicting evidence from the witness box, meaning either two or three politicians had lied on oath and would face possible perjury charges. As if all that were not juicy enough, there was also the loyal and glamorous wife, Gail, an air stewardess who looked, as one observer put it, as if she were auditioning for a part in the TV show *Footballers' Wives*.

The trial captivated the nation. As I sat through four weeks of it, until Sheridan subsequently won, I found myself playing Freud and wondering what on earth Dr J would make of it all. I found myself scribbling in my notebook: *refers to himself in the third person; grandiose sense of self-importance; external locus of control? – nothing his responsibility – everyone else's fault; requires excessive admiration? intimacy issues?? Referred to jury as brothers and sisters – v. manipulative, I think. He portrays himself as a politician who works for humanity, but I think he enjoys the power and control, a typical politician. Wife – blind trust – says she'd just know if her husband was cheating.*

Then I realised I didn't have a clue what I was talking about. So I went outside, into the sun-drenched parliament square, and wrote the story, with my all-time favourite intro:

Tommy Sheridan, the perma-tanned working-class hero and best-known politician in Scotland, leaned forward, listening intently, as a transcript of an interview with 'Christy Babe' was read to the hushed courtroom.

'He liked you to dominate him. He liked uniforms. He liked whipping just a little bit, at the top of his legs.'

Flanked by his legal team and dressed in a sharp black suit, white shirt and red tie, the man who became famous for leading the revolt against Margaret Thatcher's hated poll tax did not flinch. He remained silent and impassive.

*In the witness box at Edinburgh's Court of Session, the
testimony of a* News of the World *journalist continued: 'He
liked the feeling of ice a lot. You see, when each of us was
giving the other oral, he would get out a bit of ice and shove it
up his arse.'*

*Later, when asked whether she had documentary evidence
supporting such claims, 'Christy Babe', former prostitute
Fiona McGuire, appeared confused, before seeking guidance
from the judge: 'If you are shagging someone, what
documentation do you have for that?'*

*Listening to the exchange in the tightly packed public
gallery was Sheridan's devoted mother, Alice. Later in the
case, after hearing evidence from another woman who
claimed to have had three-in-a-bed sex with her son, she
quietly rummaged in her handbag for her well-thumbed
copy of the Chaplet of Divine Mercy. Her lips moved as she
read silently, then she closed her eyes tightly, clutched her
wine-coloured rosary beads and listened to another day of
evidence in one of the most sensational cases in Scottish
legal history.*

* * *

Immersing myself in the aftermath of the Sheridan tale provided
a welcome distraction from the fact that nearly a month had
gone by without a session with Dr J and without a reply from
David.

The last Sunday in August was another brilliant day. As I
flicked through all the papers over breakfast, I felt strangely content. Until I stumbled across a story about a survey showing that
more than half of all emails are misinterpreted.

It was now impossible to avoid facing the certainty that mine
must have been one of them. The report pointed out that only
30 per cent of communication is based on words – the vast
majority of communication between couples is nonverbal –

which is why so many emails (and text messages) are misunderstood. As I read on to the tips section, my queasiness got worse: Keep it short and sweet – don't bore someone with too much detail about your life; draft an email then edit it down to half its original length to get the important points across effectively. Oh God.

Over the previous weeks, I had been consoling myself with numerous excuses to explain his lack of reply: maybe his laptop was broken; maybe there was something wrong at my end (technological as opposed to psychological) and he hadn't even received my message; maybe he botched up an important medical case in Malawi and was pre-occupied with issues of his own professional incompetence; maybe he received so many emails that he quite simply missed mine; maybe he's not long out of a relationship – I didn't know his history – and decided he didn't want to get involved in anything just now; maybe he'd been in an accident; maybe he had fallen in love with a stunning young junior doctor who looked like Angelina Jolie; maybe he just thinks I'm nuts, and so on and so on and so on.

Later that day, after I'd wound myself up into an anxious frenzy, I decided I needed to off-load and get someone else's opinion, or more precisely, I needed reassurance. I showed the email to a kind friend who initially told me what I wanted to hear: namely, that I should stop worrying. 'Take a few steps back and consider this from the long skein of your life events,' Rachel said helpfully. 'You sent an, em, over-zealous email. It's really not a big deal. You will laugh about it in years to come, if you even remember it.'

'Thanks,' I said. 'You're so right.' She smiled but looked troubled. As if she had something heavy weighing on her own mind. 'Are you okay?' I asked.

She chewed her bottom lip. 'Do you know how many human beings there are on earth?'

It was my turn to look perplexed. 'Sorry? I mean, what? I mean, pardon?'

'There are more than 6.6 billion people in the world. That's six, six and then nine zeros. In China, there are 1.3 billion. One, three and nine zeros. Can you get your head around that? In Scotland, the population is, what, five million? The total population of Scotland is less than one-tenth of 1 per cent of the whole world. The population of Britain is three-quarters of 1 per cent of the whole world. How crazy is that? And you are just one person.'

'Okay, okay,' I said. 'I hear what you're saying. I need to get things into perspective. I'm completely, utterly irrelevant and unimportant and insignificant, I know. Thanks for reminding me.'

'I didn't mean it quite like that,' she said, still looking a bit dazed. 'It's just that I'm researching a programme about China's elderly population – expected to be 437 million by 2051, in case you're interested – and it's blowing my mind. We're all just tiny little ants. You are just one crazy little ant called Lorna who is fretting because you've sent a rather crazy email to another crazy little ant called David. He's away searching for meaning in Malawi. You're here searching for meaning with your shrink.'

I think she was having an existential crisis – I thought about giving her Dr J's number then realised that would probably only make it worse – but I took some comfort from her crazy metaphor. Not for too long, though. My anxiety returned with a vengeance later that day when Katy said: 'Did you ever hear back from David?'

'Er, no,' I said. And I steeled myself for the unpalatable truth. I decided to show Louise and Katy the email and get their thoughts. They read it, all of it, in silence. When they reached the end, they looked at each other in disbelief, then burst out laughing.

Louise, with despair in her voice, said: 'You didn't send that. Please tell me you did not send that. What exactly were you trying to say?'

'Dunno.'

Katy was slightly more constructive. 'I can't decide whether, in addition to sounding nuts, you sound completely desperate or completely disinterested.' I held my shamefaced head in my hands while Louise and Katy had a discussion about what it all meant.

Louise: 'I think, unconsciously, she may have been trying to sabotage it before anything had even started. Maybe she's still afraid of, you know, love, abandonment, intimacy, rejection etc? So she ruins it before it even has a chance to get off the ground. And then she can say it was her fault – take the blame herself – rather than risk getting intimate with someone and the possibility of him rejecting her.'

Katy: 'Hmm, she's still not very good at just sitting with strong emotions, is she? I mean, it's as if she just *needs* to act to get rid of all of them in one fell swoop.'

Oh God, I wish I'd never shown it to this pair of lunatics. 'Maybe I should send another,' I suggested. 'Saying I don't give a damn that he's not replied and I was only being friendly and I don't even like him anyway. And I never have. And he's only one small irrelevant ant in a world of 6.6 billion.'

'NO!' barked Louise and Katy simultaneously. 'Just leave it. Just try to learn to wait,' Louise added. 'What the hell have ants got to do with this?'

'He's just an ant,' I said. 'One crazy little ant in a world of 6.6 billion.' They looked at each other, deeply perplexed. I continued: 'Maybe I should send another email and tell him that? Or send one clarifying the first one? Saying, I hope I didn't sound too nuts, but –'

'NO!' they barked again. 'Just leave it. Just try to learn to wait. Try to just sit with your anxiety. And don't, whatever you do, go firing off an email saying he's just a crazy little ant.'

What, I wondered, would Dr J think? Since she'd taken up permanent residence in my head, I imagined she'd say something like: 'What goes on in another person's mind, someone who you hardly even know, who doesn't know you, who is caught up in his own life struggles, doesn't change the person you are. You are you, and if he doesn't like that, there is nothing you can do about it. You can't change who you are for someone else. What he thinks of you, based on your crazy email or anything else, doesn't matter. Surely after all the work we've done together you must know by now that the most important thing in this life is how *you* feel about you?'

I missed her and found myself longing to see her again.

September

Schadenfreude: Germany's Finest Export

Before I was psychologically torn to shreds, I thought I was quite a decent person. Yes, I had committed a terrible sin, but, apart from that, I believed that I was, on the whole, quite good. I thought I was nice, to use that bland but sometimes perfectly apposite word hated by English teachers everywhere. But thanks to Dr J, the woman I was paying to improve my life and to make me feel more comfortable in my own skin, I had discovered that this was another delusion I'd been harbouring about myself.

I wasn't all nice. There was nastiness. ('What made you think you were any different from the rest of the world's ordinary mortals?' Katy commented when I shared my latest discovery from this strange voyage with her.) I realised the cloven hoof had popped out when I found myself secretly hoping some misfortune would befall one of my friends, even though I love them all dearly and would hate for anything really bad to happen to any of them. I wasn't wishing for anything too serious. I wasn't talking major misery. Just a little heartache, a poor appraisal at work, a rejection, even a toothache or, even better, root canal treatment would have sufficed. Just some drama, crisis or scandal. Anything to make me feel a little less miserable about my own disaster-prone romantic life.

It had become blatant, horribly depressingly blatant, that David wasn't going to be replying to my crazy email any time this century. I knew he was back in town – my brother-in-law had casually dropped into the conversation that he was working in A&E at the Western Infirmary after his month in Malawi, before he moved to paediatrics later in the year. In my more pathological moments, I had concocted schemes to try to bump into him. I wondered whether my editor might like an in-depth feature about Glasgow's horrendous knife crime problem which would involve my spending the next month at, say, the Western Infirmary A&E department, shadowing a doctor called McDreamy and . . . Maybe not. Maybe the sad truth was that even after eight months of Dr J's unique psychological surgery I was still a hopeless case when it came to matters of the heart. Maybe I just had to accept that I was never going to be able to form a healthy adult relationship with a desirable and available male member of the species.

Ho hum, I thought, as I waited for a tale of woe to come my way.

I know Schadenfreude is evil, but it's also hugely underrated as a fast-acting and extremely potent pick-me-up. But there was a snag. While I longed for the refreshing tonic of other people's sorrows, I was instead confronted that autumn with a sickening barrage of good news, success and happiness.

On one single day in September, a beautiful crisp day when the trees were beginning to lose their leaves and I was already suffering from a post alcohol-induced dose of The Fear (connected to nothing concrete, just a general, free-floating anxiety), I heard that:

1) My friend Alisha was moving to Houston with her lovely husband and two gorgeous young daughters. (From where I was standing, Texas seemed exotic, even glamorous.) Alisha owned her first home and was running her own successful publishing company while she was still, officially, an adolescent. She was able to retire in her thirties to become a full-time yummy mummy.

2) Another friend was shortlisted for a prestigious placement at the *Washington Post*. I'd applied for this fellowship six years ago and didn't hear a peep, not even a polite rejection

letter. At the time, I stopped reading it for two days, in
protest.

3) A girl I went to university with, but hadn't seen in years,
   contacted me to tell me she'd written a book that was
   getting great reviews. She attached the manuscript, but I
   couldn't bear to read it in case it was original and brilliant,
   or even unoriginal but still brilliant.

4) While Rachel was going on a second date with a guy she'd
   had her eye on for ages, Emily was in a state of perpetual
   bliss ever since meeting her new boyfriend.

5) Katy revealed that her flat had practically quintupled in
   value, then casually added that she too was head over heels
   in love. Like Alisha, Katy took out her first mortgage when
   she should still have been reading *My Guy* and has almost
   repaid it. I, meanwhile, was still struggling to get a toenail
   onto the first rung of the property ladder, though I had just
   made an offer for an apartment, which was the one glint of
   hope in all this misery and despair. After years of shunning
   my nation's obsession with home ownership, I decided it
   was time for me not only to think like an adult but also to
   behave like one. I was finally prepared to become a
   mortgage slave. I was ready to make a commitment, for the
   next twenty-five years, to my bank, in return for my own
   bricks and mortar. They had agreed to lend me a 100 per
   cent mortgage, five times my salary, for a tiny two-
   bedroomed flat that was even smaller than the one I was
   currently renting.

'So who are you head over heels in love with?' I asked Katy, barely
troubling to keep the green-tinged tone out of my voice. 'You
kept all this very quiet.'

She sang back, bright and cheerily: 'Oh, I'll tell you when I see
you. I'll bring a photo.' Just before she hung up, she said: 'Oh, I

forgot to mention. I bought that Jane Fonda workout video, the original one, off Amazon. It's absolutely brilliant.' Oh no. My heart sank even deeper. She's going to get all fit and lean and look as stunning as Emily. And the few remaining single thirty-something men in the world who live in Glasgow will fancy her. 'Oh very good,' I said, and put down the phone with a sad and heavy heart.

I badly needed new friends. Less successful ones. Just when I thought things couldn't get any worse, an insensitive and grammatically-challenged estate agent called Brenda phoned and said: 'Lorna, I'm sorry to tell you this: you're unsuccessful.'

I felt an overwhelming surge of disappointment tinged with rage. After a day of other people's relentlessly good news, this was the final straw. I tried to stop them but I couldn't: my eyes filled with tears. I'd already imagined myself in my new pad. 'I'm unsuccessful. I'm unsuccessful. How bad must it be when even Brenda the estate agent can see I'm unsuc-fucking-cessful,' I was thinking. But the evil in me was only down, not out. Before too many tears had escaped, I was busily brewing unpleasant but comforting fantasies in my head: 'I hope that devious double-crossing seller who played me and the successful guy off against each other has dry rot and damp in her new place. In fact, I hope the roof falls in. And I hope the 'successful' buyer hates his new flat. I hope there are neighbours from hell. And he never gets a decent night's sleep and it's the worst decision he's ever made. And he rues the day he SNATCHED MY FLAT FROM RIGHT UNDER ME, THE JERK. And the smug seller rues the day she PLAYED ME OFF AGAINST HIM, THE BITCH.'

So I wasn't doing particularly well in Dr J's selfish and prolonged absence: picking petty fights in my head with estate agents and other players in the property market, firing off verbose emails to the man of my dreams, longing for a little misfortune to sully the perfect lives of some or at least one of my perfect friends. And I still had a full eighteen hours until my next appointment with her, the first since July.

My instinct was to avoid all happy and successful people until

I'd off-loaded onto Dr J, but no such luck. Katy was desperate to tell me all about the new love in her life, so I forced myself to meet her for dinner in Kember and Jones. 'Right, tell me everything. I can't wait to hear all about him,' I lied shamelessly. Over vast salads of chorizo, Manchego cheese and toasted almonds, she started to gush: 'He's totally gorgeous. His name's Mylo. It's spelt M-Y-L-O.' Unusual name, I thought, my spirits lifting by a millimetre – at least it's not Brad (Pitt) or George (Clooney) or Roger (Federer) or, imagine, David (Mackenzie) – as she rummaged around in her handbag. Handing me a folded piece of A4 paper, she said: 'I met him online.'

I unfolded the piece of paper and had to stop myself from letting out a high-pitched yelp of delight. She hadn't found the man of her dreams after all. The object of her affection was a dog. An abandoned greyhound – which looked grey to me, but who Katy, like all dog people, insisted was blue – who was looking for a new home.

'I've been staring at his picture for hours,' she said. 'But I just can't decide whether I should get in touch.' I could have embraced her. Katy, despite her super-confident demeanour, was also, it appeared, burdened with commitment issues. Concerning a stupid dog that she'd never even met. How totally fabulous.

A little while later, feeling much better about life in general, I felt emotionally strong enough to ask her how many times she'd done the Jane Fonda workout.

'Done it?' she said. 'I haven't actually done it. I've just watched it a couple of times with a drink, a fag and a packet of crisps.'

God I love my friends so much.

Just when I thought things couldn't get any better, Rachel texted to see if we were up for a glass of wine. 'Boys r fannies!' her message ended.

When she arrived, she explained that her second date with Angus had ended in disaster when he said, between the main course and dessert: 'Honesty's really important to me. Have you ever cheated?'

'Oh for fucking fuck's sake,' Katy said, before Rachel went any further. 'His ex must have two-timed him and he's still not got over it. And he's going to hold every other woman responsible.'

'What do you do?' Rachel said, shrugging and holding her hands out in front of her. 'Are you completely honest and tell him what he clearly doesn't want to hear? Or do you tell a little lie and give him the answer he wants?'

'It's a difficult one,' I said. 'But I'd just tell him the truth. Otherwise you're living with this big lie and the fact that you've not been honest with him becomes a bigger deal than the original transgression. If he doesn't like or approve of a mistake – and a relatively minor one at that – you've made in your past, more than he likes you as a person then fuck him, he's not good enough for you. Everyone has a past, for fuck's sake. Everyone has a skeleton in their closet. Well, everyone who's lived a bit.'

'I probably agree,' Katy said. 'Though the question really does crack me up. It's the same as "how many people have you slept with?" If a guy asks you this, he doesn't want an adult, equal relationship. He wants a little girl who he can control. The only acceptable answers for him would be: None, I'm pure and untouched – I've been saving myself for you. Or, one, but it was so awful it doesn't really count. Sorry, but the truth is, when you get to our age, most of us will have been in love before, have had really great sex before, and have probably even been involved in a love triangle. If Angus, or anyone else for that matter, can't handle someone with a past, he should probably hang about outside a school, and find an unblemished teenager to go out with. Though they're probably rarer than unicorns these days. I wonder if he's as fucking moral and perfect as he expects others to be.'

'So what did you do?' I asked Rachel.

'I told him the truth. I said I'd made a mistake, learned a lot from it and would never make the same mistake again. I explained that it was a way – not a good way, but still a way – of getting out of a relationship I didn't want to be in. I said sometimes you have to make a big mistake to figure out what's right. Mistakes are very painful, but a way of finding out who we really are. I said I know who I am now. I know what I want.'

'What did he say?'

'He went quiet and repeated that trust was a big issue for him. I said trust and honesty were very important for me too, which was why I had told him the truth. But then he said his view was once a cheater always a cheater.'

'That is such bullshit,' I said. 'I know there are some serial love cheats out there. But in my experience, every woman I know, and quite a few guys I know who've been involved in that kind of scenario, have ended up so traumatised by the whole thing, that they're probably the least likely ever to get into such a messy, screwed-up situation again.'

'I agree completely,' Rachel said. 'But that's not the way a lot of folk see it. People are pretty crap at putting themselves into other people's shoes. I was totally judgmental before I ended up in the situation myself. Anyway, I left, 'cause I couldn't be arsed trying to convince him that I was worthy of his love. Life's just too fucking short.'

* * *

The next morning was my first session with Dr J since she'd been away. As with any relationship interrupted, I felt oddly awkward and shy about going from zero to sixty again with a woman who, nine months previously, I'd never met, though who now knew more about me than any other person in the world.

I woke up an hour too early, as usual, and immediately settled into a good fret. What would she be like after this vacation: back to the silent, brooding Freudian I met way back at the beginning, or full of the kind of challenges and caustic interventions that had come as such a shock in the weeks before she went away?

'Please come in,' she said, when I arrived. I was surprised to find that I wanted to give her a hug. Instead, I smiled wryly. There was never the slightest variation to her standard greeting. I quickly calculated in my head that she had said 'Please come in' to me more than eighty times already. Never: 'Hi, come on in.' Or: 'Good morning. Sit down.' Or 'Good evening. And how are we doing today?' Always just 'Please come in.'

She had that distinct post-holiday glow about her again, with a healthy tan, but a rather stern expression on her face, and a dark and sober trouser suit to match.

'I feel a bit anxious,' I said, as soon as I lay down. She said nothing. Was the silent Freudian to be in the ascendant, or was she just lying in wait?

After a while, I ventured a compliment. 'I noticed that you have a nice suntan.'

'Hmmm,' came the reply, after a customary pause and, I assumed, consultation with the ceiling.

I'd forgotten how weird this whole process was. In the month that she'd been away, her absence had been physical only. She had taken up permanent residence inside my head. But the version I had internalised was more straightforward and predictable than the reality.

The clock ticked quietly. I noticed that I was scraping the skin around my thumbnails. The silence felt uncomfortable again, the way it had back in January. I didn't know what to say, so I just started to ramble and spent the first twenty minutes of the session telling her all about Jamaica and the Tommy Sheridan trial. As an illustration of the progress I thought I'd made, I contrasted my behaviour in Jamaica – planning ahead, being sensible – with that in Thailand earlier in the year. I also told her about my psychological assessment of the Sheridan story. 'I think he'd benefit from a good shrink,' I said. 'But he's too well defended. He'd walk out during the first session.' Predictably, she didn't say: 'Ooh, that's wonderful, Lorna. I'm so pleased to hear about this progress in your work and in your analysis of other people.' There was not a sound from behind. Maybe she was part reptile and only became active and engaged in warm weather. Now it was getting a bit chilly again after a long hot summer, was she preparing to hibernate?

I took a deep breath and decided to ask her a question: 'Did you have a good holiday?' I sank back, feeling rather proud of myself.

After a few seconds, she said: 'I believe it is more important to explore the motivation behind your question. I wonder what you're really asking?'

I thought carefully but drew a blank. I shrugged and tried again. 'I was just wondering if you had a good holiday?'

After another pause, she said: 'It is not my custom to discuss details of my personal life because it interferes with the treatment. But since it is, I believe, the first time you've ever asked a direct personal question, I have decided I am going to answer it: I had a wonderful holiday, thank you.'

Confused but also emboldened by her response, however waspish, I stepped a little further into this unfamiliar territory: 'I was wondering where you were. I thought Italy, perhaps?'

I thought I heard the faint sniff of a laugh, as if one had involuntarily escaped. 'As I have said before,' she replied after a moment, 'this is your therapy, not mine. It would be much more useful for us to talk about how you have been feeling during the past four weeks.'

There was silence for a while, which I broke by confessing that I'd had a few blips in her absence and had even been hoping for some Schadenfreude to brighten up my life. She was uncharacteristically reassuring, telling me it is a natural human emotion, very closely related to envy, but another that we all frown on and pretend not to have.

'People are crazy, aren't they?' I said in response.

She ignored this and instead confounded me with another of her question specials: 'Do you still need the failure of others to feel good about your own life? You had been making progress. I wonder if these difficulties over the past month are related to the fact that we've not seen each other for a month?'

I smiled at the ceiling, told her I didn't think therapy was *that* important to me and asked her if she knew of the Morrissey song 'We Hate It When Our Friends Become Successful'. My record for engaging her in music talk had never been a good one, so, before waiting for a reply, I added: 'There's this brilliant *New Yorker* cartoon: two slickly suited dogs drinking cocktails in a bar, and one is saying to the other, "It's not enough that we succeed. Cats must also fail."'

I laughed again (I really liked that cartoon). Dr J didn't even offer a flicker. In fact, from the quiet squeaking of her leather chair, I got the distinct feeling that she was not only unamused but also bored to the point of stupefaction.

'As I've said before, there are no jokes here,' she said eventually. 'I see that you want to devote today's session – your time and your money, and the first time we've been together in a month – to analysing a band and a *New Yorker* cartoonist.'

'He's a singer,' I corrected her. 'Although he used to be in a band.'

'A singer, a band, a cartoonist – that is irrelevant,' she said. 'My point is that you, once again, appear keen to analyse anyone but yourself.' She let this hang in the air for a few seconds before adding: 'More tactics of avoidance, more resistance. All to try to distract us from the big issue.' That reference to a reptile was decidedly premature. The woman was a tiger.

Feeling reprimanded, and smarting with mortification, I repeated her question and offered an answer: 'Okay, so today's big issue is: Do I still need the failure of others to make me feel good about my own life? Well, I'm thirty-five. Nearly thirty-six. I'm still single. I'm still living in a dingy little rented flat. My attempt at getting onto the property ladder has failed. The idiots who live upstairs think it's perfectly acceptable to play indoor football at two o'clock in the morning. I have a small and dwindling circle of single friends. Just about everyone I know is settling down, having children or moving continent or changing jobs. Getting on with their wonderful lives. While I'm stuck. In therapy. Which I'm in debt to pay for. I may have more insight and self-awareness than I did nine months ago. I may now know that I'm not the strong and confident person I thought I was. I may be in touch with the ugly stuff hidden underneath, but what good has it done me? I've probably blown it with the lovely David. So the truth is, yes, I do get a little surge of pleasure when I hear about someone, especially if that someone is smug and self-righteous, suffering a bit of misfortune. It's human, as you said. But then I am, of course, because of my upbringing, immediately struck with deep remorse for having had such bad thoughts in the first place.' I held my hands out as if to say: so there you have it, Dr J, analyse fucking that.

'Hmm. All very interesting and apparently honest,' Dr J said. 'But it's still not the big issue. This morning, you bring to my mind the kind of person who likes to spend as long as possible describing the weather and the scenery and every irrelevance under the sun, but who finds it almost impossible to get to the point. You know the kind I mean? The type of person who sings when they are angry or does housework to repress their feelings. You remind me of one of those people.'

I was caught between not knowing whether to laugh or cry. 'I'm lost, totally confused. What is really going on, as you say? I honestly don't know what you are getting at.'

Dr J was silent for what must have been a full minute. 'Now that is profoundly disappointing. The big issue is, of course: what have you been feeling about my absence? Did you miss therapy? Did you miss our time together?'

I was so taken aback, I could hardly speak. 'I cannot believe you asked me that,' I eventually managed. 'You're always saying it's my therapy, not yours. Yet you want to know whether I missed therapy. Essentially, whether I missed you.' I shook my head in utter bewilderment.

'It is indeed your therapy. Which is why it is disappointing that I had to spell out the issue. We've been working together for quite some time now. How long? Eight, nine months or thereabouts. You say you've told me things you've never talked about before. You come three times a week. It is a big part of your life. Two people locked together in an intimate relationship – or a relationship that is trying to be intimate. We don't see each other for one month and you want to talk about everything, anything – singers, politicians, sex tourists, cartoonists – other than how you felt during that time. There is plenty of action and adventure in that busy life of yours, but not one word about your feelings. Oh, and then there is this David character. The last time we met, he was on the verge of becoming the love of your life. The One. Now you say, in no more than one brief buried sentence, that you've blown it. And that's it. Not another word about him or how you're feeling about that.'

I crossed my arms and tucked my hands into my armpits. After a moment's pause, I ignored her last question and asked her something I really wanted to know the answer to: 'Did you miss me?' I tried but failed to keep the petulance from my voice.

I heard Dr J swallow hard before she calmly said: 'As I've said before, we're not trying to get in touch with my feelings. We're trying to explore yours, particularly around intimacy, abandonment and rejection. And I hope beyond hope, after all this work we've done together, that how you feel does not depend on how I feel. Do you need me to say I missed you before you can say that you missed me? Alternatively, are you only able to say you didn't miss me if I say I didn't miss you first? If I said, Lorna, do you want a hug? Would you fall to your knees and say yes, please, that's all I've ever wanted from you? Does the other person always have to make the first move with you, even after all this time?'

I blinked rapidly to get rid of the tears that were welling up, then reached down for a Kleenex to mop up the ones that had escaped.

'Why don't you give your tears a voice,' she said.

Scraping the skin away from around my thumbnail, I did just that: 'Sometimes I find this so fucking frustrating. Sometimes I find you so frustrating. Sometimes you annoy me so much that I feel as if I almost hate you. I come in here and I actually often feel okay. Better than I ever have. I actually look forward to coming here. But then you always find something else, some other blind spot and I end up feeling like shit. I feel like, no matter what I do or say, you will find something wrong with it. I feel as if I can never ever please you. Like I can never win in here with you.'

'Now that,' she said with a hint of a smile in her voice, 'is so much better. It's not a description of someone else's experience. It's not an intellectual understanding. It is simply your own feelings. Your own emotional experience. Wonderful. It would be even better if you didn't need to qualify your feelings and it is rather disappointing that you still want to please me and that you think of this as a competition. It has nothing to do with winning or losing. We're not playing a game. But it's progress, so for the moment, let's get back to the big issue: how did you feel about my absence?'

'Do you want to know the truth?'

Her quiet sigh said that she would not be providing an answer to such a ridiculously superfluous question.

'The truth is, I don't know whether I missed you. I kept myself very busy, as I always do, perhaps to stop myself from missing you. But, at the same time, you've done so much poking and probing at the inside of my head that I feel as if you are always there, either at my shoulder or actually on a little perch inside my head. I feel as if you're always with me, interrogating everything I do and say.'

'Hmm,' she said. 'It is nearly time for us to stop, but there is one other thing you have not said this morning that interests me. Have you given any thought to the question I asked you before we stopped, about what you want from this life?'

She didn't add: 'Or perhaps you've been too busy to think about that too', but I couldn't help but feel that was the insinuation.

'I have been pondering it and—'

She interrupted. 'I'm sorry. But our time is up.' She said this with a slightly sour tone. One which I interpreted as: 'At our next session, maybe it would be a good idea not to waste the first thirty minutes – time which is, remember, precious and running out and irreversible – in an orgy of irrelevance and avoidance.'

'Bitch,' I mumbled, as I descended the stairs. But I knew she was right. As usual.

* * *

'Let's go dancing this weekend,' Katy suggested. Having never been much of a clubber, I agreed on condition that we went somewhere old-school, where they play tunes by Abba and Sister Sledge. On Saturday, Katy, Rachel and I (Emily was too loved up) went for dinner in a cafe/bar called Stravaigin and then on to OranMor, a venue in the basement of a former church in the West End.

As I made my way to the bar, I met a friend of Johnnie, who told me that Johnnie had just got married. I'd often wondered how I'd feel on hearing this news, especially since, a couple of years ago, again under the cloudy auspices of journalistic purpose, I'd contacted him.

I had been doing a piece about the heady allure of contacting past lovers and the power of first love, sparked by Friends Reunited and a flurry of books on the subject. It provided a perfect excuse for me to contact Johnnie and ask for his opinion on why we split up. I can see now, though I couldn't at the time, that the very fact that I wanted to know, suggested I still hadn't laid that ghost to rest. He wrote me a long and surprisingly honest letter afterwards, saying he often looked back on the years we were together as a kind of 'golden time' and apologised from the bottom of his heart for what he did. But, he wrote, all the mistakes and wrong turns we make are part of being alive. He was immature and selfish, he said, and I was like a little girl. He said he'd recently met a woman he loved very much. I thought about the eight years I spent with him and the six it took me to get over him. He was the first love of my life. I laughed when I thought about the crazy times we had together – cycling all over Europe, trying to get his band recognised. We were like children. I was surprised now, as the sounds of Chaka Khan's 'I'm Every Woman' had Katy running to the dance floor, to feel nothing other than pleasure at Johnnie's news, and genuine happiness for him.

After a few hours of shaking our hips and strutting our stuff on the dance floor, we went back to Katy's with a guy she'd met, Stephen, who she'd been flirting with towards the end of the night, and a couple of his friends, neither of whom was fanciable, but both good fun. Someone, and the odds are that it was Katy, suggested we play truth or dare, the game beloved of adolescents and adults who sometimes like to behave like adolescents. We were still drinking wine and vodka. After running through a lot of the usual playground questions and challenges, things started to become a little more adventurous when Stephen dared Katy to strip down to her underwear and run round the block.

As a compromise she said she'd do it in her secret garden which I thought was some sort of sexual euphemism until she dangled a set of keys and invited everyone to follow her outside. Katy lives in a beautiful flat in a genteel, tree-lined nook of the West End called Hyndland. Behind the row of tenements where she lives, there is a hidden locked garden surrounded by trees and bushes, into which only residents and their guests are allowed. Although I knew about it, I'd never been inside before. Rachel, Stephen, his two friends and I followed Katy, clutching a bottle of vodka, in. As I stood, inhaling the smell of grass and the mild early morning freshness – it must have been around 4 am, I wondered what on earth Dr J would make of this.

Katy, who by now seemed to think that she was working in an upmarket gentlemen's club, gave us a big lascivious wink before performing an erotic strip-tease, slowly peeling off each item of her clothing and tossing it over her shoulder. When she had nothing on but her knickers and her platform shoes, she started to run around the perimeter of the garden waving her hands in the air above her and shouting: 'Wey-hey!' We couldn't always see her, but we could always hear her.

We were cheering her on, doubled over in laughter one minute, shaking our heads in disbelief the next. When she was on the home straight, there was a sound resembling the loud snap of a branch, a scream, followed by: 'Oh for fuck's sake. Heeeellllllpppp. I think I've twisted my ankle.'

We all ran towards her. Stephen carried her back inside, while we collected items of her clothing from the bushes. She was wincing from the pain in her foot, but insisted she was okay and didn't want to go to hospital. We decided, however, that it was time to call it a night, and went our separate ways home. Or so I thought.

* * *

The next morning, Katy phoned and said her foot was badly bruised and swollen like an elephant's.

'But I thought you said it was okay last night?' Before waiting for her to reply, I guiltily confessed that earlier in the month I'd been secretly hoping for some misfortune to befall someone. 'But obviously I didn't mean something serious like this.'

Katy sighed. 'Lorna, I know you're still coming to terms with the fact that you are a mere ordinary mortal and that the world doesn't revolve around you. If you have a bad thought and something bad happens, the chances are it's got fuck all to do with you. You're not that powerful or important. Humans, all humans, have twisted, obnoxious, selfish, stupid, childish, obsessive thoughts at times. Even good people, like your mum and dad, will have them. So will nuns and priests. But theirs will be so repressed that they probably won't even be aware of them. Hee, hee. It is only worrying when you either act on them or believe that there is a correlation between an event, i.e. my broken foot, and a bad thought you had. So shut the fuck up – this is about my foot, not you. It didn't feel so painful last night, but now the alcohol's worn off. And, well, I was, you know, Stephen and I were, er, busy shall we say, when I came back in, so it took my mind off my foot. But I think I'm going to have to go to A&E. I think I've broken it.'

'So you were, er, entertaining someone all night with a broken foot hanging out of the bed?' I laughed.

'Don't,' Katy said. 'Can you take me, please? I can't drive.' She had already called Louise to ask Scott to have a look at it, but forgot they were away for the weekend.

'Ohmigod, Katy. I don't know if I can. What if, er, you know. What if David's working?'

'Sorry?' she said.

'He's back. What if he's working?'

'Lorna, I think I've broken my foot. Please . . . I can't drive. I can't walk. I don't care who's working.'

'Okay. Okay. I'm sorry. I'll be over in ten minutes.'

Half an hour later (I couldn't decide whether to wear a little black dress, a summery frock or jeans and a T-shirt, so tried each one on around twenty times before settling on the former), I picked Katy up.

As I helped her, limping and hungover, into the car, she shot me a disapproving look. 'What took you so long?'

'Traffic,' I lied.

She looked at me with a raised eyebrow. 'Hmm. And what the hell is that you've got on?'

'What's wrong with it?' I asked, offended.

'It's a lovely dress,' she shook her head. 'For a cocktail party. But we're going to A&-fucking-E on a Sunday afternoon, which will be full of drunks and waifs and strays. You can't wear a little black dress. You look totally ridiculous.'

Katy rolled her eyes in despair and made me feel so self-conscious that we went via mine so that I could change into my jeans and a T-shirt.

I parked as near to the A&E department as I could and helped Katy from the car. As we got closer to the entrance, I had to stop. 'Sorry Katy. My pulse is racing and I'm having palpitations. I'm going to have to do some yoga breathing.'

'No you're fucking well not. I'm in agony,' Katy moaned, as she hobbled towards the door.

Just as we approached the entrance, a car (which we later found out had been hijacked) screeched to a halt, nearly running us over and creating a terrible commotion. Three young men dressed in shell-suits, Burberry caps and gold jewellery, including necklaces and sovereign rings on nearly every finger, flung the doors open and continued an angry but emotional argument over who should carry Killer, their injured pit bull terrier, into the hospital.

''E's ma dug an' ah love 'im more than ah love life itsel',' one declared.

'The dug looks deid,' another shouted. 'Killer? Killer? Ah'm gonnae kill the fuckin' cunt who did this.'

'Excuse me boys,' I said assertively. I loved being assertive. 'This is a hospital. They treat human beings here not, er, animals.'

'Shut the fuck up. Ya fuckin' snobby cunt.'

'Please don't call me that horrible word,' I retorted lamely.

'And, incidentally, I'm not snobby at all. I was born in Maryhill, you know. I'm just pointing out that this is a hospital, not a—'

'Ah mean it. Shut the fuck up, ya fat ugly cunt.'

'Fat? Did you call me fat? And ugly?' They ignored me.

'Am I fat and ugly?' I whispered to Katy as I ducked my head and scurried ignobly past them and into the relative safety of the waiting room. Katy nodded and laughed mischievously as she hobbled along.

The waiting room was packed. The three young hoodlums, who were the type known in Glasgow as neds (non-educated delinquents), barged past us and up to a triage nurse, who looked terrified despite being behind a perspex screen, and told her Killer had been run over. She explained slowly, as if she were speaking to a confused two-year-old, that a hospital was a place for injured humans and suggested that they take Killer to a vet or animal hospital.

'Fix 'im or ah'll fuckin' sue ye.'

No one sees this side of hospital life, I thought, wondering whether Kamal might want a story.

About half an hour later, after the three men and their dog had been removed by security guards, Katy (with me tagging along) was seen by a lovely nurse. Katy told her, with perhaps a shade more detail than was strictly necessary, how much she'd drunk the previous evening and all about the truth or dare streaking incident. The nurse examined Katy's foot and said she'd need an X-ray. As she was escorting us back to the waiting room, she said: 'It will be a Dr Mackenzie who will see you.' Then she winked and added: 'Wait till you see him.' Katy and I looked at each other and I couldn't stop myself from letting out a tiny high-pitched squeal.

For the next hour or so, I paced up and down in the waiting room as if I were awaiting news about the fate of a loved one or even a beloved killer dog. I bit my nails. I did some single nostril yoga breathing. I said: 'I'm going to the shop to buy cigarettes.' Katy said: 'You don't smoke.' I told her I was going to have to start, but then I realised I couldn't go then in case she was called when I was away. Every so often, I would emit a sharp burst of breath and say: 'God Almighty, I'm so fucking nervous.'

All of a sudden, a thing of beauty, dressed in green surgical scrubs, appeared through the swing doors and shouted Katy's name.

Feeling mildly intoxicated, I started making strange uncontrollable gurgling noises, and mumbling, 'Ohmigod, I'm going to faint, I'm going to faint, I'm going to pass out, help me Katy, help me Katy, please,' as I helped Katy limp towards him.

He looked completely confused as he chewed the end of a Biro. The furrowed brow quickly melted into a wide, though still slightly bewildered, smile.

'Hey, how are you?' he said, looking at me, then quickly: 'Katy. I didn't . . . obviously . . . I didn't recognise the surname. What happened?'

My heart was pounding so loud I was worried he'd be able to hear it or see it through my T-shirt. 'Hey, um, fine, thanks,' I stuttered, trying not to sound as excited as I was. 'Good, very good. But Katy's, um, she was dancing and drinking vodka and running naked around her very own secret garden and she fell over and her foot is ill,' I said smoothly, pushing her into his arms and running quickly outside.

I bought ten Marlboro Lights, sat in my car and had three in a row. It was only the second time I'd smoked since I started under-age smoking during my family crisis. (The other was when Johnnie dumped me and I chain-smoked a pack of ten.)

Half an hour later, Katy emerged from A&E with her foot in plaster and supported by crutches. She was grinning. 'He was so gentle with me,' she said dreamily.

'Stop it! Did he do the plaster himself?' I asked. 'Was he, like, touching your foot and ankle and . . .'

'Mmm hmm,' she nodded. 'It was lovely. The pain just went away the minute he touched me. He's got such lovely hands and forearms and a wonderful bedside manner.'

'Aaah. Stop! Stop! I'm going to have to break my foot or something. Here, push me off the kerb. As hard as you can.'

On the drive home, I said: 'So did he, em, say anything about, you know . . .'

She wasn't playing. 'About what?'

'You know . . .'

'No, I don't. Spit it out. Did he say anything about what? How long I'd be off work?'

'No. You know, did he say anything about mi . . . ma . . . mm . . . you know, mmme?!'

Katy smiled. 'Ah, I get it. Did he say anything about you? 'Fraid not, m'dear. He was too busy looking after moi. Plus you sent him that mental email, remember? What did you expect him to say to me – is she as nuts in real life as she sounds in black and white?'

'So he didn't say anything?'

She shook her head.

I tried to pretend I wasn't at all bothered. 'Ah well. Who cares? I didn't really like him that much anyway. Who'd want to go out with a doctor? They've all got God and messiah complexes. They'd be so busy saving everyone else's life that they'd never spend any time at home, trying to save yours. Ha ha ha.'

Katy gave me a long, sideways look. 'Yeah, it would be truly awful going out with a gorgeous doctor. If you say it enough times, you might start believing it.'

happily
ever
after?

October

It's a Sin to Say it, but it's True: They Fuck You Up

Iput down my champagne, cleared my throat and prepared to
make an important announcement.

'You know how I've got all these issues? You know how I'm,
like, damaged goods?' I asked my blissfully happy mum and dad.
We were all (my mum, dad, Louise, Scott and Lewis) out for a
family dinner to celebrate my birthday on a cold, wet Saturday
night at the beginning of October. We were in Massimo, an
Italian restaurant in Bearsden, a stone's throw from my parents'
house.

'Well, there's really no easy way to say this, but it is, apparently,
all your fault. My shrink has pretty much come right out and said
so.'

They gave me a slightly confused look, so I elaborated, barely
slurring a word.

'Lewis cover your ears. In the words of Philip Larkin: "They
fuck you up, your mum and dad. They may not mean to, but they
do. They fill you with the faults they had, and add some extra, just
for you."'

'Right,' Louise said closing her menu and making a blatant
attempt to change the subject. 'Does everyone know what they
want?'

'Do you mean from an existential viewpoint or just from the
menu?' I asked. Louise raised her eyes heavenwards and silently
shook her head.

I smiled mischievously at Lewis and continued, undeterred,

delivering my verdict to my mum and dad: 'It's not intentional and I don't want you to go beating yourselves up about this, because I know you did the best you could and I know parenting has to be the hardest job in the world. But, what I'm saying is that because you guys haven't had in-depth analytical therapy to untangle the knots from your own childhood, all the crazy unresolved issues lurking about in your unconscious, unbeknown to you, all that crazy madness has been passed on to me. I'm nuts because of you two!' I beamed, pleased as a cat bearing a dead mouse as an offering. 'Oh,' I added almost as an afterthought, 'and because of Louise as well.' I picked up my champagne glass and took another sip.

My dad momentarily took his eyes off his beloved grandson and looked at me with an intrigued smile, as if he would at least be prepared to countenance the possibility that I might be on to something. My mum, however, shook her head. 'Young lady, you need to get yourself a man,' she said.

'I am trying, mum, really trying,' I said airily, waving my champagne flute. 'But it's proving difficult because of all these issues. Maybe you could, seeing as you two are largely responsible, seeing as you were destructive, albeit inadvertently, as well as constructive, help me repay the loan I took out for therapy?'

'Shut up, Lorna,' Louise said across the table. 'You're not being funny or clever or whatever it is you're trying to be.'

'Shut up yourself,' I retorted. 'I'm just saying what's on my mind. You therapy types are always banging on about how people are reluctant to accept a truthful account of themselves and their childhoods. That they insist on viewing the past and the reflection they see in the mirror – not just the physical one but the complete psychological self-profile – through rosy-tinted shades. You should be proud of me.'

'Not everything that comes to your mind, not every issue that comes up in therapy,' she said vehemently, 'needs to be shared with the group, so to speak.'

'Not everything is,' I assured her. 'There's plenty I'm keeping to myself. Plenty. I've thought very carefully about what I am prepared to share with the group, as you say. I just think all this stuff about trans-generational transference of neurotic tendencies is dead interesting. Don't you, Lewis?'

He blew a loud raspberry – not a gentle baby one, but with pursed lips and quite a lot of force – which I think may be toddler talk for: 'Fuck off and don't involve me in your issues.'

Even though it was my birthday, King Lewis chose the venue because he wanted to 'thee Luthy'. Lucy is a very attractive law student who works part-time in Massimo and on whom Lewis, despite being just two-and-a-half years old, appears to have developed a massive crush. He greets her with a hug and a kiss, and blushes slightly when she gives him a purple lollipop and tells him he is the cutest little boy she's ever seen. 'She probably says that to all the kids so that all the gullible, besotted parents and grandparents leave her a gigantic tip,' I suggested the first time she said it, attracting widespread condemnation for my sagacity from Lewis's gullible and besotted parents and grandparents (who always leave a gigantic tip). Whenever there is a family birthday and someone says: 'Where should we go?' Lewis immediately says: 'Math-mo. Want to thee Luthy.' And, to avoid any tears, that is invariably where we end up. But I'm not complaining. Lewis knows how to pick 'em. They do a fabulous four-cheese pizza and Lucy is undeniably lovely.

In response to Lewis's Bronx cheer, his granny and granda burst out laughing before planting a big kiss on each side of his head. Naturally, he was sitting in between them. He looked from one to the other, grinned, then blew another even louder one. 'Thththbbbt!' Then another. Both in my direction. This time I suspected he was saying something along the lines of: 'Aunty Lorna, I mean it. Don't spoil my fun. Don't try and take attention away from me by talking about trans-generational transference of neurotic tendencies. No one cares about that stuff. It's sooo boring. And don't you dare try to blame my wonderful gran and granda, who are entering the winter of their lives in a state of extreme bliss (thanks to me), just because you can't get yourself a boyfriend. It might be your birthday but it's still my night. All I need to do is say a new word or count to ten or blow a raspberry or break into a rendition of 'Incy Wincy Spider' and it's all eyes on me. It's kisses and cuddles and a round of applause. They think I'm totally amazing. You simply can't compete anymore. There's a new kid on the block and it's about time you got used to it.'

'So,' Scott said, 'how does it feel to be closer to forty than thirty?'

Deciding not to take umbrage, I said it felt good. And I meant it. I thought back to this time last year: being in floods of tears at the airport, visiting my GP who suggested staying on Prozac for two years, my insane behaviour regarding Christian. The shiver-inducing feeling of shame and embarrassment that washed over me was quickly replaced with one of relief. 'It feels surprisingly good, actually. I've learned more in the past year than I have in the previous thirty-five. I may have had a bit of arrested development and been late at growing up, but hopefully I've been early at having my mid-life crisis.'

'Right,' Louise said, glaring at me, 'can we order now. Please?'

After deliberating for ages, we decided on sharing a selection of starters, then the same main courses we've been ordering since the restaurant opened, plus a bottle of red and a bottle of white. I opened my cards and presents, which had the unexpected effect of obliging me to excuse myself to go to the ladies'.

I locked myself in a cubicle and took deep breaths to stop myself from crying. Normally, despite my partiality to tears, I don't read too much into the saccharine sentimentality of greeting cards, but for some reason that night my mum's handwriting went straight to my over-sensitive lachrymose glands. 'To our wonderful daughter, Lots of love, Mum and Dad xxxxxxxxxx.'

How do you ever repay your parents? How do you adequately show your appreciation to the people who, if you're lucky, have always been there for you; who, by a strange quirk of biology, have a blind spot when it comes to your flaws? Or, if they do see them, if they are written down in black and white so that they can't be avoided, are unquestioningly forgiving and accepting. I was silently addressing these questions to the wall. But it was my internal Dr J who provided the answer, the same one she gave every time I tried to explore this mystery with her. 'You see them for what they are and you forgive them.'

This was another of the many strange ironies I'd discovered in therapy – you finally recognise your parents' flaws, you acknowledge their role in creating yours and you end up loving them even more. We live in a culture where it is regarded as a sin to criticise parents. The very idea of feeling anger towards our parents (unless they've done something awful enough to be turned into a misery memoir) is perceived as being despicable and ungrateful. Pre-Dr J, I certainly believed this. To turn round to the people who created you, raised you, would put their lives on the line to protect you, sacrificed their dreams for you, and even think, never mind say, 'Hey, guys, you fucked up' seemed to me like . . . I don't know, almost like accusing them of being war criminals or Nazi collaborators. During the first months of therapy, I would not allow myself to entertain a bad or critical thought about my mum and dad. To me, it was simply wrong, abhorrent even, to feel anger towards the people I loved.

And, initially, when Dr J suggested that I acknowledge the anger, see them for what they are and forgive them, I strongly protested.

'Forgive them?' I practically screeched. 'I have nothing to forgive them for. I owe my life to them. They sacrificed so much for us. I should be seeking their forgiveness for all I've put them through over the years. Drifting, one career crisis after another, borrowing money to pay for all sorts of courses while I tried to find out what I wanted to do with my life, going back to live at home when I had no money to pay rent, advertising my sins and failings, and they're only the things I can admit to.'

'They are your parents,' she'd said. 'They will already have forgiven any little misdemeanour. It goes with the territory. Now you have to forgive them. For being merely human. And not perfect. For making mistakes.'

Dr J had often suggested that my refusal to see my parents

realistically was part of my problem. 'It is only children who believe their parents are perfect, amazing, superhuman and better than everyone else's. And it is only children, and I'm speaking emotionally here – it has nothing to do with age – who feel that they have to try to be perfect, amazing, superhuman and better than everyone else in return. And who expect their partners, and their own children, if and when they have any, to be perfect and better than everyone else. When, in fact, there is no such thing as a human being who is perfect, amazing, superhuman and better than anyone else. With such high expectations, everyone will disappoint you, including yourself.'

But after all those months of revisiting, re-inhabiting and re-experiencing my childhood, I gradually began to understand how tangled up I'd been in that period from my early adolescence. In every relationship, not just with men, but also with bosses, colleagues, even friends, I'd played out unresolved conflicts from that time. It was the central drama in my life and, thanks to Dr J, I began to see that in many ways I had never really grown up in an emotional sense since then. I'm not using it to explain or excuse everything, but it certainly helped me understand a lot, including, for instance, my simultaneous fear of and longing for intimacy.

I went back to our table just as Lucy was bringing the starters.

'Isn't it weird?' I said, after I'd sat down, helped myself to some focaccia and olives and drowned my tomato and mozzarella salad in balsamic vinegar.

'What?' Louise said.

'Everything. Families.'

I knew this would get Louise excited. Before she moved back up to Glasgow she had worked at one of the large psychiatric hospitals in London, and done a lot of work in the field of family therapy. It was, along with eating disorders, her specialist subject. She had always maintained, much to my annoyance (until I saw it myself), that every family is dysfunctional to some extent, and that we are all in recovery from childhood. She said it was those who insisted otherwise who tended, in her experience, to be the most screwed up of them all.

Scott took Lewis to the restaurant's open kitchen to watch the chefs at work.

'You know how we had that difficult period when we were teenagers?' I asked Louise and my parents. 'Well, I just want to say I forgive you all.' I paused. 'For abandoning me.' I was grinning. 'When I was still but a child in need of love and attention.' They were all looking at me with perplexed frowns. I heard Dr J reprimanding me for trying in vain to turn this into a laughing matter. But if I don't laugh, I'll cry, I said to her.

I took a deep breath and decided to be serious. We had never as a family talked about that time. I all of a sudden wanted to know what it had been like for them. When I asked, my dad shook his head and looked down at his plate. My mum bit her lower lip. 'As a mother,' she said, 'all you want to do is protect your children from anything painful. So to see your daughter in pain is, well, I don't know, very difficult. You start worrying about your children the moment you become a mother and it never ever goes away.'

I had wanted to break the silence around this issue, but I realised that we were not the kind of family that would sit around and talk about our repressed feelings, pain and other such emotional matters. It also dawned on me that just because I wanted to bring something out into the open it didn't mean other people did. Some things in the past are, for some, just too painful to be delved into. If those issues weren't interfering with their lives, I could imagine Dr J saying, then there's no need to go back there, and people certainly shouldn't be forced to. It was only Louise who wanted to speak more about it.

She said it taught her the absolute preciousness of life. 'I was too young at the time to really grasp what was going on, but I realised pretty quickly afterwards. Which is why, for instance, I couldn't live a lie and stay in a marriage that wasn't working.'

When Scott and Lewis returned, I told Louise that, in therapy, I'd discovered I'd been angry with them all, but hadn't even been aware of it. 'How crazy is that?'

'It's not crazy at all,' she said. 'It makes perfect sense to me.

People are terrified of their own anger, especially towards family members. Which is why it has to be repressed. But once it's acknowledged and understood, and you can be more honest with yourself about your feelings, it ceases to be an issue.'

My dad topped up our glasses. I looked at him. He was immaculately dressed, as always, in shirt and tie. I thought back to some other therapy sessions during which I'd discovered the extent to which I measured myself by my father. That just about everything I did was to please him, to try to get his approval. I suppose I had perceived him to be some kind of Godlike figure rather than a flawed and complicated human who had never had a father himself and was never going to be anything other than emotionally reticent.

Dr J had asked for earliest memories and what he was like in real life and how that compared with my fantasy of the perfect father. At first I couldn't remember much, but in therapy so many hidden memories come back. My dad taught me how to ride a bike, which I'd forgotten all about. And he used to take me to the Mitchell Library every Saturday.

As my parents sat with Lewis between them, I thought about all the things I didn't know about my mum and dad, but suddenly had an overwhelming desire to know.

I didn't, for instance, know how they met. I didn't know where they got married or if they went on honeymoon. I didn't know what their dream jobs, or dream anythings, were. I was supposed to be a trained observer, curious about the human condition. Yet these two people who I'd always just assumed I knew really well, simply because they were my mum and dad, I realised I hardly knew at all. I'm not suggesting that you should be in touch with the intimate details of your parents' lives, but it just struck me as odd that, until recently, I'd thought of them as simply my mum and dad rather than multifaceted complex people who played out different roles – husband, wife, son, daughter, colleague – in different contexts.

I'd always thought of my mum as outgoing, bubbly and gregarious. Whereas my dad is, well, a typical father, a typical man.

He has that black, deadpan Glaswegian humour that I've always found very funny, but which others, perhaps Dr J included, might interpret as morose.

I remember, for example, when Louise and I were teenagers, one Saturday night we were all watching the comedienne Dawn French being interviewed on TV. She was talking about where her self-confidence came from. She recalled going on her first date. She said her dad looked at her and said something like: you look gorgeous, it is the luckiest guy in the world who is going to get you, even though she admitted she was dressed in a mini-skirt and crop top and probably looked ridiculous. My dad looked at Louise and I, who had got bored and were rolling about, fighting on the sofa, and shook his head. He laughed and said: 'It is the unluckiest two guys in the world who are going to end up with the pair of you. I'll probably have to pay someone to take you off my hands.' I still chuckle at this memory, but I could see how others, especially people like Dr J, might not find it funny. I knew my dad bragged about me and Louise to others, but would never pay us a compliment to our faces. It's just not the Scottish way.

Just before the main courses arrived, my dad turned to me and said: 'Saw you had nothing in Sunday's paper.' Although his tone wasn't accusing, the insinuation was clear: what on earth have you been doing all week? Idleness is a sin, you know. Surely you know by now that he who will not work neither shall he eat.

I got my obsessively high work ethic from my dad. 'You have good weeks and bad weeks working for a Sunday,' I said to reassure myself as much as him that my editor wasn't about to call me up and inform me that my services were no longer required.

My mum said: 'Lorna, don't listen to your dad. You should know him by now. Do you know what he said the other night?'

'What?' we chorused, while my dad smiled mischievously at Lewis before turning his attention back to his spaghetti bolognaise.

'I said to him, Owen, do you want to go out for dinner, just the two of us? And do you know what he said?'

'What?' we chimed again.

'He said, "But we went out for dinner six months ago."'

We all laughed.

'But we did,' my dad protested. Halfway through the main courses, I decided to try to find out a bit about my dad. 'Dad,' I said, 'if you could do any job in the world, what would it be?' He gave me his trademark look: sardonically raised eyebrow and furrowed brow, while winding some spaghetti bolognaise round a fork. He took a mouthful.

'I'd like to have been an interior designer, I think,' my mum said. 'I mean, I loved being a nurse, but I like making curtains and cushions and doing things like that. I'd like to have done something a bit more creative.'

'I think I'd have liked to have been a diving instructor or worked in marine biology,' Louise said.

'I'd love to have been an astronaut,' Scott said.

Lewis started singing 'Bob the Builder'.

'Dad?' I said, trying to block out the interlopers.

My dad gave me that look again before eventually saying: 'Hmm. I'll think about it.'

I tried again, using my professional guile. 'Dad,' I said, 'what are your five greatest memories? No, forget that. If your house was on fire and you could take only two things, what would they be?' He silently shook his head and looked at Lewis as if to say: 'Are you thinking what I'm thinking about your mad aunty?'

'Dad, what's your philosophy for life?' I persisted. He cleared his throat. I leaned forward expectantly. He said: 'More wine, anyone?'

Louise: 'Oh. I love things like this. Right, let me think. I think mine would probably be something about being true to yourself and remembering that, even when things are tough and life seems bleak, each day in this life is better than all eternity in the one to come. Oh, and of course, to try not to take yourself too seriously.'

Mum: 'I'm not clever enough for this.'

Me, protesting: 'Mum, you are the wisest, cleverest person I know.'

Scott: 'Mine is not to waste time sitting around talking about what your philosophy for life is.'

My dad laughed. As did Lewis.

Me: 'Why do men always try to be funny when they don't want to answer a question? Or when they're faced with the horror of trying to get in touch with their emotions?' God, I thought, I'm turning into Dr bloody J. 'Sorry,' I continued. 'Anyway, what was I saying? Yes, men and being repressed. Their feelings are put in a box and buried away and the only time they can express them is when they're drunk, on drugs or when their team scores a goal. They project all their feelings onto their sporting heroes. I mean, how screwed up is that? They can feel someone else's joy, exhilaration, pain, loss but not their own. I used to be like that before I was, you know, cured.'

My dad laughed again. Lewis copied him.

'Anyway, please, Dad, one more question and I promise I won't ask any more. What's the most important lesson life has taught you?'

Louise, my mum and Scott all spoke at once, so it was impossible to make out what anyone was saying.

Me: 'Dad?'

He looked into the distance. 'I think,' he said slowly, 'I think the most important lesson life has taught me is to remember . . .'

He paused. I was on the verge of bursting into tears with the emotional intensity of the situation and in anticipation of what he was about to say.

'It is to remember,' he continued, 'not to take my youngest daughter out for a birthday dinner next year.' Louise, Scott, my mum and Lewis cracked up.

As the main courses were cleared away, I made one final attempt to interrogate my parents.

'Okay, Dad, just one more question. The last I will ask tonight. How did you and Mum meet?'

'What?' they asked simultaneously.

'Is this an interview?' my dad said.

'No. I just don't want to be one of these people who say that they left it too late to get to know their father. I don't want to wait until it's too late and say I wish I'd asked him this. I wish I'd asked him that. I wish I knew him, etc, etc.'

My dad frowned. Again. And chewed his lip. 'Do you know something I don't?' he said.

'Well I know where we're all heading and I just don't want to wait until we get there and miss the opportunity to say the important things to the important people in my life. Sure, I'm going to have some regrets, I just don't want to add to them.'

My dad looked down at his plate.

And then, for the first time, my parents told me their own love story.

'Your dad was in hospital with a collapsed lung,' my mum explained. 'I was twenty-seven. Your dad was a year older. It was the third time this had happened and was quite common at the time in young thin men. It could be brought on just by coughing. I was working as a nurse. Your dad was the only young man in the male chest ward. All the other patients were old men. I was on night duty and all the nurses used to have a laugh and a carry-on with your dad. Can you imagine?'

We all laughed. My mum continued: 'After he was discharged he sent a letter to me at the hospital, didn't you, Owen?'

My dad, looking rather shy, nodded.

'And he kept on writing.'

'My dad wrote love letters?' I said, as if he wasn't there and to check that my ears weren't deceiving me.

They nodded, and smiled at each other.

'Seriously?'

'Seriously,' they replied in unison.

I looked at my mum and dad and felt a great overwhelming rush of love, then I quietly excused myself to go to the ladies' again.

When I came back, I ticked off one of the items on my list of things to do before I die. Over coffee and liqueurs, I blurted: 'Oh my God, I love you all so much and I'm so grateful to you, Mum and Dad, for sacrificing your own dreams to try to give us a better life. And I forgive you for not being perfect and I hope you can forgive me for not being perfect, and I'm sorry if I've been selfish and hard work at times.'

And it somehow didn't seem to matter at all that my dad responded by shaking his head, wrinkling his brow into a bewildered frown and saying: 'Lorna, please, stop being so stupid.'

***

In the middle of October, I decided that I no longer wanted to lie on the couch. It was a bright but cold Friday morning. Kelvingrove Park had turned from green to a profusion of reds, oranges, yellows and golden browns, as if someone had set fire to all the fallen leaves. It was beautiful.

Dr J's room was hot and cosy as usual and filled with the smell of rich coffee. We both had on black polo necks. Mine with jeans; hers with smart trousers. When I told her I wanted to sit, a faint smile warmed her face. 'Do whatever is agreeable for you,' she said.

I sank into the leather chair and looked out of the window behind her. The trees I could see in the distance were almost stripped bare, which made me think about what had happened to me over the past ten months.

We sat in silence, a comfortable one, for a while.

'A few sessions ago, I said that although I had more insight than I did nine months ago, I didn't think therapy had done me any good, do you remember?'

She nodded.

'Well, I don't know why I said that. You'd just come back from holiday and maybe it was my screwed-up way of saying that I did miss you.'

She smiled and nodded again.

'It's strange,' I continued, 'I feel this constant conflict between really liking you and disliking you.'

'This is normal,' she said. 'It is really the conflict between

263

getting in touch with those hidden thoughts and feelings that scare you and your impulse to keep them buried and repressed. You miss someone, you say you didn't even notice they were gone. But at least you're aware of these conflicts now.'

I told her about the family meal and we talked again about that period from my adolescence and the bizarre paradox: that I had become much less consumed with anger since acknowledging the anger I didn't even know I'd been suppressing. Even when I reflected on therapy, I could now see that, at the beginning, I hated and therefore ridiculed Dr J. She was the perfect target and scapegoat for all the rage I didn't know I had. But, since opening myself up to her, and, in particular, feeling the full force of those difficult emotions towards my family that had been repressed since childhood, my relationship with her had also begun to undergo a perceptible shift. At first, I spewed out everything, which, in retrospect, I could see was little more than a disguised form of silence. She was the authority figure and I wanted her approval. In the middle, she challenged and interrogated everything, every-thing I said, every chapter of my life to date, to separate the rosy-tinted version of the truth from reality. This was not easy and often very painful. Now, with our time running out, I felt as if I was beginning to have an honest adult-to-adult conversation with her, which, bizarre as this will sound, felt like a first.

* * *

In the middle of October I was at a conference in Glasgow about its horrendous knife-crime problem. Over a twenty-year period, the murder rate had increased drastically, making my lovely city one of the deadliest in the western world. I was hoping to get a story from it for Sunday's paper, so it was quite easy to rationalise this as the main reason for my attendance. But it wasn't.

As it happened, Scott had casually mentioned that David would be there. During my most optimistic moments, I liked to think he hadn't received my barmy email back in August. However, I also liked to think, despite the evidence to the con-trary, that I was a realist, and I couldn't escape from the fact that emails don't simply go missing. It must have appeared in his inbox. I could only imagine what he had interpreted from it. But surely, my optimistic self argued, one lengthy and wacky but not downright deranged email message wasn't enough to write me off completely.

Even with all Dr J's warnings fully in mind about my tendency to go from one love obsession to another and to elevate men I liked into superhuman positions, I still couldn't stop thinking about David. And it had nothing to do with how many boxes he ticked or anything like that. I just felt this spark, an unspoken chemistry. I still thought he was a serious candidate for the job of my Ideal Man, maybe even The One. But there was no way I could just get in touch with him. Ideal men are supposed to get in touch with you. Ideally. No matter how many obstacles you put in their way.

The best I could manage was to put myself in places where I might bump into him. The hospital and Katy's broken foot incident had theoretically been perfect, but seeing him in his greens was too much for me. Plus, Katy had refused my other suggestion of pushing me forcefully off a kerb. Now a two-hour conference about knife crime, with tea and coffee and time for discussion before and after, struck me as a glorious opportunity for our paths to accidentally-on-purpose cross once more.

In the end it was less of a bump and more of a glance across a crowded room. When he spotted me, he came over, looking gorgeous in a suit, shirt and tie, and said: 'Hey, how are you? Not doing your Florence Nightingale today?'

My heart was giving long, drawn-out thuds, which I hoped he couldn't see through my top. I didn't have a clue what he was talking about. He elaborated: 'Katy? You brought her to the hospital? Anyway, how's her foot?'

'Ah, yes. Yes. Fine. Very good. Florence Nightingale. The nurse, yes. Ha ha.' Oh God. 'Anyway,' I said, steering the conversation towards the issue of the email, which I'd decided had to be dealt with. I had to know whether he'd received it or not. And, more importantly, if he had, why he hadn't replied.

'Er, you know that email I sent you?' I said tentatively.

'The one with quite a lot of information?' he asked, rubbing his fingers over his forehead.

Shit. I realised I had no idea what I was about to say. 'Yes. Well . . . I, um, well . . .' Oh God. I'm supposed to be a journalist. I'm supposed to be able to ask people direct and difficult and acute questions. The only stupid question is the one you want to ask but don't, I remembered that wise editor at the *Herald* saying to me. (He was talking specifically about political press conferences rather than potential love interests, but it seemed a truism that could be universally applied.) Yet still I couldn't bring myself to ask him outright why he hadn't replied. So, instead, I said the next thing that came into my head. 'I didn't mean it,' I heard myself say.

'You didn't mean what?' he said, looking at me with a lovely baffled smile.

I didn't mean that my life was so fabulous that I didn't have time for a boyfriend and I definitely didn't mean whatever bits you thought made me sound nuts and stopped you from replying, I thought but didn't say.

Instead, I just repeated, in a stutter and in the vain hope that he was a mind reader and would rescue me: 'I didn't mean . . . you know . . . the bits that . . . I didn't mean the bits about . . .'

He gave a tiny laugh but said nothing. Why is it that the older and supposedly wiser you get, the more difficult this whole romantic thing becomes?

Because I was in uncomfortable territory, my body's dysfunctional coping mechanism kicked in and tried to rescue me. I looked at my mobile and pretended to have a call from my editor. 'Damn! That's my editor on the phone,' I said, then, realising my phone hadn't rung or vibrated, I quickly provided a smooth and plausible, but at the same time completely unnecessary explanation: 'My phone's on silent. Which is why you didn't hear it ringing. But I must never ignore my editor, ha ha.' Aaarrgh. I smiled and turned my back on him, feeling more incompetent than ever.

With my phone pressed to my ear, I wandered away into a corner nodding my head and saying 'yeah' and 'yeah, definitely' intermittently to no one.

When I found him ten minutes later, he'd been joined by a group of his colleagues, some journalists and a couple of politicians who were deep in conversation.

Someone in a pinstripe suit was going on about 'sensationalist journalism of the worst kind' and 'outrageous macabre voyeurism'. Another, with a florid complexion, interjected that the media had a duty and obligation to show the truth, opining that sometimes shock tactics were the most effective way of addressing problems. I was alternately smiling and nodding while gazing covertly at David. His lovely hands were cupping a mug of tea. Katy was so lucky, I thought, drifting off, to have broken her foot and had those hands caressing her foot and ankle, possibly even reaching up towards her inner thigh and . . .

Shit. Everyone was looking at me expectantly. 'What?' I said, in a panic.

In a tone that suggested he was repeating something, David said: 'What do you think?'

Oh God. If there's one thing guaranteed to bring me out in a nervous blotchy red rash, it was being asked for my opinion on something important in front of an audience of intellectuals. And it didn't help that I didn't have the slightest idea what I was supposed to be responding to.

With my face beginning to cook with embarrassment, I blurted out an answer which Solomon would have been proud of: 'Yes, I totally agree. With all of you.' I followed up my masterstroke with a magisterial nod to the assembled party, and slunk off in search of tea and biscuits.

Before he left, David said it was 'really nice' to see me again and we held each other's eyes for a moment, then he said the magic words: 'Are you up to anything exciting at the weekend?'

Was this just decency and politeness? Was he asking me out? Do I play the busy and adventurous soul I pretended to be in the email? I could say I'm climbing a mountain, going white-water rafting, doing a charity bike ride then saving a whale before bedtime. Or do I stick to the truth (watching box-set DVDs of American TV dramas because they are so brilliant that they make having a social life seem positively dull in comparison). What I opted for was: 'I'm going out with my friends.'

David looked me straight in the eyes. 'I was wondering if I could, um, maybe get your number? Maybe we could have a drink sometime?'

Oh my God. I had to stifle the high-pitched squeal that was trying to escape from my lips. Okay, okay, okay. Play it cool, girl. What do I do?

Into my head popped something I'd read earlier that day in a newspaper. It was ten profiles of thirty-something women who had found love and each was giving her advice. When I'd read it, I'd wondered what kind of stupid women read and followed this kind of nonsense. There was a little panel at the end saying that the vital thing, as far as men were concerned, was to be mysterious while at the same time flirtatious. The golden rule stated that the surest way to a man's heart was to appear aloof and uninterested. Now, in the heat of the moment, I couldn't believe I'd been so quick to dismiss what now seemed like a priceless pearl of wisdom. 'If you want my number,' I said, trying to come across as both poised and coquettishly shy, 'you'll have to get it from someone else.'

He passed his hand through his hair, frowned slightly and said: 'Um, right, okay.'

* * *

A few nights later, towards the end of October, I was once again, most inappropriately, mingling with Glasgow's great and good. David hadn't called yet, but I was determined not to fret and was instead throwing myself into other activities. That night I was among 500 guests at the Scottish Style Awards, a glitzy gala dinner held in the splendour of the recently refurbished Kelvingrove Art Gallery and Museum.

Towards the end of the night, I was standing with Rachel and a group of journalists. We were next to a table of around a dozen people. A sloshed woman – distinguishable from all the other merrily sloshed people there only by an alarming tent-like fuchsia-pink dress – staggered over.

She looked accusingly at me. 'You write that column in *Grazia*, don't you? About being in therapy and . . . other stuff.'

I nodded.

'I think it's appalling,' she said, quivering slightly. 'Every week when I read it I just . . . well, I think you should be ashamed to show your face in public.'

There was an awkward silence. I mean, always happy to meet a fan, but I've never been particularly good at handling confrontational situations like this.

I wondered what Dr J would do in such circumstances? Would she, even outside her consulting room, dare to say: 'Calm down. It's only a magazine column. I wonder what this inappropriate display of misdirected anger and hatred is really all about?'

I couldn't say that, of course, but I opted for another Dr J default: 'Hmmm.'

'No. Honestly, I'm not joking,' she said, even though no one had suggested that she was. 'Every week I read it and I . . . I just think it's shocking that you're . . .' Her voice drifted off and she shook her head to confirm how total and absolute her disgust for me was. But she wasn't finished. 'I mean, normal people don't behave like that, having affairs.'

I glanced around me. 'Sadly,' I wanted to say, 'whatever you might like to think, normal people do do that kind of thing.'

'So who's the guy?' she spat.

I shook my head. The Dr J in me said: 'Why do you care? What difference does it make to you? Do you need to focus on someone else's fuck-up to avoid thinking about your own, or to make you feel better about your own pathetic life?'

Instead I said: 'I don't mean to sound rude, but it's not only none of your business, it's also irrelevant. Unless you think it's your husband, in which case you'd be better off at home having a conversation with him, rather than taking your anger out on me.'

'Fucking home-wrecking bitch,' she slurred, before spinning unsteadily on her heel and weaving in the approximate direction of the bar.

'Hmmm,' I said, because sometimes there's no point in saying anything else.

One of the journalists asked if I was okay. I nodded, but I found myself justifying and explaining things to them. 'Part of the reason I "outed" myself, if you like, was because I had this idea, naive perhaps, that taboo subjects – like therapy, mental health, jealousy, infidelity – should be talked about rather than swept under the carpet. I'm not doing a kiss and tell. I'm not naming and shaming anyone – other than myself. All I'm saying is this happens. And, in my experience, it's an absolute nightmare. I'm not proud of it. I'm pretty sure he's not proud of it. I wish it had never ever happened. But it happens everywhere – in offices, in hospitals, in every place of work. Sixty per cent of men and 40 per cent of women, according to conservative estimates, will have an extramarital affair at some point in their lives. And one of the main reasons it happens is because we're crap at communicating with each other. That is what I was trying to say. That, and don't do it.'

She nodded and said she didn't know anyone who hadn't been affected in some way by infidelity. 'I think people like to pretend it doesn't happen because we're all living in this fantasy and it robs us, women in particular, of the perfect happy ending that we believe is our due. Sadly, monogamy is a complete myth. I think it's much better to talk about it. Then, if it does happen, it may be slightly less world-shattering than clinging to the false notion that neither you nor your own spouse or partner is capable of being unfaithful. Everyone, without exception, is capable of it.'

Later, Rachel and I were chatting. 'The other night,' I said, 'my dad phoned me. He never phones me. He said he'd been in a supermarket and noticed a woman standing reading my column in *Grazia*. He told me he went up to this woman and said, 'That's my daughter.' Imagine my dad, a sixty-four-year-old man, buying his copy of *Grazia* every Tuesday morning and, despite the subject matter, bragging to all his colleagues about it and even to strangers in supermarkets. He phoned me just to tell me about the woman in the store. Which is his way of saying he's proud of me. And that matters a hell of a lot more to me than what someone who I don't know and who doesn't know me thinks of me.' We clinked glasses and took a sip of champagne.

* * *

A few nights later, I had arranged to meet Katy in Kember and Jones for coffee and cake. Just as I was about to cross the road, I spotted Dr J sitting in a seat by the window. Seeing her out of context collapsed everything into slow motion. I felt as if I'd just caught a glimpse of my mother getting intimate with a man who wasn't my father. Dr J was with another woman, much younger. My guess was that it was her daughter. They were laughing and then, at one point, it looked as if Dr J was wiping a tear away from her cheek. Whether it was one of happiness or sadness or even a tear at all, I could only fantasise.

I texted Katy and asked her if she would mind going instead to a cafe called Tinderbox, which was on the opposite side but not directly across from Kember's. When Katy arrived, I pointed out Dr J. We spent the next thirty minutes practically stalking my therapist.

'What do you think they're talking about?' I said.

'Her favourite patient, of course,' Katy teased.

I waved this away. 'What do you think she was crying for? Maybe her daughter's just told her she's pregnant or something?'

'You don't even know it's her daughter,' Katy asked. 'It could be her young lover, you don't know, or her niece or a student. You're obviously, at some level, seeing you and your mum over there.'

'Shurrup!' I said uncomfortably, giving her a nudge.

Woman on the Verge of a Nervous Breakdown

As I walked home through Kelvingrove Park, the freshly fallen leaves crunching under my feet, I couldn't get rid of that image of Dr J. All of a sudden, the veil had been lifted. She was not a member of some mysterious rescue squad or someone who had all the answers. She had become thoroughly and alarmingly human.

November

Inside Looking Out

By the end of the first week in November, it appeared that David hadn't managed to get my number from someone else. Or if he had, he certainly hadn't got round to calling me. I berated myself now and again for playing stupid games and not simply giving it to him when he first asked, but I'd pretty much decided that I had to let the cards fall where they may. If my social and dating ineptitude had put him off once and for all, then so be it; better that he know the truth about me upfront.

In saying all this, I did have to admit that I was still thinking about him three minutes out of every five. Nuts, I know. Despite everything that Dr J had said, I hadn't managed to stop the invasion. He too had taken up residence in my head space.

* * *

As time raced by, as the weeks of the year were running out, I looked forward with increasing anticipation to each session with Dr J. It was as if I'd zipped through the first three-quarters of the year. Now, with winter here again and the end in sight, I suddenly wanted to decelerate even more and cherish every remaining session. I also felt an ever-increasing affection for this woman who had conducted the psychological equivalent of a thorough post-mortem examination on me. Though, obviously, while I was still conscious.

Although I felt an inexplicable nervousness about it, I told her that I'd seen her outside in the real world.

'And?'

In therapy you can say anything at all, no matter how stupid you think it will sound, but sometimes, even this far on, I still had to remind myself that there was no need for self-censorship. 'It made me think about *The Wizard of Oz*,' I said hesitantly. 'The bit at the end when the dog, Toto, pulls back the curtain and discovers that there is no great powerful and omniscient wizard, just an ordinary person. Seeing you outside these four walls reminded me that you are just another ordinary human – probably an imperfect one. That you don't have all the answers. That you can't save me.'

'And how do you feel about that?'

'I have mixed feelings,' I said. 'I feel as if I should be angry and as if I've been conned. But I had to remind myself that you never said you had all, or indeed any, of the answers. Or that you could save me. And nor did I say, when I first came into therapy, that that was what I was looking for. But obviously, at some level, that was exactly what I wanted, despite what my words said. I see clearly now that what I wanted was someone to give me the answers; to tell me what to do; to validate me; to save me; to, in your jargon, infantilise me. I just didn't realise it back then. So I suppose I feel a bit disappointed at the realisation that I had been expecting, unconsciously, the same perfection and Godlike qualities from you that I had expected from every other significant person in my life.'

At the same time, I said I felt a strange relief, as if in some way I had found what I was looking for: that there are no easy answers, that we are all searching for meaning and certainty in a universe that has neither. I suppose that there is nothing and no one who can remove the real difficulties and uncertainty involved in living. I gazed towards the desk, willing the framed photos facing away from me to turn around and reveal their subjects.

'You know,' I said, 'I used to pity people who believed in God. I was so disparaging of their lust to submit to an authority figure, their inability to take responsibility for their own lives, and their readiness to relinquish their power and freedom to a figment of their imagination. But I was exactly the same. I was searching for comfort, answers, meaning and certainty too. I was just looking in a different direction.'

There was silence for a while.

'The other thing that it brought home,' I said, 'was the realisation that, while my facade was being stripped away, while I was being broken down to my so-called authentic self, in many ways, what you were doing was simply presenting a facade. Because it was your job. The silences, the inscrutable face – at the beginning, I interpreted them as evidence that you were crazy or as simply rudeness, now I can see they are simply the tools of your trade. When I look back, I think it must have been so frustrating for you at times. It's so much harder to listen and say nothing than it is to talk. I wouldn't be at all surprised if you'd wanted to scream at me at times.'

She smiled. 'What happens in here,' she said unexpectedly, 'it is not real life. What goes on in this room is, in some ways, a dress rehearsal for life. A safe place for you to acknowledge the full power and force of all your feelings and emotions, all the conflicted feelings and impulses that have been repressed since childhood. If I had given you a hug when you were crying out for one, laughed at your attempts to use humour to push me away, told you what you wanted to hear, responded to you the way your good friends and family would and should, had an everyday chat with you, I'd simply have been colluding with you. Which is not my job.'

I told Dr J I'd been reading a book (*Psychoanalysis: The Impossible Profession*). It mentioned an analyst who decided to do some follow-up work on two female patients he'd treated five years previously. One woman thanked the doctor profusely, saying every night she thanked her lucky stars he was her analyst. She said it changed her life and not a day went by when she didn't still think about him and what he'd done for her. The other woman, who'd been a comparable case and had just as tempestuous and emotional a time, said the experience was okay, but couldn't say what helped her and any changes in her life would have happened anyway. The analyst said he knew right away who had had the better treatment.

'I would like to be like the latter,' I said, 'but I'm worried I'm going to be more like the first woman.'

'Who cares?' Dr J said, motionless. 'If your life changes for the better, surely that is all that matters.'

I laughed and nodded.

Dr J gazed at me for a while, then said: 'Are you worried about how this' – she gestured with her hand at the space between us – 'is going to end?'

I nodded again. 'I'm so bad at endings,' I said. 'I hate them. I'm not very good at letting things go. With my first boyfriend, I clung on for six years, though, thanks to therapy, I can see that it wasn't really him I was clinging on to. I think relationship endings are very difficult. I know guys who have packed in jobs and switched continents as a way of getting out of a relationship.'

'For once,' she said, 'I will generalise and say most people aren't good at endings. When do you ever experience a good relationship ending? It rarely happens. But therapy gives you probably the only chance you will ever actually have to work through an ending and separation and all the feelings and emotions that brings up. Every serious relationship ending – whether romantic, a friendship, a job – involves a loss, and memories of previous losses, which in turn involves a grieving process. Many people are not good at it and therefore avoid those difficult feelings of anger, frustration, helplessness, resentment, sadness and so on. But, in here, you can feel all those things and hopefully have a good experience of ending and separation.'

* * *

On Friday evening I was meeting a friend for a quick after-work drink in Babbity's. The moment I walked in, my heart sank and leapt simultaneously. If you don't think that's possible, you've obviously been smart enough and strong enough never to have fallen in love with someone you shouldn't have fallen in love with.

Christian was sitting in a corner, alone, with a newspaper in front of him, a half-drunk pint of Guinness and a neat whisky to his side. This was the first time I'd seen him since June and, even though I thought I was over him, seeing him again brought back all those mixed feelings.

I glanced quickly around the pub, saw that the friend I was meeting hadn't arrived, so walked over and stood awkwardly at the edge of Christian's table.

'Hey,' I said. 'How are . . .'

He folded his arms and slowly shook his head.

I looked at him, focusing dimly on his shoulder, not quite sure what to say. I had to stop myself from spontaneously apologising for everything and taking responsibility for his behaviour as well as my own.

'Women,' he said, shaking his head. 'That other one has fucked up my life and you're coming in a pretty close second.'

I frowned.

He told me his wife had thrown him out after she went through his mobile and discovered some incriminating text messages. He didn't say who from and I didn't ask, but I had a pretty good idea.

I sighed but said nothing.

'Anyway,' he said eventually. 'As for you, you're not the girl I thought you were.'

I thought about telling him that I wasn't a girl anymore, that I'd grown up. But I knew I'd never have the poise to carry that off. Plus, there were tears stinging my eyes. Instead I said: 'And you aren't the man I thought you were either. As wrong and dysfunctional as it was, I fell in love with you and, again, as wrong as it was, it broke my heart when you started messing about with Charlotte.'

He looked down at his drink.

I gazed at him with a mixture of sadness and regret.

'We both screwed up,' I finally said. 'We both behaved like arrogant, selfish teenagers. Both of us. We're both guilty.'

'Yeah, well,' he said, 'it doesn't matter anymore anyway. I'm fucking off out of this shit-hole of a country. None of this would've happened if I hadn't moved up here. I'm fucking off back down to London.'

'I am sorry,' I said. 'I'm really sorry. For the part I played in this.' Should I be apologising? My onboard Dr J asked. Well, yes. I wasn't taking the blame for his part, but I was genuinely sorry for mine. I looked at him one last time and said 'Good luck.'

I decided to wait outside for my friend and suggest going elsewhere. As I waited, I noticed a young, attractive blonde heading into the bar. She bore a passing resemblance to Charlotte, but looked, if anything, even younger. I immediately assumed she was going to meet Christian and a mixture of metaphors, as well as emotions, flooded over me. Something about old dogs and leopards, new tricks and spots. And the thought that some people would probably never change.

But as I began to shake my head, my internal Dr J made another appearance, warning me against making assumptions and jumping to conclusions about anyone. Don't see and believe only what you want to see and believe. All that does is reinforce your own prejudices and stop you from having to think too hard. See the facts, and acknowledge that the rest is nothing but your own narrow-minded, pre-conceived bias. Whether the girl was going to meet Christian, I'd never know.

* * *

The next week I was down in London for a meeting at the *Observer*. I had stopped going down every week or even fortnight – I think that had been another symptom of the mess my life had been in – and this was the first time in a couple of months I'd been in the office. As I walked from Farringdon underground station, I thought about how much I'd changed since the beginning of the year, when I was an anxious wreck every time I set foot in the building. There was nothing in it that was scary. All the terror, I could see now, was within me. It seemed to have gone completely. I didn't feel nervous at all. At the editorial meeting, I pitched a couple of ideas, gave one or two of my own opinions on other stories, listened to other people's views, but didn't automatically think they were right and I was wrong.

Later, I went for lunch with Kamal and some of the other journalists at The Coach and Horses. Again, memories from last year came flooding back. This was where I had frequently got drunk and wept and ended up missing all those flights.

'So, how are you doing?' Kamal asked.

I told him that, in my entire adult life, I'd never felt better; that the money I'd spent on therapy was the best I'd ever spent.

'I feel – and I know this will sound dead corny,' I said, 'but I feel as if I've found myself. I've discovered who I really am. I feel ordinary, average. I'm no longer pretending or trying to be someone or something brilliant that I'm not. Before, what people thought of me was far more important than either what I thought of them or what I thought about myself. I was, in a way, apologising for breathing. Everything I did or said was only good or right when approved by others. I lacked the autonomy to form my own opinion or judgment about anything. And I mean anything. Even the cinema. I'd go to see a film and come out paraphrasing what David Denby or Anthony Lane or Philip French had written about it. I still read them, of course, because they're all brilliantly written and observed. But I don't necessarily come out thinking what they thought.'

He smiled. Someone else asked if I was going to turn into one of those therapy bores, like the fitness or diet zealots, or born-again Christians, who believe it is their mission to spread their own particular brand of the gospel to the masses.

I laughed and admitted that I had entertained a fantasy about how differently people would behave in relationships with partners, parents, children, friends and colleagues if they had a good dose of in-depth analytical psychotherapy. 'Just think,' I said, 'in this brave new world, there would be no divorce, no infidelity, no crime and no wars, because everyone's hidden jealousy, control, power, co-dependency, approval, and mummy and daddy issues would be explored and worked through. But it was when I started to think it might solve the obesity crisis and lead to world peace that I realised I'd gone too far. I decided that I wasn't going to become a self-appointed authority on what is best for someone else. Therapy worked for me, that is all. Faith, running marathons, dieting, flower arranging – they work for others. Each to their own. As long as you're not breaking the law or thrusting your views down anyone else's throat, then who bloody cares?'

'I hate all this navel-gazing,' someone else said, 'it just seems so self-indulgent. I think it creates problems where none exist and forces generally healthy people into unhealthy introspection. To turn tiny insignificant problems into major ones.'

'I can see why people think it's self-indulgent and selfish,' I said. 'It was exactly what I thought when I first went into therapy. I felt terribly guilty about it because I thought, compared with the "real" problems some people face, I had nothing to complain about. Human beings have a duty and responsibility to others, but they also have one towards themselves. I think, if therapy makes someone a better, stronger person and improves their relationships with others, then that is a worthwhile endeavour and it has knock-on benefits. I look back at what I was like. I was on Prozac, so I was partly responsible for the UK's £290 million annual anti-depressant bill. I'd been involved in a disastrous relationship, which had hurt other people. I was inhibited towards work. Now, I'm no longer on Prozac, I'm much freer and more productive at work. And although I know you can never say never – I used to say it and proved myself very wrong – but I am as certain as it's possible to be that I won't ever get into another relationship like that.'

'But all these things, worries and fears, are just the quotidian problems of life,' he said. 'There *was* nothing really wrong with you.'

'On the outside there was nothing wrong with me, but the inside was a completely different story,' I said. 'And I think it's like that for quite a lot of people. As a society, we spend a fortune on gym memberships, yoga, health foods, diets, massages, expensive clothes etc. As long as it's on the physical side, it's fine. But people are terrified of anything to do with mental health. It's seen as selfish if you try to make yourself a better person on the inside. I was probably hovering close to the edge for ages, then something happens to tip you over, and, as a result, I ended up in therapy and discovered that everything I thought I knew about myself was wrong. I had all this stuff going on below the surface that I wasn't aware of. That's what this kind of therapy is all about. It's not about getting guidance from a wise counsellor, or someone telling you what to do, or having a cosy chat with a pseudo-friend, or learning how to think positively. In fact, it's the opposite. It's delusional to think positively all the time. Life can be tough – it's one challenge after another. The kind of therapy I'm having is about making some of the invisible motives that drive us all visible. Which, in turn, makes it easier to enjoy the good things in life and negotiate the difficult things.'

After lunch, I said goodbye and, giving myself plenty of time as usual, made my way to the airport. Now, reading the paper, people-watching, gazing out of the window at the passing scenery required no concentration. Life is so much better, I thought, now that I am no longer running, I live it in slow motion.

* * *

On a wild November morning when the wind was howling outside Dr J's window, I finally answered the question she'd asked me back in July about what I want, what I really, really want from life. The looming end of therapy forced me to address all her killer questions.

Initially, I told her that, although I'd given it a great deal of thought, I found it difficult to say aloud.

When she asked why, I said: 'In case it doesn't happen and then I'd have to deal with monumental failure. I'm not at all superstitious, but I do have a feeling that you shouldn't speak aloud what you want most, otherwise it won't happen.'

She allowed a quiet laugh to escape, as if to say, you people out there in the real world really are a strange and crazy bunch. 'If you don't have a destination, you can never fail to get there, but you will end up drifting along forever.' She suggested that it might be easier to start by saying aloud what I don't want.

'That's easy,' I said. 'I don't want to be with someone I don't really love. I don't want to be with someone who doesn't really love me. I don't want to be like that old spinster I read about in my mum's local paper, who fell out of her bed and, having no living relatives or friends in the world, lay on the floor until a neighbour noticed her curtains hadn't been opened for two days and phoned the police. I don't ever want to be involved in another love triangle. I don't want to miss the chance to have children, although, in saying that, if it doesn't happen I feel I'd be much more able to handle it than I would have been before. I don't want to do a job I don't enjoy. I want to . . .'

And what I didn't want suddenly became the things I would like in life. I'm aware, of course, that in life you don't always get what you want. But I also realise that you stand a much better chance if you actually acknowledge what they are, and have realistic expectations about what difference they will make to your life.

There were three things.

'Since I was a teenager, I've secretly dreamed of writing a book,' I said. 'I've started hundreds of times over the years, but have never managed to get beyond about four pages. It was always that thing about not being good enough. I always lacked the courage to continue, but I'd like to give that a real go, to see if I'm capable of making that dream a reality.'

She nodded. 'And what difference do you think that will make to your life?'

'Other than fulfilling a dream, none at all,' I replied.

'The second thing: well, I've learned that you can get your heart broken even when you're doing your hardest to stop that from happening. I realise now what I don't think I did before: that two human beings trying to get along in an intimate relationship is always going to be complicated and full of ups and downs. There's always going to be conflict, internal and external. I used to think that to fall in love would be self-destructive because loss, and the searing pain of loss, was inevitable. But now I realise that loss is part of life. I feel better equipped to deal with that. I understand now that attachments, and plenty of them, are the indispensable ingredients of a full life. I think people should be with other people, that this journey through life is better shared, even if it does involve conflict and risk heartbreak, because the alternative is far too lonely.'

Dr J looked at me. Her expression was hard to read. 'And the third?'

'The last thing is to stand on my own two feet and be true to myself. Which I know means having to be brave, having to be daring.' I took a deep breath. 'I think it's almost time to stop.'

'Yes it is,' she said, looking at the clock.

* * *

The next morning, Scott called me to let me know that David had asked him for my number the previous evening. I had to stop myself letting out a gasp of excitement. But there was a slight problem: I'd lost my mobile the previous day, told everyone, and had only just found it again.

'So what did you say?' I asked Scott.

'I told him you'd lost your phone,' he said.

'But I found it this morning.'

'Well, how was I supposed to know, last night, that you were going to find it this morning?'

'Shit. Did you give him my landline?'

'No.'

'Why not?'

'Well, he didn't ask for it.'

'You could have given it to him anyway,' I fumed.

'Er, you could have given him your number in the first place and we wouldn't now be in this utterly ludicrous situation. He said he asked you for it a couple of weeks ago at that conference, but you said something like you couldn't give him it and that he had to get it from, em, someone else. Which sounds completely fucking bonkers, but then, you are a woman, so . . .'

'Now he's going to think I'm not into him,' I sighed. I hung up, mumbling to myself: 'Guys are useless. Useless. Completely frigging useless.'

Since I hadn't solicited my friends' advice after receiving the email in Jamaica, and managed to botch that up, I decided to call an emergency summit with them to debate whether I should ask Scott for David's number and call him.

'Absolutely,' said Rachel. 'He emailed you and made the effort to get your number. Guys' egos are much more fragile than ours, remember. First you told him you didn't want a boyfriend, then refused to give him your number. Then, when he asks for it, Scott tells him you've lost it. He'd be mad to think anything other than that you're not interested and are trying to let him down gently.'

When she finished, Katy said: 'Well, normally, I would say absolutely NOT! Guys like to be the pursuer. They like to feel that they have chased and caught. So under normal circumstances I would say, if he wants you, he'll try again. But he's made quite a lot of effort, so I would say go for it. What's the worst thing that can happen?'

December

Into the Wild Blue Yonder

A few days later, on Sunday, I received an anonymous text message. It contained a comment relating to a story I'd written for that day's paper. The article in question was about politicians ripping off the taxpayer in an expenses and property scam. It wasn't Watergate, but it was as close as I was ever likely to get to exposing any political corruption. And if I'm being really honest, I can't even take full credit for it. Contrary to the popular opinion that hacks are all hard-nosed, every-man-for-himself types who would rather sell their grannies than help a competitor, I was greatly assisted by a benevolent member of the political pack. He found me wandering alone along the labyrinthine corridors of the Scottish Parliament in search of a good story. I told him how much I hated covering politics. He said he found it thrilling, dramatic and addictive, and pointed me in the direction of a minor expenses scandal.

Earlier that Sunday morning, a rather guttural voice message from a withheld number was left on my phone, warning me to steer clear of the subject or risk getting my legs broken. I didn't realise Scottish political journalism was so fraught with danger. Outraged by this *Sopranos*-style intimidation, though also secretly quite excited at the prospect of being embroiled in a tense real-life political/newspaper drama worthy of a Sunday-night mini-series, I'd immediately contacted my editor. 'My life is under threat,' I said. 'I might need a bodyguard.'

He said he was in the middle of Sunday lunch with his family but told me that, if there were any more calls, I should let him know and we'd consider contacting the police. How sensational, I thought, making a mental note to tell Louise in the hope that she would tell Scott who would in turn tell David, who would hopefully feel compelled to come to my rescue. (I hadn't yet found the courage to take my friends' advice and ask Scott for his number.)

Now, only a matter of hours later, I had this text message. It said: 'Scandalous story. U better watch your back!' My back? Were they going to break that too? Would they start with the legs and work up? How did these hoodlums operate anyway? The story wasn't even all that shocking: we weren't talking millions of pounds. Just a few thousand. I reread the text message. Scandalous story. How rude, I thought.

I noticed the message wasn't from a withheld number, like the earlier phone call, but it still wasn't one I recognised.

I guessed (ignoring my internal Dr J, shaking her head and saying no guesswork) that it had to be from the same person, who I fervently hoped was a weirdo or a government sympathiser and not a vendor of concrete overcoats. He was probably the kind of jerk who gets his kicks from harassing fearless journalists who are only trying to make the world a better place for everyone, I thought. Pissed off, I decided to be assertive and take matters into my own hands. I dialled 141 followed by the number winking on my mobile's caller ID screen.

A disembodied male voice said: 'hello'. It was friendlier and breezier than I'd been expecting from the phantom phone freak of Charing Cross.

I took a deep breath. 'Yes, hi,' I said, calmly but firmly, 'I mean, hello. I've just received your text message.'

The voice indicated it was about to say something, but I cleared my throat, loudly, to interrupt: 'I just wanted to let you know how sad and empty your life must be if all you have to do with your time is send abusive messages to journalists who are simply doing their jobs, exposing political scandal and hypocrisy on behalf of the Great British public.'

I paused and smiled to myself. Being assertive gives you such a great buzz. There was silence from the other end. So I carried on, emboldened: 'I don't know who you are – a government sympathiser, perhaps, or one of the beneficiaries of the type of corruption I am determined to expose – but a bully like you doesn't scare me. You can leave as many threatening voice messages and send as many texts as you like. You can threaten to break my legs. It won't stop me on my quest to uncover political scandals of this kind and get value for money for . . . for . . . the Great British taxpayer.'

Just as I was wondering how on earth I'd managed to miss all the drama and excitement of Scottish politics, The Voice said: 'Lorna?'

'Yes?' I replied stonily.

'Lorna. It's David.'

!?#!?!?#!?!?#!?

'I never, um, meant . . .' His completely bewildered-sounding voice drifted off.

'Nnnn . . .' I felt as if someone had pointed a stun gun at my forehead and pulled the trigger. Oh. My. God. Almighty. Oh. HolymarymotherofGodAlmighty. Is this really happening? Will I ever stop landing myself in the merde with this guy?

'I really didn't mean to cause any offence,' he said. 'I just . . . I'm trying to remember exactly what I said now. I just meant, you know, it was a good story, but one that some people might not be very happy about. Oh God. It wasn't meant at all . . . And, um, I swear I only sent that one text. I haven't left any voice messages. Or threatened to, er, break your legs.'

'Oh,' was all I managed to utter. I was too stunned to ask him how he got my number or to explain about the threat I'd received earlier, which had probably influenced the way I'd interpreted his text. Nor did I have the wherewithal to ask him why he didn't sign off with D, x, or David, to give me a clue as to his identity.

'Oh,' I said again. When it dawned on me that I really had to say something more substantial, I managed a string of single syllables: 'Oh. Kay. Right. Well. Good. Bye. Then.'

'Yeah, er, bye,' he said.

I wandered through to my kitchen and contemplated putting my head in the oven. Instead, I poured myself a large glass of Sauvignon and spent the rest of the night cross-examining myself, every question beginning with the words why, why, why, and all ending with the same inevitable answer: because you're a horse's ass.

* * *

Later, to distract myself from myself, I called Louise. Deciding it would be too embarrassing to divulge details of the David disaster, I shifted attention to the genuinely threatening voice message. 'One of the perils of my job, I suppose,' I said finally, trying to sound brave and courageous rather than melodramatic.

Louise didn't appear too alarmed about this. In fact, she sounded as if she was trying to stifle a laugh. 'Here,' she said quickly, 'Scott wants to speak to you.'

'What happened?' he asked.

I told him. Only when he put on his exaggeratedly thick Glaswegian accent to offer his concern and condolence ('Aw, man, that's pure terrible, by the way') did the penny plummet.

'I. Am. Going. To. Kill. You,' I said and I wasn't joking.

Scott and Louise were in hysterics.

'I absolutely cannot believe you did that,' I said. 'You've no idea the problems it has caused.'

'What do you mean?' he asked.

'I nearly called the police,' I said lamely. 'I told my editor and . . . oh, never mind the rest. It's too unbelievably bloody nightmarish.'

Before I hung up to seek solace in the dregs of my Sauvignon, I managed to say to Scott: 'Just out of curiosity, did David ask you for my number again?'

'He didn't ask,' Scott said, 'but I gave it to him anyway. Last week. I forgot to tell you.'

'How can you forget something like that?' I asked, beginning to really want to murder my brother-in-law.

'I'm a guy,' he said. 'I have other more important things on my mind. Why, has he called you or something? You owe me one if he has.'

'No, you owe me one,' I said, 'big time.'

It's Scott's fault that David and I are not together, I thought later as I listened repeatedly to 'Lonely This Christmas' on my iPod. And Katy also deserved some of the blame for not *forcing* me to contact him last month. If they hadn't jeopardised my chances at true love, I have no doubt we'd be starting the count-down to the festive season at the beginning of the road pointing in the direction of happily ever after.

I suppose it's partly that political journalist's fault too. If he hadn't given me the story, none of this would have happened. I wondered why people were so determined to destroy the beautiful thing that could have been between David and me. Maybe Scott secretly fancied me, and Katy no doubt wanted me to stay single until she got a boyfriend or a dog to keep her company, I thought, taking Freudian reductionism a step too far.

I understand that learning to take full responsibility for your own life predicament is one of the key aims of therapy. I also understand that not scapegoating is an ideal. But lofty ideals are not always realistic or achievable.

Grrr. It had been a bleak day. Threats of actual bodily harm followed by repeated humiliation would be enough to harsh anyone's mellow. The only positive slant I could put on it was to say that it acted as a valuable reminder that, no matter how good you're starting to feel about yourself or things in general, in spite of all the happiness life can afford, one fact always remains: life is at the same time full of inescapable tragedy – old age, sickness, death, boys.

* * *

For the next few days, I managed not to think too much about my unromantic life by taking my entire family plus Katy to Aviemore in the far north of Scotland. ('No,' I told my internal Dr J, 'before you ask, I'm not trying to get Lewis a bigger, better Christmas present than anyone else.') It was a couple of weeks before

Christmas and was for an *Observer* winter wonderland travel piece. We had contemplated Lapland, but decided to save that until Lewis was old enough to fully appreciate it. Or at least until he was old enough to be told, repeatedly, how lucky he was and how grateful he must be for the rest of his life because not all the children in the world were as fortunate as he was.

Even for what we had planned – meeting Father Christmas and his elves in their workshop in a forest in the Scottish Highlands, seeing reindeer in the wild, going dog sledding with Siberian and Alaskan huskies, staying in a log cabin with a real fire – he had displayed a remarkable lack of interest.

For almost a month, we had all been trying to get him into the Christmas spirit. We'd practically forced him to play with toy Santas and snowmen. We wore antlers with flashing lights on our heads. We sung 'Jingle Bells' and 'Rudolph the Red-nosed Reindeer' with cruel repetition. We managed to work ourselves up into an unprecedented festive frenzy, but he had remained impassive and unimpressed. Nothing had been able to distract him from his then obsessions: big lorries, ambulances, fire engines, trains and Shrek.

It was only after we set off late one Friday afternoon, on our mini-expedition to find Santa, that Lewis began to show a suitable level of excitement. Worryingly, this was just after I narrowly avoided a head-on collision with two red deer. Louise, Lewis and I had started out earlier than everyone else, the plan being that we would complete the journey in daylight. Everyone else had to wait until they finished work. The near miss happened on the A9, around forty miles south of Aviemore, in a wild blizzard that had reduced visibility to around five metres. One second, the road ahead – all five metres of it – was clear, the next two deer were sprinting across it, pausing momentarily only to stare into the car. Louise and I let out a scream as I slammed on my brakes to avoid them. We swerved into the middle of the road. If I hadn't been travelling so slowly or if there had been a car behind us or heading towards us from the other direction, then I think we may have been on our way to meet our maker.

I pulled into a lay-by. Lewis was in his car seat giggling hysterically, unaware that we'd all just had a near-death experience. Or I don't know, maybe he was aware of it, and that is how toddlers respond when their whole lives flash by in front of their eyes. Louise and I, meanwhile, were a little less effervescent. We just gazed silently ahead for a while, then gave each other a hug. We completed the rest of the journey at around five miles an hour, arriving within five minutes of everyone else, even though we'd left Glasgow two hours before them.

By the time we were shown to our woodland lodge at the foot of the Cairngorm Mountains, there was a thick blanket of snow on the ground. It was unusual for this time of year and we couldn't believe our luck.

Lewis ran into the lodge and found a letter from Santa, saying he'd be dropping by in the morning, and a plate of carrots. Although at home my nephew rarely touched the organic vegetables his mum lovingly cooked for him, he picked up the dirtiest one on the plate and took a large bite out of it.

'Aw, they're for poor Rudolph and his friends. What are they going to eat?' Louise asked him despairingly.

He looked at her for a moment, then spat the chewed-up orange remnants carefully back onto the plate.

The next morning, Scott announced that there was a very special visitor on his way to see Lewis. We all peered out at the snowy paradise. Through the glistening pine trees, a lovely old bespectacled Santa emerged, with his skis flung over one shoulder. He was ringing a hand bell and shouting: 'Ho ho ho!'

My mum, Louise, Katy and I were jumping up and down with excitement. 'This is amazing. Amazing. Absolutely amazing,' I kept repeating. Lewis studied us all with a thoughtful frown, then he yawned.

But as soon as Santa sat down, he jumped onto his knee and gave him a hug and kiss. 'A fire fengine,' he gasped, after ripping the paper off his gift. Out of the blue, Lewis, still hugging Santa, started singing: 'Jesus' Love Is Very Wonderful'. There was a slightly awkward silence.

'Who taught him that?' Scott, a committed atheist, asked, glaring at my mum, who had disappeared into the kitchen.

'Oh my God. The baby's been brainwashed. You'll never get him back. It's too late,' I shouted, for dramatic effect and in a weak attempt to get my own back on Scott for the voice message prank.

The next twenty-four hours were blissful: we went to Loch Morlich with Murdo, an outstandingly good *Observer/Guardian* photographer, to get shots of Lewis and Santa. For hours, Murdo arranged and rearranged his lighting reflectors and flash guns while Lewis posed with Father Christmas with the cool of a catwalk veteran. At the end of the photo shoot we went to see the Cairngorm reindeer herd, the only free-ranging herd in Britain.

After dinner that night, as we walked back through the pine trees to our cabin, it magically started to snow again. Lewis decided that he didn't want to hold anyone's hand. Nor did he want to be carried. Instead he tucked his hands into his duffel-coat pockets and sauntered very slowly home with his proud dad on one side and his besotted granda on the other.

My mum, Louise, Katy and I walked ahead, but stopped every now and then to watch them, and to listen to the crunch of snow underfoot and inhale the resiny smell of the ancient Caledonian pine trees. 'Can life get much better than this?' I asked no one in particular. I knew there and then that this was one of those occasions – that used to be so rare but were becoming ever more frequent in my life – when neither the past nor the future was important. All that mattered was savouring every second of the present moment, and knowing, really knowing that these are the good old days, right here, right now. And no fake mafia members or embarrassing encounters with men were going to spoil them for me.

* * *

Back in Glasgow, a few nights later, after I decorated my new Christmas tree, I made a three-course dinner for myself: roasted red onion, rocket and Parmesan salad followed by sirloin steak with pepper sauce, frites and roast vegetables with rosemary, and finished off with a large helping of Ben & Jerry's Cookie Dough ice cream. Now, so far so piggy, but otherwise fairly insignificant, you might think, but it wasn't. For two reasons. First, last year I didn't bother putting up a Christmas tree, much to my mum and dad's sadness. I just thought, what's the point? I live alone. No one will see it. (Apart from me, of course, but that didn't count.) You go to all the hassle of putting it up. Then a few weeks later you have to take it back down again. Last year, it seemed to be a pointless waste of time, even though the only other thing I was doing with all that precious time I was so worried about squandering was moping around in tears wondering what the point was in anything. This year, I went from one extreme to the other. I'd bought the biggest tree I could squeeze into my small living room. At seven feet, placed on a low table, it almost reached the ceiling. I also bought the most beautiful decorations I could find. I put it up far too early so that I could get as much enjoyment from it as possible, and invited my girlfriends round one night for mulled wine and mince pies, to admire the tree and to watch *It's a Wonderful Life*.

The other not insignificant thing about that particular gluttonous night was the gluttony itself. In the three years I'd lived in that flat, apart from the occasional (okay, annual) Thai meal I made for friends, I'd never cooked a decent meal, especially not for myself. If someone else wasn't making dinner for me, I oscillated between takeaways, snacks and, when the guilt kicked in, salads, soups and fruit smoothies.

As I went back for a second helping of ice cream that night, I remember thinking that, unless I was out for dinner with family or friends or being cooked for by someone else, I had rarely derived so much pleasure from simply eating. Although I felt that therapy had in many ways helped me grow up, in other respects I often felt like a child again, as if I were starting afresh: many things, especially the simple things, that I had long taken for granted, I now seemed to approach with a sense of baffled wonderment. I was, for instance, recently painting a picture with Lewis and for some reason was more amazed than he to watch blue and red making purple, and red and yellow becoming orange. 'Look at that,' I'd said. 'Amazing. Amazing.' When he looked at me, confused, I said: 'Wait till you discover it second time round.'

Later that night, I went back to my notebook, right back to the beginning of the dreaded *Notes on a recovery*.

On that first, long, rambling twelve-page stream of consciousness entry, which I wrote in between tears and sips of gin and tonic at the airport, I'd outlined, among other things, some of my reservations about therapy. They included comments like: 'surely no one can ever know a person better than they know themselves; a stranger cannot sort someone out better than an individual can sort themselves out; I already know myself – I've been introspective since adolescence.'

The idea that I really, truly thought I was self-aware back then now made me cringe on one side of my face and laugh on the other. I'd actually been quite clueless. By the time I got to thirty-five, I'd built up a thick layer of armour that had become no more protective than a sheet of tissue paper. No amount of solitary navel-gazing or bibliotherapy or new challenges or new jobs or new men or new continents would have enabled me to see through my facade. It had taken the utterly unique and peculiar relationship with Dr J to do that.

How do I know that a charity trek in the Himalayas or a solitary Buddhist retreat or going back to church or immediately replacing Christian with a new model wouldn't have had the same effect? Well, the only completely honest answer is that I will never know what impact any of those things would have had on me. But what I do know is that none of those things would have provided me with the opportunity to explore the way I behaved in relationships. Neither would they have forced me to look into my unconscious and discover some of those deeply hidden factors that were driving me. No one, other than a neutral, non-judgmental, well-trained individual who has no emotional connections to you, can do that. People had asked me over the past few months what the difference is between therapy and talking to a really good friend or family member. I'd discovered that it could be like comparing country and western music with punk rock. They are completely different.

I had read somewhere that the therapeutic relationship constitutes the mould-breaker: it is the relationship after which every other one will be different. I'd yet to put that to the test with a man, but I certainly felt I had much healthier, and more honest, mature relationships with my family, friends and colleagues.

* * *

One evening in mid-December, I stopped at an advert while reading the *New Yorker*. Not something I'd normally do. There was a photo of Roger Federer, which made me think immediately of David. It wasn't that he hadn't been on my mind. In fact, I'd spent quite a lot of time lately gazing at a picture I found of him online looking very rugged and handsome. Yes, I had Googled him. And, yes, I bought a copy of *The Sportswriter*. Just knowing that the book lay, or at least had lain, next to David's bed made reading about Frank Bascombe even more enjoyable than it would have been without that special connection. Anyway, the advert. It wasn't just the picture of Federer and David's resemblance to him that caught my eye. It was the tag line running underneath it. Let's not talk history yet, it said. Yes, I thought, let's not talk history yet. As Lysander said to Hermia (and as everyone knows), the course of true love never did run smooth. Maybe all of these little hurdles have been sent by Cupid to test the strength of our feelings for each other. I was getting carried away again, I know. I'm not supposed to believe anymore in fairy tales and fate and my gran's favourite sayings: 'What's for you won't go by you' and 'Good things come to those who wait' (or, depending on the situation: 'He who hesitates is lost' and 'The early bird gets the worm'. No wonder I've been confused in the past). I turned back to the magazine advert, which went on to describe Federer as the kind of person that seldom comes along.

Well, I thought, amazing tennis players aren't the only rarities in life. The opportunities to find true love are also relatively few and far between. Gorgeous doctors like David Mackenzie also seldom come along. I knew intellectually, rationally, that only fools let these golden opportunities pass them by. I was also beginning to get it emotionally too, enough to spur myself into action.

I called Louise, gave her a sanitised version of the text message incident and asked her if she had any ideas as to how I could 'accidentally' bump into David some time very soon. She phoned me a while later and said he was having a few beers in a pub called The Ben Nevis that Friday as it was his last day at the Western Infirmary before he moved to another hospital in Glasgow to do paediatrics.

My lovely friends, Katy and Rachel (Emily was on another romantic mini-break), agreed to accompany me on the proviso that we went to a few other places first. I think they rightly presumed that watching me make an idiot of myself again didn't constitute enough entertainment for an entire evening out.

By the time we arrived at The Ben Nevis, which is another of Glasgow's fabulous whisky bars with the feel of a cosy and intimate living room, it was after 10 pm.

As soon as we walked through the door, I quickly glanced around but couldn't see him. There were a few small groups, some couples, a few men on their own, but definitely no David. There was that horrible surge of disappointment you get when you go somewhere with the sole purpose of seeing someone, and realise that it's not going to happen. I tried to pretend to Katy and Sarah that I wasn't too bothered, even though I knew it was as obvious as wailing: 'He's not here. Wah.'

Just as we sat down, at the only free table, the front door opened. It was him, wearing only a T-shirt even though it was freezing outside and looking as gorgeous as ever. Katy and I were sitting with our backs to the wall, facing the door. She kicked me under the table. He saw us and came right over, picking up his half-drunk pint from the bar where one of the groups of people was standing. He must have been outside, on the phone – he had his mobile in his hand.

I introduced him to Rachel and the three of them swapped some idle chat about Christmas plans and preparations. Shit, why can't I speak to him? My default position, despite everything, still seemed to be to concentrate so hard on not giving the impression that I thought he was gorgeous that I ended up appearing all formal and not particularly interested. After a few minutes and a slightly awkward pause, he said he'd better get back to his friends for a bit.

At the end of the night, we all spilled out onto the pavement. David asked where I lived, which was only five minutes from the pub, and said he'd walk me home.

When we arrived at mine, we leaned against the wall for a bit, not saying very much.

He took my hand, then, just when I thought there was going to be another of those lovely kisses, he looked at me with a slight frown.

'Look, um, I . . .' he swallowed hard.

I didn't say anything.

'I really really like you,' he said. We looked at each other for a while. At times like this, the processor in my brain works in excruciatingly slow motion. It's only afterwards that I think of all the right things to say. In the heat of the moment, if I'm not rambling incoherently, I just stand and stare, taking it all in but probably looking either deeply medicated or deeply deranged. Was I meant to say: 'And I really really like you'? I didn't. I just bit my lower lip and frowned.

He took a deep breath. 'I just thought that maybe you weren't that into it. You know, with the email and the text and stuff.'

I still didn't say anything but felt a nasty prickling in my thumbs.

'And I've kind of started seeing someone,' he said.

I froze. Determined not to let my face betray my feelings, I probably just continued to look slightly confused. I remembered Louise telling me ages ago that she knew several girls had their eye on him. I've missed my chance, I thought, as the events of the last few months flashed before me: telling him I didn't want a boyfriend, refusing to give him my number and, to cap it all, the insane text fiasco. For fucking fuck's sake, I've missed my chance.

From what seemed like some distance, I heard him say: 'It's very early days but I don't want to, you know . . .' He was still frowning as he used his hands to help him find the words he was looking for. 'I don't want to get into any two-timing scenario. Even though it's very early days, it's not the way I want to go. I've been there, done that and it just ends up a horrible, messy situation that's not fair on anyone.'

Before I could tell him how I really felt, my instinct for self-preservation took over. 'No, no, no, no worries,' I stuttered. 'It's cool. I've kind of started seeing someone else myself anyway.'

'Oh,' he said.

I rambled for a while about rubbish then gave him a peck on the cheek, turned round and walked into my flat, wondering whether, where matters of the heart were concerned, I would ever be able to say what I mean and mean what I say.

* * *

It was time to stop. Some people remain in this kind of therapy for years and it is easy to see how it could become addictive, but I was conscious now of having a choice: between becoming my own parent or remaining an eternal child, merging with one superior force or another and forever seeking someone else's approval and validation and authority. I wanted to try standing on my own two feet. By this, I didn't mean avoiding relationships; I know that joining another is not always the same as abandoning yourself.

My last session with Dr J took place on an ice-cold Thursday morning, just over a week before Christmas. A light snow was blowing around in a gusty wind. I wrapped myself up and walked through Kelvingrove Park, feeling a weird concoction of emotions.

I looked around the waiting room for the last time, taking a final glance at those photographs which were now seared anyway into my mind's eye: the beautiful snow-capped mountain range, the rugged and isolated Hebridean beach and the breathtaking

Loch Lomond. As usual, the smell of coffee was so strong I felt as if I was drinking a mug.

I was greeted with my usual 'please come in'. I gave her my usual smile and she responded with a very unusual smile, which brought an all too familiar sting of tears.

'I want to thank you,' I said, before any had the chance to escape. 'I want to really thank you for helping me to become a much better friend to myself and hopefully, as a consequence, to other important people in my life. I had no idea, in the beginning, how much I must have disliked myself, or how much anger I had buried away inside of me.'

She smiled again.

'I can't believe,' I continued, 'that in the beginning I thought you were cold and unfriendly.' This made me think of that Talmudic saying, about seeing things not as they are but as you are. 'Though I didn't realise it at the time, I came in here, to therapy, looking, yet again, for approval and affirmation and love. When it wasn't forthcoming, I thought you were awful and decided I wanted to quit.'

'And then?' she said.

'And then,' I replied, 'I don't know what happened, but thank God I persevered. For the first time in my life, I really, really persevered, not with some external challenge – I'd done that before, half-marathons, triathlons, solitary travel, an A to Z of different careers, difficult work assignments, being in a relationship, staying single, testing my limits. For the first time, I persevered with getting to know myself, the ugly bits as well as the good, and with being entirely, brutally honest with myself, which was a hundred times more difficult than any of those other projects.' I fell silent, gazing out of the window behind her. The snow was falling more heavily now, making a quiet ticking sound against the glass.

'You worked very hard here,' she said. 'You made a commitment and you stuck with it even when there were times – and they were very clear to me – that you struggled to be here, and didn't want to be here, exploring things that were uncomfortable for you and finding things out about yourself that weren't particularly pleasant.'

I laughed a little. She raised her eyebrow as if asking me what was amusing.

'It is just the weirdest, weirdest experience I've ever had,' I said. 'I really thought I knew myself before I came in here. I didn't at all. I was just thinking that at the beginning when I sat outside your door thinking that I didn't really need therapy because there wasn't anything really wrong with me, I was all over the place. I see everything differently now. Everything. I remember thinking therapy was for the weak and needy and selfish. Now I realise there is no such thing as a human being who isn't at times weak and needy and selfish.'

We sat in a strangely comfortable silence for a few minutes.

After a while, I told her that, before I'd come into therapy, I didn't have a clue that, as human beings, we are all born into remarkable conflict. There is the severe conflict that begins in the second year of life, between dependency and autonomy – of wanting to be looked after and protected and wanting to be free. This tug of war persists at some level throughout life. In some cases (such as mine), it became so extreme – abandonment or engulfment – that it was disabling. There is also the conflict, which again starts in early childhood, between our pleasure-seeking nature and our fear of punishment and guilt. Inside everyone, to some degree, there is a conflicting drive to be acquiescent, conciliatory and to rebel. And there is the never-ending internal fight between the rational and irrational. This is closely related to a fear, which everyone has at some level, of losing control and being overwhelmed by your impulses. It is why people often do crazy things to give them the illusion of being 'in control'.

Most of us learn to behave rationally; the irrational thoughts are too terrifying that we have learned from an early age to keep them hidden from ourselves. The trick, I now think, to a happy, fulfilling, authentic life, has nothing to do with positive thinking and challenging negative thoughts. It is, I think, much healthier to get in touch with all of those 'negative' and irrational impulses that we have been told are bad and simply allowing ourselves to feel them. I don't quite understand why this makes them much less of an issue, but it does.

'What do you think has been the biggest or most significant change for you?' Dr J asked after a while.

I thought about this for a long time. I remembered someone comparing the process to the end of *A Midsummer Night's Dream*, when the human characters wake up and rub their eyes and aren't sure what has happened to them. They have the feeling that a lot has occurred – that things have somehow changed for the better – but they don't know exactly what caused the change. It's been said that psychoanalytic therapy is like that for many patients.

I told Dr J this and said I could relate to it. 'I think there have been subtle changes, but at the same time it feels as if it is a completely different person who is about to stumble out of here from the one who stumbled in twelve months ago. I have grown up. I understand that life cannot be controlled. That there is going to be good and bad. I just feel much better equipped to deal with whatever comes my way.'

She nodded. 'I notice many changes in you,' she said.

'I feel as if I've made peace with myself. I also feel that I'm no longer racing through life, searching for someone or something to make me feel happy and content. I'm no longer so critical or judgmental of myself or of other people. Every single day now, I feel lucky to be alive. Which I'm sure probably sounds utterly ridiculous. But that is how I feel. And when I have those inevitable days when things go wrong or something bad happens, I feel much less catastrophic and reactionary about it. I feel able to sit with uncomfortable or seemingly irrational emotions, whether they are jealousy or anger or fear or sadness or loneliness or guilt or boredom or just free-floating anxiety. I can feel the full extent of them but not necessarily act on them. Whereas before, I was so afraid of them, that unconsciously I must have pushed them immediately into a box and buried them. But without even being aware that that was what I was doing. Avoidance was my *modus operandi*. I just didn't realise it.'

Dr J nodded again, as I continued reflecting on the most bizarre year of my life.

'I remember reading somewhere that Paul Federn [a famous analyst of Freud's day] apparently used to say to women patients that he couldn't promise them too much, but he could promise that they'd be prettier. I don't think my physical appearance has changed, but I feel about two stone lighter. As if all that baggage that I was carrying around with me has been raked through, dealt with and discarded. And as if this big heavy protective layer that I wore to defend myself is no longer needed. Again, it seems paradoxical. I would've thought I would be more vulnerable without it, when in fact I feel much less vulnerable than I did a year ago. I no longer constantly feel the need to prove or justify or defend myself or apologise for everything. I've accepted myself, faults and all. Accepted my ordinariness. I feel as if I no longer do things to please other people or am fearful of other people's opinions.'

'I wonder how you're feeling about this ending,' she said eventually.

'Again,' I said, 'it's strange. I feel a mixture of emotions. There is a bit of anxiety about giving up what had become such a solid crutch. Over the past few months, whenever something difficult or challenging has happened, I've always had the comfort of thinking, I'll take that to therapy, and I realise I won't have that anymore. But I'm also looking forward to it; to trying to live without a crutch.'

I also told her that I'd read that therapy, like writing a poem, is never completed, only abandoned.

She nodded. 'Just because you won't be coming here three times a week anymore, just because the therapy has ended, it doesn't mean that the process is ended. For some people, they don't make sense of a lot of what has happened in therapy until months or even years after it has finished.'

I nodded and told her I'd imagined the ending so many times in my head over the past few days. I'd imagined giving her a hug and I'd thought about buying her a gift. I'd also glanced around the room to see if there was anything she wouldn't miss that would remind me of her. I told her that it had even crossed my mind, fleetingly, to put the copy of the 1985 *National Geographic* from the waiting room, which I'd glanced through three times a week for the past year but never read, into my bag. I'd even thought I'd like to record a session (I didn't), just so that I would be able to hear her voice again.

She gave me a knowing smile. 'We have just a couple of minutes left now,' she said. 'So I want to say again that I think you have worked very hard here and I can see a different person from the one who came in here at the beginning of the year.'

'Until I stumbled in here,' I said, 'I thought life was too short and too precious to waste valuable time exploring who we really are: why we feel what we feel, fear what we fear, think what we think, do what we do, and, probably most importantly, how we behave in our relationships with others – friends, partners, colleagues, parents and children. Now I think life's too short and too precious not to.'

She stood up and walked with me to the door, something she'd never done before.

We looked at each other silently for a moment. I was still thinking about wrapping my arms around her when she raised her hand and put it on my shoulder in a kind of semi-hug.

'I wish you all the very best,' she said, with the warmest smile I'd ever seen from her, 'and I hope things go well for you with your journey and with your dreams.'

'Thank you,' I said, putting my hand on her forearm. 'Thank you very, very much.'

I stood outside her apartment block and watched the light but chaotically falling snow for a few minutes. Then I walked away slowly, knowing that I wouldn't be seeing her again.

Epilogue

Later . . .

I found out what Katy meant when she said back in January that there are more ways to live happily ever after than to get married and have kids. After years of procrastinating, she tackled her commitment issues and finally got a dog. Not Mylo the abandoned greyhound – she missed her chance with him. But she discovered that there are plenty more dogs in the kennels. Bella provides endless unconditional love and Katy has never been happier. Emily has met her Mr Darcy. He proposed and she said yes. Rachel is pursuing her dream of making a documentary. For King Lewis, the world as he knows it is about to end. He is soon to be de-throned by the arrival of a little brother or sister. My parents, on hearing this news, cracked open a bottle of champagne before performing an impromptu paso doble around Louise and Scott's kitchen.

No more avoidance, get to the point. (Thanks, Dr J.)

And so . . .

I thought, ah, what the hell. I decided to tell David how I felt about him. Not in too much detail, as that would, understandably, have sent anyone running and screaming in terror for the hills. I'd gone on some other dates, but when I closed my eyes and opened them again, I was always disappointed it wasn't the lovely doctor sitting there opposite me. I didn't want to spend the rest of my life wondering 'what if' or regretting that I'd never been more honest with him. Yes, he'd mentioned there was someone else, but I'd heard that it had fizzled out. So I decided, for the first time out in the real world, to take my cards away from my chest and lay them down on the table.

The moment of truth came at the end of another big night out that Scott had kindly orchestrated (during which I made a point of nursing only one glass of wine, like an athlete in training). Outside in the pouring rain, when everyone else had gone home, I turned to David and said: 'I think I kind of quite like . . . er.' Stop hiding behind froth. I quickly corrected myself. 'I mean, I like you.'

He gave me his usual curious, slightly mysterious smile. I didn't have a clue what was coming. All I knew was that Roger Federer wished in vain to be so handsome.

He took me in his arms. He snogged me senseless, carried me off into the sunset – (I mean to the nearest city centre taxi rank) – and we all lived happily ever after.

Er, no. It didn't exactly go down like that. Real life isn't like Hollywood, at least not where I live, in Glasgow.

Instead, there was a moment's slightly awkward pause. He said he liked me too. But then he said he thought we'd missed that sliver of opportunity that permits two complicated adults to get it together. And, he said, he had some issues of his own to work out. Which may, I am well aware, have been a polite way of saying I'm way too nuts for him.

I had a moment of instant, devastating regretification. I wished I'd never asked. I felt embarrassed, humiliated. I wanted to burst into tears or to turn the clock back or say 'ha ha, I was only joking'. But I didn't. I nodded wisely, went home, drank some wine, shed some tears and smoked three cigarettes. I crept off to my bed, hid my face behind my hands and called him a complete jerk for refusing to give me the happy ending I so badly wanted. For a while, I tried to comfort myself with the fiction that I didn't really care because I didn't like him that much anyway and there are plenty more fish in the sea and what's for me won't go by me. And so on, and so on, and so on, until I fell into a light and restless sleep.

The next morning, with the combined effects of rejection, crying, alcohol and nicotine, I felt even worse. As the day wore on, the feelings didn't wear away. Eventually, I realised I was sick.

Not in the head. I had a cold and sore throat. I stumbled out of my bed only to get hot drinks and medicine. My flat felt, especially in illness, like a little pocket of isolation. I spent the next three days in my bed, envying all the happy couples of the world. Dispensing with the temporarily soothing bromide about not giving a damn, I allowed myself to feel the full force of rejection and all the emotional discomfort that comes with it. It wasn't pleasant. It was horrible. Before Dr J entered my life, I'm pretty certain I wouldn't have been able to handle it. I'd have reacted to get rid of it. I'd have avoided it, ignored it, distracted myself from it, made a joke about it, run away from it, pretended it didn't exist, or fired off a couple of mental emails to David, saying one thing but meaning another. In fact, before Dr J, I probably wouldn't have taken the risk of getting rejected in the first place. Instead, I'd have wasted years daydreaming about David and me living happily ever after.

A few days later, my cold almost gone, I woke up and looked out of my window. It was a bright sunny day. I went for a walk in Kelvingrove Park and was surprised to feel not only relieved but also happy and optimistic about the future. All the uncomfortable feelings had passed. Sure, I would have liked for things to have been different. But not every dream can come true. I really was on my own two feet now: no Dr J, no crazy crush to sustain me, just a chance to be my own mother and father.

I sat on a bench and hugged myself. Of all the lessons I learned during that bizarre journey with her, I think the most valuable was about not suppressing or denying emotions and not leaving important things unsaid or only partially said. I know now, thanks to her, that attempting to avoid uncomfortable or difficult feelings – whether of loss or love or rage or jealousy – leads to greater and longer-lasting pain.

I felt light and I noticed what was missing. Fear, anxiety, insecurity, anger, self-hatred, guilt. All the things that had weighed so heavily inside me since adolescence, most of which I hadn't even been aware of. I realised that I hadn't just accepted myself, I liked myself, imperfect and flawed as I am.

Woman on the Verge of a Nervous Breakdown

I found myself smiling like a lunatic at complete strangers and saying 'Morning, lovely morning,' simply because I felt so lucky to be part of this utterly crazy, remarkable, wonderful thing called life. So one dream didn't come true. So what? I had others to be getting on with.

Acknowledgements

There are a lot of people who helped to make this dream a reality. So, I want to give many, many thanks to many, many people . . .

I am indebted to Rupert Heath, agent extraordinaire, for his time, suggestions, enthusiasm, intelligence and wit. He had a vision for the book before I did and it would not exist without him.

I am immensely grateful to everyone at John Murray for their tremendous support, enthusiasm and assistance. Eleanor Birne, my editor, was fantastic to work with and offered many sensitive and thoughtful suggestions; Helen Hawksfield, her patient assistant, was wonderful, as were Nikki Barrow, James Spackman and Roland Philipps. Thanks also to all those who work energetically behind the scenes.

I am also extremely grateful to Jill Schwartzmann at Random House in New York for her insightful suggestions, and to those who worked so hard in foreign rights.

Although I have made a joke about it in these pages, I came very close to the edge one day at the *Observer*. I don't think it could have been a pretty sight and I will never forget four people who took time out from putting together a national newspaper to help me: Kamal Ahmed, Lucy Rock, Jan Thompson and Viv Taylor. I'm extremely grateful to them and also to Ruaridh Nicoll, Tracy McVeigh, the reporters and everyone else at the *Observer* for their friendship and support over the years.

Many thanks to Jane Bruton and Vicki Harper at *Grazia* for suggesting the column, 'Conversations with my Therapist', and to the many readers who said they found it helpful or just enjoyable.

Over the years, I have worked with and shared a glass of wine (i.e. got completely trolleyed) with a lot of journalists. Many of them have, without their even realising it, been inspirational as well as great company. I want to thank in particular Bill McDowall and Iain Gray, formerly of the *Herald*. They were the first real newspaper people I ever worked with and, at last and for the first time in my life, I had found a job I loved. I'm also grateful to Mark Douglas-Home who was a great editor to work for, and to Kevin McKenna, who was fantastic to work with and is also a very good friend. Thanks also to Tom Gordon and to BH.

Immense gratitude to a certain psychotherapist whose unique and baffling form of medicine helped save my life. 'Hmmm. A tad melodramatic, don't you think?' I can hear her say. Possibly. But still, I hate to think what kind of mess I'd be in now if I hadn't sought help.

I feel lucky to have some truly great, loyal and supportive friends – women who I have shared a lot of laughter and a lot of tears with, and, of course, talked a lot of drivel with in The Wee Pub. I'm eternally grateful to all of them – in particular, Katy, Kay, Susan and Elaine, for their friendship and constant support, especially during the writing of this book.

I want to thank my family for giving me permission to write a bit about their lives. Louise is my harshest critic but also my best friend and I didn't realise until recently how fortunate I am to have her as a sister. I also want to thank Scott for allowing me to treat their home as my own, and for providing lots of lovely meals, wine, poker games and good chat. And, of course, thanks to them for bringing that wonderful bundle of joy into the world. I'm grateful to King Lewis for making me an aunty, easily the best thing that's ever happened to me.

The two people who require thanking above all others are my mum and dad.

When I told them about the book, they could so easily have said: 'Nervous breakdown? Therapy? Anti-depressants? Other stuff? Good Lord, what on earth are we going to say to our neighbours, our friends, the family, your gran?' But they didn't. They opened a bottle of champagne and have given me not only their support but also never-ending encouragement. They are strong, honest and amazing people. They have also, thank God, got a great sense of humour. I feel blessed to have them as my mum and dad.

The author and publisher would like to thank the following for permission to reproduce copyright material: extract from 'This be the Verse' by Philip Larkin, from *High Windows*, published by Faber & Faber Ltd, (1947); extract from *Totem and Taboo*, standard edition, volume 13, by Sigmund Freud, reproduced by arrangement with Paterson Marsh Ltd, London.